American Academy of Religion
Dissertation Series

edited by
H. Ganse Little, Jr.

Number 29

JOHN WESLEY AND AUTHORITY
A Psychological Perspective
by
Robert L. Moore

JOHN WESLEY AND AUTHO

Robert L. Moore

John Wesley and Authority: A Psychological Perspective

Scholars Press

Distributed by
Scholars Press
PO Box 5207
Missoula, Montana 59806

JOHN WESLEY AND AUTHORITY
A Psychological Perspective
Robert L. Moore

92
W 515 mo

80090834
Library of Congress Cataloging in Publication Data

Moore, Robert L
  John Wesley and authority.

  (American Academy of Religion dissertation series ;
no. 29)
  Bibliography: p.
  1. Wesley, John, 1703-1791. 2. Methodist Church—
Clergy—Biography.   3. Clergy—England—Biography.
4. Authority. I. Title. II. Series: American Academy of
Religion. Dissertation series · American Academy of
Religion ; no. 29.
BX8495.W5M64   287'.092'4   79-13709
ISBN 0-89130-290-5
ISBN 0-89130-291-3 pbk.

Printed in the United States of America
1 2 3 4 5
Edwards Brothers, Inc.
Ann Arbor, MI 48104

FOR ELIZABETH

TABLE OF CONTENTS

Chapter

PREFACE

It has been said that John Wesley sought to bring together aspects of theory and practice which were seemingly irreconcilable. When one gets to know John Wesley, one becomes certain that at least for him there was no real difficulty in understanding how it all "went together." In a similar vein, the reader of this monograph may wonder what Joachim Wach has to do with John Wesley, psychology with *Religionswissenschaft*, general systems theory with philosophical hermeneutics. I can assure the reader that, at least in my own mind, it all "goes together." Indeed, this study was conceived as an integrative endeavor from its inception. I have attempted to illustrate the manner in which certain arbitrary boundaries, now influential in the religious academy, may be transcended through a reconstruction of our theory of interpretation. An assumption underlying the following discourse is that the time has come for the development of a post-modern hermeneutics of culture and personality which can enable us to move beyond the disciplinary myopia of the modern era. It is my belief that in hermeneutical inquiry we must undergo a creative regression through which we may rediscover the ancient insight that character and cognition are closely related, that charity must precede understanding.

I wish publicly to thank Professor Don S. Browning for providing me with the example of a scholar who knows how to "take care" in both the academic and personal involvements of life. Professor Jerald Brauer offered his valuable time and generous encouragement during the final period of research and writing. Professor Donald Capps was instrumental in the choice of my topic and provided much of the initial impetus for my research.

I am especially grateful to Dean Joseph Kitagawa and Professor Bernard Brown for their understanding and assistance during the critical final days of my work on this project. I hope in the days and years ahead to prove myself worthy of that great trust which the Divinity School bequeaths to all of its graduates.

CHAPTER I

INTRODUCTION: THE HERMENEUTICAL TASK AND METHOD

In spite of the immense contribution of Joachim Wach to
the scholarly study of religion one can discern little current
interest in his work. This apparent lack of awareness of the
importance of Wach and his work is all the more puzzling given
the fact that both the issues which he addressed and the methodological problems which he raised remain not only timely but for
the most part unresolved. This study begins with attention to
the continuing significance of Wach's vision for the future of
Religionswissenschaft.

The problem of authority in religious leadership was one
of the many issues which attracted Wach's scholarly interest.
In his monograph, *Sociology of Religion*, Wach devoted a chapter
to developing a typology of patterns of authority in religious
leadership.[1] In this study he outlined ways in which the authority of different types of religious leaders (e.g., founder, reformer, etc.) is manifest in the particular institutionalizations
of religious community issuing from their leadership.

Although his approach is self-consciously "sociological"
in its focus on communal and institutional formulizations, Wach
interweaves into his discussion a suggestive commentary on other
dimensions of religious experience and expression. As evidence,
for example, that his interest in the problem of authority in
religion transcends the narrowly sociological, note the following statement: "Reformers differ from prophets psychologically,
sociologically, and theologically."[2] A scrutiny of Wach's discussion of authority reveals that he believed observable parallels
exist between the "psychological type" of a religious leader and
his style of exercising authority, his theological formulations,
and the organization of the particular religious institutions
with which he is engaged. Although this idea is an important
recurrent theme in *Sociology of Religion*, Wach never pursued an
intensive study of these apparent parallels in the structure and
dynamics of authority. Wach's work is replete with many such
suggestive leads which he failed to follow up in subsequent works.

Richard Scheimann has noted that:

> Wach felt he had to choose between two alternative
> ways of expending his energies: (1) to engage in
> methodological inquiries and to elaborate a compre-
> hensive theory of *Religionswissenschaft*'s 'nature'
> and 'tasks' as a hermeneutical science; or (2) to
> leave the edifice of his scientific theory unfin-
> ished and to employ it, in fragmentary form, in
> sustained interpretations of entire religious cul-
> tures. He chose the first alternative.[3]

According to Scheimann, Wach hoped that others would take
his often schematic suggestions and interpretations and in the
process of "sustained interpretation" discover the value of his
work for the community of religious scholarship.[4] The present
work studies intensively the career of one religious leader with
regard to how his style of authority is expressed psychologically,
theologically, and sociologically. This "sustained interpretation" of the career of one leader, if supplemented by similar
studies of other leaders, could figure as a beginning toward
establishing the usefulness of Wach's insights in understanding
concrete materials in the history of religion.

As a focus for this inquiry I have chosen the life and work
of the English reformer and evangelist John Wesley. One of the
major considerations for such a study is the availability of
biographical as well as autobiographical resources. Albert
Outler, one of the foremost contemporary Wesley scholars, has
noted that "we have more autobiographical data from John Wesley
than from any other figure in church history."[5] This richness
of data and documents, Wesley's prominence in eighteenth century
religious history, and the central role of the problem of authority in Wesley's cultural milieu and career combine to make the
choice of John Wesley an appropriate and promising one.

An Inquiry into Method: *Religionswissenschaft* and Psychological Interpretation

The basic interpretive method for this study is psychohistorical, largely based on the seminal work of the psychoanalyst Erik H. Erikson. One of the fundamental tenets of Erikson's
methodology is, of course, that continuities can often be discerned between the dynamics of an individual's personal identity
and those of his ideology and institutional relationships. This

obvious parallel between the assumptions of Wach and Erikson
could be offered as a superficial answer to any query regarding
the appropriateness of Eriksonian method for this study. Wach,
however, had grave reservations regarding the use of psychological interpretation in religious inquiry. Before proceeding
further, the reasons for these reservations must be examined in
some depth. I am convinced that these reservations, once appropriate, no longer constitute sufficient grounds for inordinate
suspicion of psychological inquiry in *Religionswissenschaft*.
On the basis of the following discussion of the historical and
theoretical grounds for Wach's concern I argue that the time
has come for a full acceptance of psychological research as an
important resource for the "general science of religion."

It may seem strange to call attention to the widespread
distrust of psychological interpretation in religious studies
at a time when there is a renewal of interest in the uses of
psychological theory and methodology. It should, however, be
quite clear to us that given the current state of "interdisciplinary" inquiry in the religious academy, a renewal of interest
in a neglected problem area by no means suggests that the methodological issues which have plagued similar research in the past
have now been resolved. The very use of the term *Religionswissenschaft* is an embarrassing reminder of our disorderly conceptual
and methodological "house."[6] I am using the term as it was
understood by the much revered but all too rarely read Wach.

In the introduction to Wach's monograph, *The Comparative
Study of Religions*, Joseph Kitagawa defines *Religionswissenschaft*
as "a field of study which embraces three main divisions: hermeneutics (or the theory of interpretation), the study of religious
experience, and the sociology of religion."[7]

> Wach's starting point was the assumption that subjec-
> tive religiousness is objectified in various expres-
> sions, and that these expressions appropriate definite
> structures which can be comprehended. The study of
> such structures of religious expression is one of the
> primary objectives of *Religionswissenschaft*. In this
> sense it is a descriptive science, following Dilthey's
> notion that a descriptive science 'is one whose units
> and laws are found by empirical analysis, or close
> examination of what is actually given in experience.[8]'

Wach himself pointed out a number of ways to study religion
under the general rubric of *Religionswissenschaft*: one can do

historical studies, phenomenological studies, sociological studies, and *psychological* studies.

> The quest for knowledge of the interior aspects of
> religious experience wherever and whenever that ex-
> perience may occur constitutes another legitimate
> approach. Individual and group feelings, together
> with their dynamics, have to be explored. This is
> the task of psychological interpretation. Although
> the more recent decades have shown an appreciable
> cooling of the fervor once displayed by the advocates
> of the psychology of religion at the beginning of the
> twentieth century, today the various schools of depth
> psychology and psychoanalysis offer clues to the un-
> derstanding of the unconscious and its workings. The
> writings of Grensted, Allport, Horney, Menninger, and
> Fromm--to mention only a few contemporaries--have ap-
> plied Freudian and Jungian theories to the study of
> religion.[9]

Wach believed that psychological interpretation was necessary for a full understanding of religious phenomena and that
such inquiry should be integrated into religious research along
with other equally important interpretive methodologies:

> Interpretation of expressions of religious experience
> means an *integral* understanding, that is, full lin-
> guistic, historical, psychological, technological, and
> sociological enquiry, in which full justice is done
> to the intention of the expression and to the context
> in which it occurs, and in which this expression is
> related to the experience of which it testifies.[10]

In spite of these protestations as to the importance of
psychological interpretation, a closer scrutiny of Wach's work
reveals the grave reservations with which he viewed such inquiry.
He believed that the materialistic and positivistic assumptions
of modern psychology led almost irrevocably to a "psychologism"
which interpreted religion in a reductionistic manner. This
opposition to psychological reductionism manifested itself in
a critique of the Freudian analysis of religion in his essay,
"Das Religiose Gefuhl," published in 1931.[11] As early as 1924
Wach indicated his suspicion of psychological interpretation.

> The lay adherent of religion is easily convinced, not
> for example, that religion is an elementary, 'eternally
> human' phenomenon, but that it is made up of certain
> impulses, strivings, notions and agitations. It is
> especially a kind of repressed sexuality. And though
> it is not expressed, there is a little word written
> above the whole description: 'only.' The psycholo-
> gizer knows no more beautiful word. He is happy when
> he has discovered that something is 'only' something.[12]

Wach was committed to the need for scientific analysis of
religious phenomena yet was convinced that such analysis did not
require the destruction of the object of investigation. For him
limits should be built into hermeneutical method:

> ...in order to avoid dissolution of actuality and of
> values. *There are no natural limits;* only those of
> tact, respect and shame, most unmodern virtues. *The
> setting of limits is a limitation, but without limi-
> tation there is chaos.* If we want to build a 'formed
> world' we must learn to honor the forms of things.[13]

For Wach, practitioners of psychological interpretation
seemed unaware of the limitations of a psychological perspective.
Consequently, they did not "honor the forms of things." Enthusiasm for the practice of the psychology of religion as a sub-
discipline of academic psychology had already begun to wane,
and Wach's reservations were an added impetus for the continued
eclipse of psychological investigation within *Religionswissenschaft.* Since Wach's death in 1955 the term *Religionswissenschaft* has increasingly been identified more narrowly--and less
accurately--with the discipline currently referred to as the
history of religions. Indeed, at present there seems to be little
communication between those scholars involved in the "scientific
study of religion" and the practitioners of the "science of religions."

It is my purpose to focus on one of the major factors which
led Wach to formulate his influential reservations about the use
of psychological interpretation: Wilhelm Dilthey's ill-fated
search for an adequate psychology. I then outline Erikson's
psychohistorical method which, I argue, renders Dilthey's difficulties and his "solution" obsolete both in itself and in its
subsequent influence upon Wach and *Religionswissenschaft.*

From Psychology to Hermeneutics: The
Frustrated Vision of Wilhelm Dilthey

The irresponsible stewardship of the intellectual legacy
of Wilhelm Dilthey ranks as one of the great tragedies in the
history of the sciences of man. Unfortunately, his direct influence has been most limited in Anglo-American scholarship.[14]
When we do hear of him it is usually in sketches either too brief
or intensely polemical in nature. Indeed, most are unaware not

only of the fundamentals of Dilthey's work but of his substantial
influence upon Weber, Husserl, Heidegger and others. The renewal
of interest in hermeneutics has, however, heightened awareness
of Dilthey's foundational work in that area. In his recent monograph, *Hermeneutics*, Richard Palmer has noted Dilthey's contribution:

> After Schleiermacher's death in 1834, the project of
> developing a general hermeneutics languished....Near
> the end of the century, however, the gifted philoso-
> pher and literary historian Wilhelm Dilthey (1833-
> 1911) began to see in hermeneutics the foundation for
> the *Geisteswissenschaften*--that is, all the humanities
> and social sciences, all those disciplines which inter-
> pret expressions of man's inner life, whether the ex-
> pressions be gestures, historical actions, codified law,
> art works, or literature.[15]

Eugene Gendlin, in a discussion of Dilthey's views on the
"Human in Culture and History," has summarized the philosopher's
approach to the interpretation of these human phenomena:

> The observable, expressed or objectified, is to be
> studied in its own inherent human significance.
> That means it is to be studied in accordance with:
> (1) the human structural-functional context of
>   thought, feeling and purposing;
> (2) an objectified, shared context of such ex-
>   perience in social-cultural historical data;
> (3) centering around the investigator's own inner
>   context of experiencing, the understanding of the
>   objectified contexts;
> (4) a kind of category of thought that is adequate to
>   describing the dynamic, changing, interrelating,
>   value-filled character of experience of life.[16]

Thus, according to Dilthey, this dynamic process of interaction constitutes the basis of both the culture and the personal
experience of the individual. Social and cultural phenomena are
"objectifications of life," with life understood as the interaction of the polymorphous *life-units*. Life is a "temporal
stream of inter-individual commonness whose forms are here for
us in their expression."[17]

The human individual in Dilthey's thought is the focus or
"crosspoint" of social and cultural systems. The individual
acquires his own symbolic universe with its structured modalities of experience through learning in social groups. Even
"before he learns to speak he is already a historical being."[18]

The individual, nevertheless, is not merely a passive *tabula rasa* on which society imprints its designs. He integrates the different systems as he internalizes them and "carries them creatively."[19] Thus he is capable of both active adaptation as well as passive internalization and can make his own imprint on the socio-cultural systems in which he lives and acts. For Dilthey, this creative action by individuals marks their participation in the ongoing process of creating the constellations of meaning which constitute human life. It is in the context of this historical process that all cultural, social, and personal phenomena are significant, and Dilthey's chosen life task was the development of a method of interpretation which could comprehend the myriad dimensions of that ongoing process.

Though Dilthey had envisioned an integrative approach to the understanding of culture and personality, he was frustrated in his attempt to formulate theory and method adequate to his task. H. A. Hodges in his monograph, *Wilhelm Dilthey: An Introduction*, has called attention to an inconclusiveness present in all of Dilthey's attempts to arrange the human studies according to a coherent system. He notes a curious development and change of emphases in Dilthey's theory:

> Thus in the *Introduction to the Human Studies* of 1883 the whole edifice is made to rest on psychology, which together with the generalizing social sciences receives much more space than biography and historiography. Yet‛ at the end we are told that the synthesis which some would seek in sociology is really to be found in history, written "philosophically," i.e., with full consciousness of the results of the special sciences, and the aesthetic and cultural values of history are stressed. In the *Critique of Historical Reason* of 1910 the human studies are made to arise out of lived experience by way of autobiography, biography, and history, the generalizing sciences of society are recognized as important but subordinate, and there is considerable doubt as to where psychology comes in and what it is to be like. Much is heard of hermeneutics, which is given a place not altogether unlike that which mathematics holds in the natural sciences.[20]

In order to understand this shift in emphases, we must address ourselves briefly to three questions: (1) What type of psychology did Dilthey reject; (2) What type did he envision; and (3) Why did he turn away from giving psychology such a central role in the human studies?

In his masterful study, *The Philosophy of Wilhelm Dilthey*, Hodges notes that Dilthey rejected the suspicions of Kantians and Hegelians toward the use of psychology in the human studies. He found, however, promising new directions in the use made of psychology by the British empiricists whose work

> stood for an attempt to integrate psychology with the other empirical sciences, in recognition of the fact that the human mind lives and works in the physical world, whereas the Germans were too apt to run off into metaphysical speculations and to seek in the soul of man the key to the understanding of all that is.[21]

But the British psychology also had weaknesses which Dilthey never accepted. It sought to imitate physics, with Hume, for example, using a mechanical model which failed to do justice to either the instinctual or the spiritual in human experience. Too narrow in scope and confined to a study of the processes of human cognition, it neglected the instinctual and volitional experiences of man. Finally, it tended to treat "the individual as a unit prior to, and in essence unaffected by, his union with others in society."[22] Dilthey believed it was possible to develop a psychology without these weaknesses, a psychology which would give a coherent account of mental life in purely descriptive and empirical terms. Hodges has summarized Dilthey's assumptions regarding mental life:

> Mental life, he thinks, is a functional unity which cannot be reduced to or built up theoretically out of non-functional units. This is where he parts company with sensationalism, and also with Brentano, whose position is only superficially like his own. The real unit of mental life is not a sensation or feeling, or even an isolated 'intentional act' with its 'content,' but a total reaction of the whole self to a situation confronting it. Every such reaction (called by Dilthey an *Erlebnis*) includes elements of three main types, viz., cognitive, affective, and conative, and these follow and depend upon one another in a definite order which constitutes the ground-rhythm of mental life. Cognition comes first, then feeling, then conation.[23]

In Dilthey's system, these relations between the three elements in human mental life are called the "structure" or "structural system" of the mind. The possibility of developing a "descriptive psychology" rests on his belief that this structural system is actually given in "lived experience." For Dilthey, psychology was the systematic elaboration of the self-knowledge which begins in common experience.

> Since the structural system is one of living function, our knowledge of it will not be altogether like our knowledge of inanimate objects...it will depend on the possession of an eye for the structural type. It will 'always retain something of the living, artistic process of understanding.' Indeed, one of its methods for sounding the unconscious depths will be the study and interpretation of those manifestations of human achievement which Dilthey calls 'objective mind,' those 'permanent forms with firm outlines' in which so much that has sunk from memory into unconsciousness is still expressed for all to read. It is here rather than by introspection that the approach to the unconscious should be made.[24]

According to Dilthey, such a "descriptive and analytical psychology" would, in order to be adequate, have to: (1) begin by describing the structures of mental life, showing how the various "spheres" are related to one another in the ongoing process of lived experience; (2) explain the dynamics of "mental development" through which the structural system grows increasingly refined and complex in the creative adaptation of the person in his physical and cultural environment; (3) clarify how the individual is both integrated into and differentiated from the various social systems that make up his communal existence; and (4) formulate an understanding of how men come to share basic uniformities and yet develop unique individual characters, including within this task the development of a psychological typology of the various character types.[25]

Dilthey's grand design for such a psychology on which to base the human studies was to remain little more than that. He found the available psychological theory and methods inadequate for the task, and consequently could not formulate the comprehensive "structure-psychology" that had been his goal. Increasingly, "structure-psychology" took on a less central role in his writings, and the focus of investigation moved from the "structures of mind" to the "understanding of expressions of lived experience." In his later years, he viewed the human studies as based not on a comprehensive psychology but on the discipline which defined as its task the understanding of expressions--hermeneutics. Psychology, while still suggestive and illuminating and still an important tool, was only one of many resources useful in interpreting lived experience and its expressions.

Dilthey's Legacy to Wach:
The Flight From Psychology

Richard Scheimann has illuminated Wach's indebtedness to
Dilthey for the fundamentals of his theory and method.[26] From
the above discussion it is obvious that Wach's orientation toward
psychology and hermeneutics--and that of many later practitioners
of *Religionswissenschaft*--must be understood in the light of the
work of the later Dilthey. Wach retained Dilthey's never-surren-
dered conviction that psychological methods *might* prove useful
in the interpretive task but, like Dilthey, found existing psychological theories and methods inadequate. Although Wach accepted psychology as one among many methods, the problematics
involved in its application led him to place his fundamental
methodological eggs in other baskets. Therefore in Wach's work
the promise of psychological method remains unfulfilled. It is
our contention, however, that the work of Erik Erikson offers
the fundamentals of a methodology which enables psychological
interpretation to make its own distinct contribution in the
context of a more comprehensive hermeneutics. In order to support our contention, we must: (1) introduce and discuss the
fundamentals of Erikson's method; (2) show its relevance for
investigating the structure and dynamics of authority in our
research; and (3) place his fundamental method in a wider theoretical perspective.

Reclaiming the Vision: The Promise of Erik
Erikson's Psychohistorical Method

Clearly, the publication of *Young Man Luther* marked an
important advance in Erikson's development of a psychoanalytic
approach to the interpretation of culture and personality.[27]
The present task is to discern the basic intent and structure
of his psychohistorical methodology.

For the scholar seeking an introduction to the methodology
of psychohistorical study, a survey of the relevant literature
proves frustrating. Psychohistorians, I believe, prefer to
offer concrete examples of their investigations for illustrative
purposes rather than discussing their endeavors in the abstract
language of methodological statements. Erikson himself embodies
this abhorrence for abstract, and perhaps over-simplified,

theorizing. One searches his writings in vain for a clear and concise outline. Therefore the following discussion represents my own reconstruction of his aims and method from scattered, often obscure, references. In this reconstruction of the major topography of his project, we must examine the following passage from *Young Man Luther* in which Erikson by using the reformer as a concrete image presents his insights into what he has called the "metabolism of generations":

> Each human life begins at a given evolutionary stage and level of tradition, bringing to its environment a capital of patterns and energies; these are used to grow on, and to grow into the social process with, and also as contributions to this process. Each new being is received into a style of life prepared by tradition and held together by tradition, and at the same time disintegrating because of the very nature of tradition.[28]

Erikson is not satisfied with the idea that human individuals are mere pawns, passively reacting to societal and cultural conditioning. From his point of view societies optimally facilitate the development in the individual of what recent ego psychologists have called "ego-activity."

> But the social process does not mold a new being merely to housebreak him; it molds generations in order to be remolded, to be reinvigorated, by them. Therefore, a society can never afford merely to suppress drives or to guide their sublimation. It must also support the primary function of every individual ego, which is to transform instinctual energy into patterns of action, into character, into style—in short, into an identity with a core of integrity which is to be derived from and also contributed to the tradition. There is an optimum ego synthesis to which the individual aspires; and there is an optimum societal metabolism for which societies and cultures strive. In describing the interdependence of individual aspiration and of societal striving, we can describe something indispensable to human life.[29]

It should be clear from this passage that Erikson understands his psychohistorical investigations to be deeply grounded in and a significant development of his earlier research into the dynamic interaction of selfhood and culture. Following the above statement of intention he notes that an earlier book, *Childhood and Society*, was a program of studies which "might

account for the dovetailing of the stages of individual life
and of basic human institutions." He then states that *Young Man
Luther* "circumscribes for only one of these stages--the identity
crisis--its intrinsic relation to the process of ideological re-
juvenation in a period of history when organized religion dominated ideologies."[30]

Although there are many suggestive discussions in the monograph specific to the understanding of Luther and his culture,
the most concise and illuminating portrayal of the processes
operating in this "metabolism of generations" is found in Erikson's essay, "Ego Development and Historical Change":

> Beyond this, however, the observer is aware of the
> fact that what he conceptualizes as id, ego, and
> superego are not static compartments in the capsule
> of a life history. Rather they reflect three major
> processes the relativity of which determines the
> form of human behavior. They are:
> (1) the process of organismic organization of bodies
> within the time-space of the life-cycle (evolu-
> tion, epigenesis, libido development, etc.);
> (2) the process of the organization of experience by
> ego synthesis (ego space-time, ego defences, ego
> identity, etc.);
> (3) the process of the social organization of ego or-
> ganisms in geographic-historical units (collective
> life plan, ethos of production, etc.).
> The order given follows the trend of psychoanalytic
> research. Otherwise, although different in structure,
> these processes *exist by and are relative to each other.*
> Any item whose meaning and potential changes within
> one of these processes simultaneously changes in the
> others.[31]

Erikson goes on to state that the undue accentuation of
any of these processes arising from loss of mutual regulation
and balance can lead to enslavement by the id, by ego defenses,
and by historical conditions.[32] But his central concern in
Young Man Luther, and in *Gandhi's Truth* as well, is to show
not only this pathological side but also the personal and cultural synthesis which can occur when the cultural moment is
ripe and the creative, adaptive and synthesizing capacities of
the human organism (especially certain uniquely sensitive and
insightful ones) can be brought into play.

We can say, then, that Erikson's program of psychohistorical
research focuses on three major tasks. First of all, he discerns and attempts to map out the structures and dynamics of the

on-going historical life process, the "metabolism of generations," with its three major components. Secondly, he illustrates the creative human capacity to adapt, to synthesize
creatively the polymorphous elements of the different systems
of the historical process—and, in addition, outlines some of
the basic elements which are necessary in such attempts at adaptation. Finally, he describes the manner in which the process
of cultural change occasionally precipitates a conflictual crisis
in the socio-historical milieu, a crisis which potentially can
be solved by a given historical personage because of his special
sensitivity to the pattern of the cultural situation.

This sensitivity is, according to Erikson, born out of
the similar (one might say "congruent") pattern of conflict
grounded in the microcosm of his individual development. Erikson
seems to believe that such an individual, due to the congruence
between the microcosm of his personal conflict and the macrocosm
of the cultural conflict, is enabled to be the "cultural ego"—
one who in struggling with his own conflict is able to resolve
the deepest crisis of his socio-historical milieu.

Given the integral grounding of Erikson's psychohistorical
research in his earlier studies, we should not be surprised that
his method of approaching the interpretation of a historical
personage is likewise grounded in his standard clinical approach
as a practicing psychoanalyst. I would posit that his article
"On the Nature of Psycho-Historical Evidence: In Search of
Gandhi," ostensibly intended to clarify his methodology, is
virtually incomprehensible if not read as a continuation of or
sequel to his previous article, "The Nature of Clinical Evidence."[33]

In the latter article, Erikson illustrates his clinical
method by describing the case of a young man plagued by disturbing dreams. In the course of successive interviews with the
young man the therapist (Erikson) collected a growing amount of
clinical data in the form of remembered experiences that the
patient had had with a number of significant persons in his life.
Everything said by the patient in a given hour was linked with
the material of previous appointments. According to Erikson,
the therapist assumes that the synthesizing function of the ego
associates material together, though it may be remote in history,
separate in space and contradictory in logical terms.

In Erikson's view the therapist in interpreting the clinical
material does not approach it aggressively or actively try to fit
the material into his diagnostic schema. Rather, he approaches
the material with a "disciplined subjectivity," with a "free-
floating attention" which "turns inward to the observer's ruminations even as it attends the patients 'free associations' and
which, far from focusing on any one item too intentionally, rather
waits to be impressed by recurring themes."[34]

After sketching the relatively passive, expectant mind-set
of the therapist, Erikson goes on to characterize the nature of
his "clinical evidence." Positing that the patient during the
therapeutic encounters will have produced a sequence of themes,
thoughts and affects which seek their own concordance, he suggests that

> these themes will, first faintly but ever more in-
> sistently, signal the nature of the patient's mes-
> sage and its meaning. It is, in fact, the gradual
> establishment of strategic intersections on a num-
> ber of tangents that eventually makes it possible
> to locate in the observed phenomena that central
> core which comprises the 'evidence'.[35]

In the case in question, Erikson was able to discern an
"evidential continuity" as it manifested itself in patterns
arising out of many different sectors of the patient's life,
not only in his dreams, but in many different significant relationships: those with his mother, grandfather, therapist, etc.
These patterns at various times and relational coordinates were
found to be congruent with regard to their structural and dynamic
configurations. This congruence in the dynamic patterning of
the patient's life process was the key for understanding the
conflicts of the patient, and the basis for an orientation from
which to plan therapeutic intervention.

In his article, "On the Nature of Psycho-Historical Evidence: In Search of Gandhi," Erikson reiterates again, for the
psychohistorian as well as for the therapist, the importance of
a disciplined subjectivity which "turns inward to the observer's
ruminations even as it attends" to the data under scrutiny.
Erikson is concerned to emphasize that the psychohistorian must,
as does the therapist, include as a part of the discipline in his
"disciplined subjectivity" the capacity to discern the presence
of the phenomenon of counter-transference. Counter-transference,

Erikson assumes, is going to be present in the psychohistorical study. The question is whether it will become an important source of insight or a fatal source of interpretive distortion. As Erikson has put it,

> even as we demand that he who makes a profession of
> 'psychoanalyzing' others must have learned a certain
> capacity for self-analysis, so must we presuppose that
> the psycho-historian will have developed or acquired
> a certain self-analytical capacity which would give
> to his dealings with others, great or small, both the
> charity of identification and a reasonably good con-
> science.[36]

We should not assume from the above comments, however, that the method of disciplined subjectivity is exhausted by an aware-ness of the uses of counter-transference. Certainly, though Erikson does not make this explicit here as he did in the article on clinical evidence, the disciplined subjectivity of the psycho-historian should include that same sensitivity to thematic con-tinuity which is reflected in the clinician's approach. The capacity to see analogues or parallels between patterns of be-havior in different arenas, both temporal and relational, of a person's life is as necessary for the psychohistorian as for the clinician. At any rate, we can be sure that the character-istics of disciplined subjectivity refer in general to that heightened capacity for sensitivity to thematic continuities in intra-personal and inter-personal dynamics which is realized through a long period of supervised clinical training and experi-ence. It is, however, unfortunate that Erikson's writings on this important topic include an incomplete, albeit suggestive, treatment of this concept.

In this article Erikson includes a schema which, though present in principle in the previous article, receives more emphasis here: the necessity to keep in focus the juxtaposition of the history in the person with the person in history.[37] Here he emphasizes again the dynamic interaction of the self and its cultural-historical milieu, keeping both the interpreted and the interpreter continually in such a dialectical focus.

In the light of the above discussion we are enabled to summarize the major elements of Erikson's interpretive methodo-logy. He begins with a multidimensional process conceptuality which includes all the personal and social dynamics affecting

and affected by the individual. These interrelated processes
range from the biological to the cultural. The interpreter approaches his data with a disciplined subjectivity which, while
ever conscious of counter-transference and other nuances of
intra-personal and inter-personal dynamics, allows his "free-
floating attention" to play over the clinical or historical
data. The patterns and configurations in the data impress themselves on the awareness of the interpreter, and, by a process
of thematic analysis, the interpreter discerns the various in-
dices at which the patterns and configurations intersect, or
again, are found to be structurally and/or dynamically analogous,
parallel, or congruent. The central themes or modal patterns
thus derived constitute the basic evidence of the interpreter
from which he can build his interpretation.

I have in the foregoing discussion suggested that Erikson's
work fulfills the projections for Dilthey's "psychology of the
future," the descriptive and analytical psychology. Others have
noted the possibility that psychoanalysis, even that of Freud,
may be a step toward meeting Dilthey's requirements. As early
as 1939 Max Horkheimer observed: "We shall here raise a different question, whether in spite of the opposition between the
naturalistic principles of Freud and the historical principles
of Dilthey, the theory of psychoanalysis does not meet some of
Dilthey's requirements."[38] Horkheimer points to a number of
interesting parallels between Dilthey and Freud including assumptions about the nature and dynamics of the historical process
of the individual-in-culture and of the symbolic processes underlying both poetic fantasy and hallucination. However, the agreement between them, Horkheimer believes, lies "above all in the
conception of a coherent totality of meaning (*Sinnzusammenhang*)
in each individual existence, a totality which develops itself
in the struggle between the individual human being and his environment."[39]

To my knowledge, Horkheimer never continued the investigation of the similarities between Freud's psychoanalysis and
Dilthey's projected psychology. I came upon Horkheimer's comments after becoming convinced that Erikson's ego psychology
together with his clinical and psychohistorical method fulfills
the vision of the early Dilthey. The task of presenting in a

systematic fashion the grounds for this assertion, of course, is
beyond the scope of this study. Such a task would entail--as
suggested above--not only comparing Dilthey and Erikson in depth,
but also examining the relationship between Dilthey's work and
that of Freud, Jung, Adler, and the subsequent psychoanalytic
tradition. The parallels are, however, obvious. Both seek to
understand man's lived experience by examining closely the expressions or objectifications of that lived experience; both use
an intuitive mode of sympathetic understanding as a central interpretive technique; both describe the dynamic interaction and
mutual activation between the individual and his culture; both
see developmental stages in human life and world-views; both
see a correspondence between psychological states and ideological
characteristics; and both see the study of the role of the "great
man" as a useful entree into the complex issues of cultural crisis
and change. Like Dilthey, Erikson stresses not only the defensive
but the adaptive and creative aspects of the human personality.
Following Hartmann, Erikson emphasizes the necessary "fit" between the human organism and its "average expectable environment."[40] From our perspective this emphasis represents an extension of insight into the formation of what Dilthey, Weber and
others have called the *Sinnzusammenhang*.

Certainly an important step forward, more by clinical psychiatry as a whole, but surely focal in Erikson is the grounding
of the development of the intuitive capacities of the observer/
interpreter in long hours of disciplined, supervised reflection
upon one's involvement with oneself and others. The discovery
that the sensitivity of the interpreter can be trained and honed
is a significant discovery and advance beyond Dilthey's herme-
neutics--especially if the interpreter is concerned that his own
"archeology of the subject" will prevent the substitution of
projection for exegesis.

Yet Erikson's clearest advance beyond Dilthey is in the
area of the dynamics of human development. Dilthey was quite
clear that realization of a "descriptive and analytical psychology" would entail explaining the dynamics of "mental development"
through which the "structural system" grows increasingly refined
and complex during the creative adaptation of the individual.
While he saw man as a psychophysical unity who developed in

stages both organically and ideologically, he never filled in
the suggestive outline with a discussion of the relationship of
the various components and discernible steps in the processes of
human development. Erikson's epigenetics provide a much more
specific, comprehensive, and therefore more satisfactory treatment of these processes. It is here that Erikson's ego psychology has made its most important contribution to the methodology
of cultural interpretation. Erikson grounds the source of psychic
energy solidly in the biology of the human organism, and then
clarifies the manner in which this energy is mediated through
certain structural givens and patterned additionally in interaction with the social world. As we have seen above, he has
used these insights to present a more comprehensive "metabolism
of generations" than did Dilthey.

Psychohistory and the Problem of Authority

A general model and method of interpretation must, of
course, be appropriate to the particular problem under investigation. We have stated the problem as that of investigating
possible parallels in the structure and dynamics of authority
as manifest in the personality of a religious leader, in his
thought, and in his institutional relationships. Is Erikson's
method applicable to the problem of authority? In answer to
this query, we note that a scrutiny of *Young Man Luther* reveals
that the investigation of Luther's "authority problem" is in
fact the fundamental theme of the monograph. This theme is
evident throughout the work, but nowhere is it more clearly
put than in the chapter, "Obedience--To Whom?" Erikson notes
there the overriding centrality of the problem of authority in
Luther's milieu, both familial and cultural:

> This conflictedness of Martin's early education,
> which was *in* and *behind* him when he entered the
> world of school and college, correspond to the con-
> flicts inherent in the ideological-historical uni-
> verse which lay *around* and *ahead* of him. The theo-
> logical problems which he tackled as a young adult
> of course reflected the peculiarly tenacious pro-
> blem of the domestic relationship to his own father;
> but this was true to a large extent because both
> problems, the domestic and the universal, were part
> of one ideological crisis: a crisis about the theory
> and practice, the power and responsibility, of the
> moral authority invested in fathers: on earth and in

heaven; at home, in the market-place, and in politics; in the castles, the capitals, and in Rome.
But it undoubtedly took a father and son of tena-
cious sincerity and almost criminal egotism to make
the most of this crisis, and to initiate a struggle
in which were combined elements of the drama of King
Oedipus and the passion of Golgotha, with an admix-
ture of cussedness made in Saxony.[41]

In a similar vein, Robert Coles, in discussing *Young Man
Luther*, understands the Oedipal drama described by Erikson in
terms of authority conflict. Note the following illuminative
passage:

> If Luther did anything for Western man he helped him
> examine once again the priorities of his various alle-
> giances. Whom do we obey, and with what degree of com-
> mitment and order? Luther first challenged, then dis-
> obeyed the authority of authorities, the Pope;...Luther
> had a 'problem'; he was rebellious, outspokenly so....
> Clearly, Erikson will have to 'deal' with Luther's
> struggle to obey; with his disobedience; with his per-
> sistent and extraordinary defiance in the face of the
> Pope's censure; with his urge to speak that defiance
> ....[42]

We could continue documenting in Erikson's writings the
centrality of the problem of authority and the applicability of
his method for interpreting parallels between patterns of authority in the religious leader's psychological development, his
thought, and his institutional relationships. It should suffice
here, however, to note that Erikson's work has not only provided
us with a basic interpretive model appropriate to the study of
authority in religious leadership. He has, as well, made significant strides in the application of that method to the *specific
problem* to which this study addresses itself.

Erikson and the Problem of Reductionism

In the foregoing discussion I have attempted to make it
clear that the fundamentals of Erikson's theory and method in
reality constitute a *verstehende Psychologie* which is by no means
alien to Wach's most basic methodological commitments. The question will inevitably be raised, however, as to whether Wach's
criticism of reductionistic psychologizing does not apply to
Erikson's work. Doesn't the scientific materialism of Erikson's
spiritual father, Sigmund Freud, manifest itself in Erikson's

theoretical and methodological orientation? Erikson has never clearly disassociated himself from the metapsychological mythology of Freud, nor has he expressed any intention of doing so.

Don Browning in a recent article, "Body and Existence: A Problem in Interpretation," addresses precisely this problem.[43] He notes that there are at least two ways of reading Erikson. Indeed, one can read Erikson and find evidence that he is truly in the camp of the "psychologizers." But Browning believes that Erikson's theory and method lends itself to another reading which precludes classifying Erikson as just another reductionistic psychologizer:

> Our point is this: Erikson is ambivalent. Sometimes he appears to be discerning the meaning of a human phenomenon by reducing it to its earliest infantile origins. Insofar as Erikson does this he has not moved beyond the reductionistic tendencies common to most psychoanalytic interpretations. I am suggesting that Erikson should be read in another way, a way I believe is entirely consistent with the totality of his thought. Actually Erikson does not reduce human symbolic phenomena to infantile origins so much as does he seek for the modal analogy which unites and weaves together different levels of symbolic meaning--infantile and adult, cultural and individual, religious and personal. Basic archetypal modes and learned variations of these modes constitute the analogical nucleus which holds together the various dimensions of symbolic reality.[44]

Browning clearly believes that Erikson's interpretive methodology can be separated from the more crass elements of Erikson's metapsychological mythology--those based on scientific materialism and leading to reductionism--and that in Erikson's work can be found the fundamentals of a method adequate to the *sui generis* nature of cultural and religious phenomena. In summary, it is Erikson's fundamental theory and method, not his Freudian myth, that meet the requirements for an adequate method as stipulated by Wach.

Browning's thesis has received some convincing, though indirect, support in the publication of the recent monograph, *Ego and Instinct: The Psychoanalytic View of Human Nature--Revised,* by Daniel Yankelovich and William Barrett.[45] They argue that the clinical research and interpretive method of psychoanalysis not only *can,* but *must* be freed from the scientistic and reductionistic metapsychological tenets of Freud. In their view,

the Freudian metapsychology can never be reinterpreted radically
enough to give an adequate theoretical and conceptual framework
for what actually occurs in psychoanalytic practice and interpretation. This inadequacy of Freud's metapsychology is grounded
in its foundation on an outmoded view of physics and of scientific
theory and method in general. Yankelovich and Barrett posit that
an adequate metapsychology must take into account modern physics
and scientific theory. Following the maxim that "ontology dictates epistemology," they procede to offer a heuristic sketch
of what an adequate metapsychology might look like.[46]

The ontology of human being and becoming to which they point
consists of what they call "constitutive principles," principles
which focus on the structure and dynamics of human experience.[47]
Accordingly, an event "cannot be reduced to the sum of its parts
nor explained away by reference to its origins."[48] The most
fundamental law of nature expressed in human life is "the tendency to form new wholes or structures."[49]

> This coming into being of new gestalts is the princi-
> ple of creativity in nature...no description of human
> experience is possible without taking this phenomenon
> into account--as is well recognized in certain branches
> of psychology. Gestalt psychology, holism, the or-
> ganismic point of view, and even systems analysis, all
> insist upon the irreducibility of wholes to their con-
> stituent parts....We are proposing a radical extension
> of holistic thinking to cover virtually every aspect
> of human experience, from the most minutely elaborated
> personality traits to the broadest social institutions.[50]

The authors then move on to summarize their conclusions
and proposals for an adequate theory of the constitutive principles of human nature:

> In brief, then, human experience is characterized by
> the dynamic development of synergistic structures
> over time, no one structure being reducible to the
> other...biologically rooted tendencies...must en-
> counter fortunate environmental circumstances to
> permit the fundamental structures of personality
> to develop. This interactive process goes on through-
> out the whole of life.[51]

The new metapsychology must present a clear theory of a
developmental maturational schedule including a theory of
structure formation.

In psychoanalytic theory, the concept of a maturational schedule is suggested both by Anna Freud's
line of development and Erikson's epigenetic principle. But Anna Freud holds her view within the
traditional metapsychology, and Erikson has developed
his own principle without at the same time challenging
the orthodox metatheory. For this reason, the power
of such concepts has not fully emerged; only when
psychoanalysis is cleared of its old philosophical
base will this all-important concept of a maturational
schedule be free to generate the sublety, depth of
understanding and detail of documentation that it war-
rants....We propose to link the concept of a maturational schedule with a theory of learning and structure formation to form a single constitutive principle.[52]

In the above statement, Erikson is damned with very faint

praise. When, however, one notes the basic lines of their

emerging argument in the text and their heavy dependence upon

Erikson as a resource, one is led to question how far their

"ontological reconstruction" has in fact gone beyond Erikson.[53]

Moreover, we would assert that Erikson's interpretive method as

presented above exhibits the fundamentals of the "epistemological

reconstruction" which Yankelovich and Barrett call for. They

view psychoanalytic "explanation as a special kind of descrip-

tion."[54] In psychoanalytic interpretation as in historical

interpretation, what has been denoted "causes" are "really more

or less systematized descriptions of social structures and events

interlinked in time."[55] If a description is to have explanatory

power, it must: (1) "show a tightly disciplined selectivity"

which is based on a thematic analysis of patterns seen against

the backdrop of the person's current maturational needs and at-

tendant "problem" in adaptation;[56] (2) present the case or event

at several levels of generality at the same time, including

references to concrete incidents unique to *this* particular per-

son and viewing these incidents against the background of data

relevant to the general patterns which have been established

regarding behavior of others in an analogous situation;[57] and

(3) it must address the question of *purpose* as well as *process*.

The interpreter

not only asks how the process unfolds but why. The
adaptive point of view in psychoanalysis describes
why a person's behavior or style helps him to cope
with the world and its demands: it thus functions
as an ultimate explanation of why a person behaves
as he does.[58]

It is hard to see how this approach differs in any significant way from that which Erikson has offered. Browning, I believe, would argue as I would that the fundamentals of the "reconstruction" proposed in *Ego and Instinct* are already implicit in the work of Erikson and that many, if not most, of the criticisms made of Erikson's theory and method are in fact based on the narrow and reductive reading of Erikson's works.[59] This is not to say, however, that they do not point us in a helpful way to the tasks of developing the implicit aspects of Erikson's approach and of offering a more adequate "covering theory" and conceptuality for the fundamentals of his interpretive method. I will return to these and other issues in the last chapter of this work. It will suffice here, however, to indicate that I conclude on the basis of the above discussion that the fundamentals of Erikson's interpretive theory and method can be separated from the scientistic and reductionistic assumptions of the Freudian metapsychology. Wach, I conclude, would be able to accept Erikson's psychosocial as I employ it as a valid and appropriate basis for the task of investigating religious phenomena.

At this point, however, we must table the theoretical argument and turn again to the problem which led to these methodological inquiries: the problem of authority as it is manifest in the life and thought of John Wesley.

John Wesley and the Problem of Authority: The Structure of the Study

In order to complete this study three steps must be taken: first, it must be asked whether patterns of authority relations can be discerned in Wesley's search for selfhood, and those patterns, if any, will have to be described and illustrated; second, the same question will be asked and answered with regard to his thought and institutional relationships; and third, any parallels or continuities which may be found between the various configurations must be isolated and interpreted.

The second and third chapters will deal with the first of these tasks by focusing on the question of how Wesley changed from a defeated and despairing, unsuccessful missionary pastor to a powerful and effective field preacher and founder of a religious movement in the course of a few months.

The fourth chapter will address the second task by raising the question of how Wesley came to be both accused and praised, depending on one's perspective, as being a "Papist" on the one hand, and a Calvinist on the other. I will give particular attention, among other themes, to Wesley's viewpoint toward Calvinism.

In the fifth chapter I will complete the necessary analysis and data gathering for the second task by focusing on the ever-problematic question of Wesley's ambivalent relationship with the institution and authority of the Anglican church.

The last chapter will address the third of the necessary interpretive tasks and offer analysis, conclusions and implications related to the problem of authority and initiative in religious leadership. It will conclude with my own heuristic reconstruction of a "covering" conceptuality and systematic orientation which will address both the constitutive ontological and epistemological principles implicit in Erikson's theory and method as it relates to the problem of interpretation in personal, cultural and religious phenomena.

CHAPTER II

THE ACTIVE SELF: FROM ASPIRATION TO RESIGNATION

The place of John Wesley in the religious history of the
West is a secure one. A major figure in eighteenth century
English religion, his career as an evangelist, reformer, and
founder of an important religious movement has had an influence
reaching far beyond both his century and his country. Few men
of the England of his day have received such widespread and
continuing interest. With only a few exceptions, Wesley has
had more biographies and other studies written about him than
any other Englishman of the eighteenth century.[1] Given the
interest of the psychohistorian in personal documents, it should
be reiterated that we have more autobiographical data on Wesley
than on any other leader in the history of the Christian church.[2]
Beginning with his first "conversion" in 1725 he kept a narrative record of the meaningful events of his life. Add the richly
autobiographical correspondence and it becomes clear that Wesley
is an ideal subject for psychohistorical investigation. Indeed,
the historical importance of the figure and the accompanying
availability of personal data invites the scholar to undertake
a full-length psychohistorical narrative of the entirety of the
leader's life.[3] The purpose of this chapter and the two which
follow represent a far less ambitious undertaking. In these
essays we will carefully limit our focus to certain interpretive
problems which, though of fundamental importance to any larger
psychohistorical study of Wesley, relate closely to the problem
of authority in Wesley's life and thought. Let us turn now to
the first of these interpretive problems and to the psychohistorical analysis from which we hope to glean insights into the
structure and dynamics of authority in the life and thought of
John Wesley.

The Interpretive Problem

In his critical and comparative study of Wesley biographies
written since 1850, Herbert Loring has noted that the principal

25

areas of Wesley's life which have led to conflicting interpretations by biographers have been:

> ...the King William episode, the 'sinner' at Charter-
> house, the nature of Holy Orders, the identity of
> Varanese, the conversation with Spangenburg upon
> arriving in Georgia, the Sophie Hopkey affair, the
> conversion of 1738, field-preaching, the Grace Murray
> affair, Mrs. Wesley, and Wesley's funeral services.[4]

Our analysis in this chapter will deal with materials which
have relevance to the interpretation of all of these areas, but
which will focus on the important interrelationship between two
of them: the conversion of 1738 and the beginning of field-
preaching. The eminent Wesley scholar Albert Outler, in a response to a query regarding important issues in a psychohistorical analysis of Wesley, has posed the interpretive problem which
will occupy us in this chapter:

> Your real problem, I would suggest, is to explain
> how it happened that Wesley's achievement and im-
> pact up to his 37th birthday (June, 1739) were
> negligible; if he'd died at any time before, he'd
> not rate even a footnote in the history books.
> After that--wow! But what happened, and how?
> Aldersgate doesn't explain it, really--moreover
> there are no decisive mutations in the substance
> of his theology or his large assortment of bias
> and predilections. It was a full year after Alders-
> gate before 'the real Mr. Wesley' (i.e., the leader
> of the Revival) stood up. And all the rest of his
> life, he retained a neurotic character-structure
> that would be a shrink's happy hunting ground....[5]

Outler, in his *John Wesley*, has summarized the conclusions
which underlie the above statement.[6] While other biographers
and Wesley scholars have emphasized the Aldersgate experience
as *the* turning point in Wesley's life, Outler notes that the
experience is actually one of a series of significant experiences
and is "neither first nor last nor most climactic."[7] The Aldersgate experience was followed by a "long series of spiritual up-
heavals and frustration which lasted well into the spring of
1739."[8] According to Outler, it was the journey to Bristol
which brought Wesley to the "threshold of his true vocation."[9]
Wesley's field-preaching at Bristol was met with an almost un-
believable positive response. The great crowds were obviously
deeply affected by his preaching, and the experience marked not
only the beginning of the Revival but the full maturing of the

revivalist as well.[10] Outler has characterized this change in
Wesley:

> It is most impressive to observe the marked effect
> this success at Bristol had on Wesley's spiritual
> equilibrium. Up to this point the story is full of
> anxiety, insecurity, futility. Hereafter, the in-
> stances of spiritual disturbances drop off sharply
> and rarely recur, even in the full records of a very
> candid man....For the next half-century, in failure
> and in triumph, tumult and peace, obloquy and fame,
> the picture rarely varies: a man with an overmaster-
> ing mission, acutely self-aware but rarely ruffled,
> often in stress but always secure on a rock-steady
> foundation.[11]

Outler has posed the question for us by describing the remarkable changes which took place in Wesley's life in the months
between his return from Georgia and the beginning of the field-
preaching. Our task in this psychohistorical analysis is to
offer some insights into the "how?" of this transformation.

Erikson and the Interpretive Conceptuality

Those familiar with Erikson's studies of Luther and Gandhi
are aware of the usefulness of his concepts and insights in the
interpretation of the formation of personal and vocational identity. Clearly, in Erikson's terminology, the events which Outler
has described mark the formation of Wesley's mature "ego-identity." Let us examine briefly some of the psychological and
historical dynamics which are involved in the formation of such
a mature ego-synthesis or ego-identity.

Erikson has summarized the three elements of the process
by which a person's individuality comes into existence and main-
tains continuity over time:

> The first of these...is the *biological process*, by
> which an organism comes to be a hierarchic organiza-
> tion of organ systems living out its life cycle.
> The second is the *social process*, by which organisms
> come to be organized in groups which are geographi-
> cally, historically, and culturally defined. What
> may be called the *ego process* is the organizational
> principle by which the individual maintains himself
> as a coherent personality with a sameness and conti-
> nuity both in his self-experience and in his actuality
> for others.[12]

While the interaction of the processes described here apply
to all stages of the life cycle, our attention will be focused

on the interrelation of these processes in the individual's task
of *identity formation* in adolescence and early adulthood. For
Erikson, the concept of *personal identity* means more than simply
an individual's name and station in the community. It includes
a subjective sense of continuous existence and coherent memory.[13]
And the broader term psychosocial identity points to a more complex integration of elements at once subjective and objective,
individual and socio-historical.[14] Not only does one have to
develop the subjective sense of identity--a sense of sameness
and continuity as an individual, but this sense of being aware
of one's individuality and continuity as a self must be shared
and confirmed by others in the objective, external world. For
Erikson, the development of a mature psychosocial identity requires:

> ...a community of people whose traditional values
> become significant to the growing person even as his
> growth assumes relevance for them....Psychosocial
> identity thus depends on a complementarity of an in-
> ner (ego) synthesis in the individual and of role
> integration in his group.15

The development of a psychosocial identity cannot be completed before adolescence and becomes indispensable at the end
of adolescence when:

> ...the grown-up body grows together, when matured
> sexuality seeks partners, and when the fully de-
> veloped mind begins to envisage a historical per-
> spective and seeks new loyalties--all developments
> which must fuse with each other in a new sense of
> sameness and continuity.16

At this time identifications made in childhood must find
some successful integrative alignment with urgent, yet often
tentative, new self-identifications and role choices. The magnitude of this synthesizing task as experienced by the individual
leads to what Erikson has called an "identity crisis."[17] Identity, therefore, is not merely the sum of childhood identifications or simply an additional set of identifications. Identity
formation begins:

> ...where the usefulness of identification ends. It
> arises from the selective repudiation and mutual as-
> similation of childhood identifications, and their
> absorption in a new configuration, which in turn, is
> dependent on the process by which a *society* (often
> through subsocieties) *identifies the young individual,*

recognizing him as somebody who had to become the
way he is, and who, being the way he is, is taken
for granted.[18]

Thus, while the end of adolescence is marked by an overt
identity crisis, identity *formation* cannot be said to begin nor
end with adolescence. Rather, it is a lifelong process of development which is largely unconscious to both the individual
and his society and which has roots which reach back to the
earliest beginnings of self-recognition and mutual recognition
in infancy.[19]

The growing child must develop a sense of awareness that
his "individual way of mastering experience, his ego-synthesis,
is a successful variant of a group identity," one in accord with
the group's space-time and life-plan.[20] The self-esteem engendered by this growing sense of mastery in the synthesizing task
gradually grows into the "conviction that the ego is capable of
integrating effective steps toward a tangible collective future,
that it is developing into a well-organized ego within a social
reality."[21] The process of identity formation, then, emerges:

> ...as an *evolving configuration*--a configuration
> which is gradually established by successive ego
> syntheses and resyntheses throughout childhood; it
> is a configuration gradually integrating *constitu-*
> *tional givens, idiosyncratic libidinal needs,*
> *favored capacities, significant identifications,*
> *effective defenses, successful sublimations,* and
> *consistent roles.*[22]

In order to differentiate this maturing configuration of
identity from simple personal identity, Erikson has named this
emerging psychosocial identity *ego-identity*.

> Ego-identity then, in its subjective aspect, is the
> awareness of the fact that there is a self-sameness
> and continuity to the ego's synthesizing methods,
> *the style of one's individuality,* and that this
> style coincides with the sameness and continuity
> of one's *meaning for significant others* in the
> immediate community.[23]

Thus the emerging ego-identity bridges the early childhood
stages, "when the body and parent images were given their specific meanings," and the later stages of adolescence when "a
variety of social roles becomes available and increasingly co-
ercive."[24] Here the objective aspect of the task of the formation of ego-identity becomes critical. The individual must find

an appropriate *ideology*, a systematized set of ideas and ideals
grounded in a communal orientation, which can lend support to
the developing wholeness of identity; and an appropriate role
to which he can commit himself and find, in the development of
a personal and/or professional vocational identity, an outlet
for those developing capacities for loyalty and competence which
Erikson has termed *fidelity*.[25]

> Fidelity, when fully matured, is the strength of dis-
> ciplined devotion. It is gained in the involvement
> of youth in such experiences as reveal the essence of
> the era they are to join--as the beneficiaries of its
> tradition, as the practitioners and innovators of its
> technology, as renewers of its ethical strength, as
> rebels bent on the destruction of the outlived, and
> as deviants with deviant commitments.[26]

Thus the formation of ego-identity is based on a new set of
processes of identification, with both significant persons and
ideological forces, giving importance to the life of the individual by relating it to a living community and to ongoing history, and engaging the newly developed individual identity with
some communal solidarity.[27] Here, then, life history intersects
with history, individuals are confirmed in their identities, and
societies may be regenerated in their life style. To enter history, according to Erikson, each individual must find an identity
--personal and vocational--which is in some way consonant with
his own childhood and perceived traditions, and with an ideological promise in the perceptible historical process.[28]

The onset of the identity crisis marks the coming of the
time when the individual feels forced to choose between the
various available and socially meaningful models for a workable
combination of his identification fragments. Now his ego must
subsume in fewer and fewer images and personified *Gestalten* the
fragments and loose ends of all infantile identifications.[29]
The usefulness of the various models which he has at his disposal
depends on the way in which they simultaneously meet the requirements of his maturational stage, his own style of adaptation or
ego-synthesis, and the demands of his culture.[30] The prime danger
of this crisis is the threat of *identity confusion*, the state of
being bewildered by the plethora of images and feeling unable to
formulate an appropriate and workable synthesis.[31] And the more
numerous the available models for personal, occupational, sexual

and ideological commitments, the more difficult the task of formulating an appropriate and workable ego-identity.[32]

According to Erikson the onset of identity confusion can
manifest itself in:

> ...excessively prolonged moratoria (Hamlet offers an
> exalted example); in repeated attempts to end the
> moratorium with sudden choices, that is, to play with
> historical possibilities, and then to deny that some
> irreversible commitment has already taken place; and
> sometimes also in severe regressive pathology....[33]

In Erikson's terminology, a *moratorium* is a period of delay
granted to an individual by his society in which he does not
have to take on irrevocable adult commitments. It may be characterized by provocative playfulness or deep, if transitory, commitment by the youth. It may not be consciously experienced as
a temporary commitment; rather, the individual may feel deeply
committed and learn only much later that what he had taken so
seriously was in fact only a period of transition. When he is
ready--and hopefully not before--the moratorium ends in a more
or less ceremonial confirmation of commitment on the part of
society.[34]

The final identity, as formulated at the beginning of responsible adulthood, is superordinated to any single identification with individuals of the past and to any fixed model for
identity. It includes all significant identifications, elements
of one or more identity models, and picks up the threads of
various aspects of the cultural and familial traditions of the
individual.[35] The final synthesis, then, is firmly grounded in
the identifications, models, and traditions of the individual's
past. Yet through the process of identity formation he has been
able to transform them, to make them his own in order to fashion
a unique and reasonably coherent whole.[36]

The process described above, then, is a conceptualization
in psychological terminology of the personal and religious pilgrimage which culminated in Wesley's commitment to the vocational
role of evangelist and leader of the Methodist movement. We
turn now to a reconstruction of the significant family tradition
which set the stage for Wesley's quest for identity and of the
events which can illuminate the unique structure and dynamics
of that quest.

Family Tradition: The Political Milieu

John Wesley once told his friend Adam Clarke that "If I
were to write my own life I should begin it before I was born."[37]
It is quite obvious that we too must begin before his birth.
Some of the most important persons and events for understanding
the development of his identity are, not surprisingly, found in
the lives of his grandparents and parents before the time of his
birth. We could not, of course, even begin here to sketch in
any depth the lives and personalities of his grandfathers, to
say nothing of the complex and intriguing Samuel and Susanna
Wesley. We can, nevertheless, relate a few traits and events
which can help us illuminate the influence prior generations
had on the life of our subject.

The history of England, both religious and political, in
the century preceding the birth of John Wesley could be characterized as a century of intense authority conflict. This conflict had roots deep in the tapestry of the prior history of
Europe, and became profoundly manifest in England with the break
of Henry VIII with Rome. Under both Henry and his daughter
Elizabeth (1558-1603) countless Englishmen were executed over
the question of the proper allegiance in matters religious and
political. During the reign of Elizabeth the lines of authority
conflict took on a new front. In seeking to unite the English
nation in an anti-Roman direction, she had allowed a freedom of
belief and practice within the Anglican church which soon led
to the growth of a strong Puritanism.[38] The increasing strength
and dissenting policies of the Puritans issued in 1567 in a
split in the Anglican church, with the Puritans separating and
beginning to hold services in small private groups.[39]

Under James I (1603-25) and Charles I (1625-49) an open
struggle against Puritanism became official Anglican church
policy.[40] The policies of the Crown increasingly came to be
interpreted as moving toward "Popery" and led to the Great
Rebellion (1642-49).[41] In 1649 Charles I was executed and
Cromwell became the Puritan dictator. Yet in 1660 the pendulum
moved back again, and the authority of the monarchy was restored
with the beginning of the reign of Charles II. Charles renewed
Queen Elizabeth's Act of Uniformity in 1662, followed it by the
Conventicle Act of 1664, and the even harsher Five Mile Act of

1665. These were frontal attacks on the Puritans, designed to re-establish Anglican authority, to break up Puritan congregations, and to keep Puritan ministers away from their former parishes.[42]

The successor of Charles II, James II, moved too far toward Roman Catholicism for comfort and was dethroned by the revolution of 1688. William of Orange, a Protestant, changed the direction again in 1689 by issuing the Toleration Act.[43] Yet intense authority conflict continued. The name "Non-Jurors" came to characterize those who did not believe that William of Orange had succeeded legally to the monarchy. Again the question of allegiances took its toll as many clergymen refused to take the oath of loyalty to him and suffered in a manner much as the dissenters before them.

William's successor, Queen Anne, once more began to promote a "High Church" line and the position of dissent was once more threatened as High Church leaders such as Sacheverell questioned the validity of the Act of Toleration and the legality of the current ecclesiastical practice.[44]

That John Wesley's family and personal history was embroiled in these events of acute authority conflict in the English society will become evident in the following brief account of events in the lives of his grandfathers and parents. The authority conflict between the established church and dissent, between Jurors and Non-Jurors became an important part of Wesley's family tradition. Let us now turn to an examination of some of the "agents" of that tradition.

The Grandfathers

John Wesley's unorthodox approach to ministry had been brought to the attention of the Bishop of Bristol, and John was summoned before the Bishop to give an account of his actions. The young minister gave his defense, emphasizing his Biblical justification for his ministry, his determination to conform to the practice of primitive Christianity, the fruit of visible results, and the central aim of conversion. The Bishop's response was to let the young man leave unhindered in his work.[45]

Those familiar with the career of John Wesley the evangelist might well think the account of the above event to refer to

the encounter of Wesley with Joseph Butler, Bishop of Bristol,
in 1739. In fact, the event recounted above is a much earlier
encounter between Wesley's grandfather and the then Bishop of
Bristol, Gilbert Ironside, in 1661. Wesley's biographer Martin
Schmidt has noted that the event not only can be looked upon as
a prelude to the grandson's later encounter, but that the theological and ecclesiological themes expressed during the interview
are in many ways parallel to those of the grandson.[46] That the
later John Wesley had access to information about his grandfather
seems clear. According to Nehemiah Curnock, it is probable that
he may have used an empty book of his grandfathers to write down
his own first attempts at journal keeping.[47] Adam Clarke has
also suggested that it may well have been the example of the
grandfather that led young John Wesley to begin keeping a journal.[48] It is certain, at any rate, that Wesley published the
account of his grandfather's encounter in his own journal, sup-
posedly from family papers.[49]

For our purposes it should suffice to relate a few biographical notes on the life of John Wesley senior. Born the son of a
minister and physician, Bartholomew Wesley, in the year 1636,
the first John Wesley matriculated at Oxford in 1651 and studied
theology and the Oriental languages.[50] After receiving his B.A.
(1655) and his M.A. (1657), he became affiliated with a Separatist
congregation in Melcombe Regis. Receiving a commission from the
group, he became a traveling teacher and preacher in the surrounding communities. In 1658 he became minister of the church at
Winterbourne Whitechurch.[51] As he was without episcopal ordination, this was a congregational "call" which was in keeping with
the local practice of the time. But two years later came the
restoration of the Stuarts, and a faction within his congregation
raised a question with the Bishop of Bristol regarding the legitimacy of his ministry. The encounter noted above was a result
of this complaint. A complete account of the dialogue of the
interview is found in Clarke's *Memoirs of the Wesley Family*.[52]
Though he had been promised that he would not be disturbed, the
pressure upon him continued to increase until in August 1662 he
had to leave the church. He found a small congregation at Poole,
Dorsetshire that desired to have him as its minister, but soon
the Conventicle Act outlawed even that post. Repeatedly arrested,

he continued his ministry as a traveling teacher and evangelist. Schmidt indicates that as a result of the hardships brought about by continuing persecution Wesley died a premature death in 1670.[53]

The maternal grandfather, Samuel Annesley, though in a much less dramatic way, was also prophetic of the famous grandson. One of the central intentions of the Act of Uniformity was to prevent any further ordinations of Presbyterian ministers in England. Some leading Puritan ministers were intimidated by this prohibition, but not the grandfather of John Wesley. He continued the practice of ordaining presbyters in secret until after the revolution of 1688, and on June 22, 1694, he undertook the first public ordination of dissenting ministers in his meeting house at Little St. Helen's.[54] John Wesley was also going to find himself in a position in which undertaking presbyterian ordination seemed required by the circumstances and justified theologically--though also a flagrant violation of established ecclesiastical law. On September 1, 1784, John Wesley himself began to ordain ministers for the work of his movement in America.[55]

Born in 1620, Samuel Annesley was a member of a prominent aristocratic family, and, like the two John Wesleys, was an Oxford graduate. Ordained in 1644, he was made a naval chaplain by the Earl of Warwick.[56] After leaving the fleet he had a surprisingly successful ministry at Cliff in Kent with a congregation notorious for its "scandalous conduct."[57] He then moved to London and served successively the Church of St. John the Apostle and St. Giles, Cripplegate, two of the largest Puritan congregations in the city.[58] Soon, however, he too suffered the consequences of the Act of Uniformity and was ejected from St. Giles in 1662. Unlike most in his situation, he was independently wealthy and did not suffer economic hardship.[59]

After his ejection, he preached for a number of small groups of dissenters and soon became the pastoral leader of a congregation at Little St. Helen's. There he was successful in erecting a meeting house in which the group could hold their worship and other meetings.[60]

Samuel Annesley continued to be a prominent leader in dissenting circles until his death in 1696.[61] Like his famous grandson, he undertook a great deal of charitable work with the

poor and sought to distribute Bibles and other literature to those
who had none.[62] He also published a volume of sermons dealing
with the Puritan theology of conscience and the conscience-guided
life.[63] John Wesley was later to indicate his appreciation for
the views of his maternal grandfather by publishing many excerpts
from his sermons in *A Christian Library*, which according to
Wesley represented "...the choicest pieces of practical divinity
which have been published in the English language."[64] No doubt
Annesley's daughter Susanna, the mother of John Wesley, was the
chief agent of the transmission of his influence to John Wesley.
With this introduction, then, let us turn to the children of
dissent, Samuel and Susanna Wesley.

Samuel and Susanna: Renegades from Dissent

Although both Samuel Wesley (1662-1735) and Susanna Annesley
(1669-1742) were reared by courageous and committed dissenters,
neither was content to remain within the camp of the Puritans.
Samuel at first seemed to be following in the footsteps of his
father by beginning studies for the ministry at a dissenting
academy. Given an assignment to vindicate the righteousness of
the cause of dissent, his research seemed to him to be a defense
--not of dissent--but of the Anglican church. Instead of facing
the wrath of his Puritan relatives, he quietly packed and left
for Oxford. Soon Samuel Wesley was hurling literary harpoons
at dissent and its academies from the secure, high Anglican foundation of Exeter College.[65]

It has been suggested by some scholars that Samuel's real
motive for leaving the ranks of dissent was that he was ambitious, and believed that real possibilities for success lay in
the Anglican communion.[66] But whether it was ambition or the
appeal of the zealous royalist orthodoxy of Oxford with its rich
intellectual apprehension of the seventeenth century Anglican
tradition, Samuel soon became a loyal Anglican and an, if not
fanatic, then at least stern and often undiscerning opponent
and critic of dissent.[67]

Whatever his reasons for leaving dissent, he found a willing
compatriot in rebellion in the person of Susanna Annesley, the
daughter of London's leading dissenter. They had met at a wedding in 1682 when Susanna was still in her early adolescence,

but was already manifesting the independence and precocious mind in religious matters that were to mark her adulthood.[68] Impressed by the cocksure young Samuel and by the intellectually impressive way in which he presented the case for Anglicanism, she left her father and his dissent to convert to the Anglican church and marry Samuel in 1688.[69]

If Samuel was ambitious for a life of ecclesiastical preferment, and if Susanna believed the pretty picture which had undoubtedly been sketched of their future together, both were to be cruelly disappointed. After a brief stint as a naval chaplain, he was appointed to the small living of South Ormsby in 1690 and then to Epworth in 1695.[70] Even when the living of nearby Wroot was added, the living was a poor one indeed. The couple was to spend the remaining thirty-eight years of their life together in this obscure, poorly endowed assignment in the backwaters of the realm.[71] Susanna was soon to discover that the Samuel she had chosen to marry was neither as gentle nor as effective a minister and provider as the first Samuel in her life. Though certainly possessed of a modicum of scholarly and poetic talent, she discovered that Samuel Wesley also possessed an arrogant manner and bearing which far surpassed in its claims the extent of his real talents and virtues.[72] Even a fair and objective appraisal (which most have not been) must present her husband as a tremendously domineering yet ineffective man whose insensitivity to both his parishioners and family knew no bounds.

An impractical man, and from all accounts an extremely poor ecclesiastical tactician with regard both to the hierarchy and to his own parish, he found himself in a remote, undesirable parish, so poor that his family was always deep in debt and often hungry, and with parishioners that, given his personality and opinions, hated him with a venom. This hatred went so deep that the parishioners—when unable to express their feelings sufficiently violently with him and the family—would maim his dogs and farm animals.[73] They even went so far as to, during fits of rage, set the crops and rectory afire in an attempt to burn them out.[74]

In the midst of all this, Samuel remained the poetic dreamer, living more in his fantasies of greatness as a scholar or missionary than in the harsh realities of his parish or family responsibilities. He lived to see his "scholarly writings" and "poetry" published and circulated and hoped at some future date to escape Epworth for the mission field.[75] These dreams were bought at a high price to his family. His income, though small, would have been sufficient, through careful management, for even his large family. But such mundane matters were not for him, and were left to his wife Susanna along with the responsibilities of raising the steadily growing family.[76]

It is not surprising, then, that Susanna's ability and independence in such a situation would add much to an already potent formula for domestic dissension.

Authority and Parental Conflicts

In order to illustrate the way in which issues of authority and legitimacy, manifest in myriad ways, were the foci of conflict in the family circle, we must examine three important areas in which the conflict became intense: the religious, the parental, and the political.

In theological matters Susanna and her husband seldom entered into severe conflict. Both were orthodox in their positions, and a mutual respect facilitated their discussions. Ecclesiastical practice, however, was a different matter. Samuel's rejection of dissent had manifested itself in a rigid and unbending scrupulousness in terms of Anglican canon law. He applied the most insignificant detail of prescribed practice in his parish without regard for the discomfort or inconvenience it caused his parishioners, their sympathy for a freer style in the mode of dissent, or for their traditional hatred of heavy-handed authority of any kind.[77] Susanna was far more pastorally inclined and sensitive toward the parishioners. Her rejection of dissent, though irrevocable in most areas, was not so totalistic in character that she could not bend the rules when human need or the perceived will of God seemed to call for it. In later years her flexibility would influence John Wesley in his willingness to use practices which reeked of dissent.[78]

But in the Epworth parish such flexibility and sensitivity was suspect. When Samuel left for Convocation in 1710, he left an incompetent curate in charge of the parish.[79] Susanna began to hold a small prayer meeting on Sunday evenings for her children

and servants. During these meetings she would lead the singing
of Psalms, read prayers, and deliver a short sermon usually taken
from the files of her husband.[80] The services, however, soon
became extremely popular with the parishioners, and soon more
were attending her services than those held by the curate on
Sunday mornings. The curate soon complained to her husband,
and Samuel wrote to reprimand her, saying that there was no precedent for such practice, that the meetings smacked of a dissenting conventicle, and that they jeopardized the regular worship
of the church.[81]

She answered this charge by pointing to the good that was
being done, to the increase of good will among the parishioners
toward the church and its ministry, and by asserting that the
meetings could in no way be harmful. She closed her defense
with the following appeal to her husband:

> Now, I beseech you, weigh all these things in
> an impartial balance. On the one side, the honour
> of Almighty God, the doing much good to many souls,
> and the friendship of the best among whom we live;
> on the other--if folly, impiety, and vanity may
> abide in the scale against so ponderous a weight
> --the senseless objections of a few scandalous per-
> sons, laughing at us, and censuring us as precise
> and hypocritical. And when you have duly considered
> all things, let me have your positive determination.
> I need not tell you the consequences if you deter-
> mine to put an end to our meeting. You may easily
> perceive what prejudice it may raise in the minds
> of these people against Inman especially, who has
> had so little wit as to speak publicly against it.
> I can now keep them to the church; but if it be
> laid aside, I doubt they will never go to hear him
> more, at least those who come from the lower end of
> the town. But if this be continued till you return,
> which will not be long, it may please God that their
> hearts may be so changed by that time, that they may
> love and delight in His public worship, so as never
> to neglect it more. If you do, after all, think fit
> to dissolve this assembly, do not tell me that you
> desire me to do it, for that will not satisfy my
> conscience: but send me your positive command, in
> such full and express terms, as may absolve me from
> all guilt and punishment for neglecting this oppor-
> tunity of doing good, when you and I shall appear
> before the great and awful tribunal of our Lord
> Jesus Christ.[82]

Thus, in effect, Susanna was defiant and would not discon-
tinue the services unless he would put his full priestly and
husbandly authority on the line in a command for her to desist.

She indicated that while she would obey the full force of his authority--recognized by her as legitimate--she felt herself claimed by a higher authority, an authority which he would have to face and answer to if he ordered her to stop the meetings.[83] Though he did not approve of her actions, the very forcefulness of her challenge put an end to his attempts to stop them. When he returned from Convocation the effectiveness of her work was evident in the good will which, from that point on, smoothed the relationships between the Wesley family and the Epworth parishioners.

Other conflicts were not so brief in duration or so easily resolved through Samuel's reluctance to do battle. A constant source of friction between the parents was their conflict over the exercise of parental discipline and authority.[84] In our discussion below of John Wesley's experience as a child in the Epworth parsonage, we will examine in some detail Susanna's account of the method she followed in the education of her children. It should suffice for our purposes here to note that she had developed a careful and comprehensive approach to rearing her children which stressed subduing the onrush of impulse and inculcated into the child an unquestioning obedience to a consistent and fair authority. Her method was expressed in a routine for every hour of the child's day and in rules which the child could grasp and to which he could accommodate himself. The very clarity of the rules for behavior and the patient consistency with which she enforced them were designed to help the child to develop his own capacity to reason and choose obedience, and, through obedience, certain approval. Elsie Harrison has captured for us Samuel's response to his wife's method:

> In this miracle effort of salvation for her children Susanna Wesley could look for little help from her good husband. On the contrary he had an unfortunate habit of putting sand in the workings of her dear, delightful method. He stalks between the lines of her letters as the agent of Bolshevism. Now Susanna had her fixed rules for the children's conduct, but her impetuous spouse would lose his temper and frighten her little Methodists quite out of their wits.[85]

That this disagreement on how to exercise parental authority would have influence on the children is without doubt. We will come back to this discussion when we characterize John Wesley's experience in the family circle.

With regard to political issues, the parents found themselves, if anything, disagreeing more violently than in other
areas of contention. Samuel and Susanna found themselves on
opposite sides in the controversy over the legitimacy of the
claim of William of Orange to the throne. John Wesley's own
words testify to the importance of this disagreement:

> Were I to write my own life, I should begin it
> *before I was born*, merely for the purpose of men-
> tioning a disagreement between my father and mother.
> 'Sukey,' said my father to my mother, one day after
> family prayer, 'why did you not say *amen* this morning
> to the prayer for the King?' 'Because,' said she,
> 'I do not believe the *Prince of Orange* to be King.'
> 'If that be the case,' said he, 'you and I must part;
> for if we have *two* Kings, we must have *two beds*,'
> My mother was inflexible. My father went immediately
> to his study; and, after spending some time with him-
> self, set out for London; where, being *convocation man*
> for the Diocese of Lincoln, he remained without visit-
> ing his own house for the remainder of the year. On
> March 8th in the following year, 1702, King William
> died; and as both my father and mother were regard as
> to the legitimacy of *Queen Anne's title*, the cause of
> their misunderstanding ceased; my father returned to
> Epworth, and conjugal harmony was restored.[86]

John Wesley's concise and calm account belies both the
intensity of the conflict and his own anger about it. In a
letter to a friend Susanna expressed her worry over her husband's
departure:

> ...I'm more easy in the thoughts of parting because
> I think we are not likely to live happily together
> ....I have six very small children, which though he
> tells me he will take good care of, yet if anything
> should befall him at Sea we should be in no very good
> condition....I've unsuccessfully represented to him
> the unlawfulness and unreasonableness of his Oath;
> that the Man in that case has no more power over his
> own body than the Woman over her's; that since I'm
> willing to let him quietly enjoy his own opinions,
> he ought not to deprive me of my little liberty of
> conscience.[87]

In fact, when Samuel returned home after some months, he
intended to stay only long enough to pack more of his things.
But the parishioners chose the time of his arrival to commit
arson and the rectory was set on fire.[88] The attending crisis
interrupted his plans, and, after a tenuous "reconciliation,"

he remained with his family. Nine months later John Benjamin Wesley was born on June 17, 1703.[89] It is hard to believe, given Susanna's account and the circumstances leading to the "reconciliation," that "conjugal harmony" either preceded or followed the episode.

John Wesley learned of these circumstances leading to his birth from his father in London on November 30, 1733.[90] That John was angered by this is evident by his interpretation of the manifestations of the family poltergeist as being intended to bring home to his father the sinfulness of his desertion of his wife in 1702: "I fear his vow was not forgotten before God."[91]

We have characterized the emotional climate of conflict in the Epworth parsonage. We now turn to the experience of John Wesley in that home.

Wesley's Experience in the Family Circle

We are fortunate to have Susanna's own summary of the method which she used to raise her children in order that we might better understand what John Wesley's experience was like as an infant and young child. The following sketch of her method will illustrate both the severity and the consistency of the maternal authority.

From birth the lives of the children were ordered according to a regular routine. There were definite times for eating, sleeping, and having a change of linen. At approximately one year of age, Susanna explains, "they were taught to fear the rod, and to cry softly, by which means they escaped abundance of correction which they might otherwise have had...." They could "eat and drink as much as they would," at mealtime, but were "not to call for any thing....Drinking or eating between meals was never allowed unless in case of sickness...."[92] After their supper, they were washed by seven o'clock and in bed by eight. Obedience was the fundamental foundation and goal of child development:

> In order to form the minds of the children, the
> first thing to be done is to conquer their will,
> and bring them to an obedient temper. To inform
> the understanding is a work of time; and must with
> children proceed by slow degrees, as they are able

to bear it: but the subjecting the will is a thing
which must be done at once, and the sooner the better; for by neglecting timely correction, they will
contract a stubbornness and obstinacy which are hardly ever conquered....When a child is corrected it must
be conquered....And when the will of a child is totally
subdued, and it is brought to revere and stand in awe
of the parents, then a great many childish follies and
inadvertences may be passed by....I insist upon con-
quering the will of children betimes, because this is
the only strong and rational foundation of a religious
education....[93]

Susanna was quite self-conscious regarding the religious
implications of her method. She noted that self-will is the
root of sin, and that the parent that encourages it is laying
the foundations of the child's damnation:

This is still more evident if we farther consider that
religion is nothing else than the doing the *will* of
God, and not our own; that the one grand impediment
to our temporal and eternal happiness being this *self-
will*, no indulgences of it can be trivial, no denial
unprofitable. Heaven or Hell depends on this alone.[94]

Mrs. Wesley also noted a number of "by-laws" which were observed by her, several of which are of interest to us here.
First, to prevent lying, a law was made if a child would confess
his transgression of a rule and promise "to amend" he would not
be beaten. Second, that no "sinful action" would ever remain
unpunished. Third that no child would ever be scolded or beaten
twice for the same fault, and, if they did not continue the error,
they were not to be upbraided regarding the transgression later.
Fourth, that every act of obedience would be praised and often
rewarded according to the merits of the particular case. And
that fifth, if a child did anything with the intention to please
or obey, even if the act lacked success in its intentions, the
obedience and intention should be noted and the child helped in
order to do better in the future.[95]

This discipline of the will was complemented by a discipline
of the mind manifest in an organized program for the education
of the child which occupied six hours of his day. This program
emphasized reading, writing, and religion. We shall see in a
later chapter how Susanna's role as tutor in theological matters
for John Wesley would reach far beyond the confines of the Epworth
nursery. If she was conscientious to a fault in her efforts with
all of the children, the following event led her to be even more
conscientious with John Wesley.

On the night of February the ninth, in the year 1709, the
Epworth parsonage was again on fire. This time it was unclear
whether the cause was arson or simply carelessness on the part
of Samuel Wesley. Nevertheless, the fire was not discovered in
time, and the entire family came close to losing their lives in
the holocaust. The fire spread so fast and the heat was so intense that no real attempt was made to rescue young "Jacky" from
his bedroom--although his father did kneel and commit the child's
soul to God.[96] Thanks to the efforts of a friendly parishioner,
however, young John was spotted at his bedroom window and pulled
through to safety. His mother, overwhelmed with thankfulness at
his "miraculous rescue," thereafter referred to him as the "Brand
plucked from the burning," and when she was alone made pious vows
on his behalf: "I do intend to be more especially careful of the
soul of this child."[97]

And careful she was. It should be helpful at this point to
reflect on the special meaning that John was coming to have for
his mother. Her dreams about having her own "Samuel" follow in
the illustrious ministerial tradition of her first "Samuel"
(though in a different communion) had undoubtedly been cruelly
broken by the time of John's miraculous rescue.[98] In this "divine intervention" Susanna believed she had a sign--a portent
of John's future stature as a man of God. If she had not been
able with all of her ability and commitment to enable Samuel
Wesley to carve out a place of importance for himself, it had
been because of weaknesses in his character. With care, she
might be able to form a character in John without those debili-
tating weaknesses.

We have already noted the impatience of Samuel Wesley with
his wife's rigorous and consistent method of child-rearing.
Harrison has characterized his response to the personality traits
which this method was creating in John:

> ...the star pupil, John Wesley himself, had an un-
> comfortable time with his father, for he got both
> beaten and laughed at for observing the rules too
> well. His mother had taught him to reason out
> everything, with the result that he debated every
> step of the way forward and made a man like his
> father very angry. A poet cannot be expected to
> tolerate too much reason. He would thunder at the
> child, 'You think to carry everything by dint of
> argument,' and turning to his mother he followed

up his advantage in that trying strain of crude ban-
ter: 'I protest, sweetheart. I think our Jack would
not attend to the most pressing necessities of nature
unless he could give a reason for it.'[99]

No doubt this early experience of conflicting styles of
parental authority would constitute the beginnings of not only
his special style of mastering experience, his ego-synthesis,
but also some of the basic parameters of his integrating task.
During his experience under Susanna's method, John Wesley seems
to have learned his lessons well. His personal style as a "Methodist," compulsive, over-organized, perfectionistic in his attempts
to obey "legitimate," "just," and consistent authorities was determined at an early age by this relationship. His sense of
having a destiny, some special mission in religious leadership
was also fostered by the mother, leading to his strong belief in
the providential element in his personal history.[100]

V. H. H. Green has noted that the dominance of Susanna led
to an intense dependency upon her in all of the Wesley children,
and that though "In some respects the brothers were less tied,
more especially Samuel as the eldest; but even in their development the powerful, loving, counselling and warning figure of
Susanna Wesley was never far away."[101] He concludes that "two
features, the femininity of his early environment and the thorough
training to which he was subjected by his mother, were of the
first importance in John Wesley's development."[102] We will see
in the next section of this essay how these two ingredients were
to set the stage for a continuing struggle with the maternal
authority in Wesley's life. Yet we do not want to minimize here,
as many biographers have done, the importance of Samuel Wesley
in his son's developmental economy. The scholarly, poetic, vola-
tile, unorganized and imminently unpredictable figure of his
father must have elicited a response from young John that had
elements of both *mysterium tremendum* and *mysterium fascinans.*
If it was impossible for John to have an unambiguously positive
response to Samuel, neither was the response completely negative.
Though all of the children suffered under the capricious and
often heavy hand of the father's authority, neither they nor
their mother were willing to deny the formal legitimacy of that
authority and its claim upon them. If not an effective head of
the household, he was a powerful presence for the children

emotionally and had to be dealt with in their struggle to develop appropriate and autonomous ego-identities. We will see
below how John Wesley's own integrative task included not only
the problem of struggling with a dominant mother, but also that
of neutralizing the problematic potency of the capricious father
while also finding a place for him in his emerging identity.

Wesley and Conflict with Maternal Authority

John Wesley liked being with women. No doubt his early experience in the home had contributed to his enjoyment of female
companionship, since until the birth of Charles in 1707 the
household was predominantly female.[103] His older brother Samuel,
Jr. was away at boarding school, and so John's early years were
spent in a home dominated by his mother, and, since his mother
did not like for her children to mix with the other children of
the parish, his playmates were for the most part his seven sisters.[104] V. H. H. Green has suggested the following as a manifestation of the influence of the sisterhood:

> There was a decisive streak of femininity in John's
> character....His neatness, his meticulous, at times
> fussy, concern with detail, his personal sensitivity,
> his histrionic approach, must have been in part con-
> ditioned at this early age. While he was well-liked
> by his fellow-men, he seems always to be more at home
> in female society.[105]

These relationships with the women of his home allowed an
intimacy without danger of passion or desire. Susanna had always characterized temptation to sinful willfullness as a personified female:

> I am verily persuaded that the reason why so many
> seek to enter into the Kingdom of Heaven but are
> not able is there is some Delilah, some one beloved
> vice, they will not part with....[106]

Schmidt has noted the influence of two devotional books on
Susanna Wesley. Both Lorenzo Scupoli's *Spiritual Conflict* and
Henry Scougal's *The Life of God in the Soul of Man* were books
which emphasized the goal of perfection in human life.[107] And
in both the will and the body must be subjected to reason and
spiritual discipline. Susanna heard their warnings to be ever
committed to the struggle for perfection and to withdraw from
the things of the world, and she passed these concerns on to

her children and especially to John.[108] The passions of the
flesh and human sexuality, of course, ranked high among the
temptations and were especially to be guarded against.

Wesley left his Epworth home for Charterhouse, where he was
to become a foundation scholar, in 1714.[109] There is little information about Wesley's experience at this boarding school, although Green has concluded in his *John Wesley* that the experience
"has not modified to any perceptible degree the predominant
influences of home life."[110] Wesley left Charterhouse in 1720
and matriculated at Christ Church, Oxford, one of the most pres-
tigious colleges in the university.[111] In the following chapters
we will focus our attention on Wesley's experience at Oxford
with regard to his theological development and his early experiments in religious leadership. Here, however, our attention
continues to trace the strand of Wesley's relationships with the
opposite sex.

While at Oxford, Wesley delved deeply into the study of
early church history and patristics. He no doubt found that
their views on sex were, if anything, even more severe than
those of his mother. Not only did they view as sinful sexual
relations which could in any way be termed promiscuous or irregular, but they included even the slightest thing that might en-
courage "carnal feeling."[112]

Being away from Epworth at college, however, was not all
study. While at Oxford he became a part of a group of young
men and women of his age which became a source of great enjoyment for him. The friends were for the most part from the
Cotswold villages of Stanton, Buckland, and Broadway.[113] The
center of the group was the Kirkham family. Mr. Kirkham was
the rector of Stanton, and his children, Bob, Sally, Bett, and
Damaris were among John's closest friends.[114] They were all
very religious, and Sally introduced him to some very challenging
devotional literature. He had more than devotions in mind,
however, as is evidenced by his diary entry of April 14, 1725:
"First saw Varanese (his playful nickname for Sally). May it
not be in vain!" Soon his mother's warnings seemed not to apply
to this relationship, and Sally's combination of youthful attractiveness and religious commitment led to John's falling very much
in love with her.[115] He began to entertain thoughts of marriage,

but since he had only recently been ordained and was expecting soon to be made a fellow at Oxford, he was hesitant to raise the question with Sally. She had already been engaged to the local schoolmaster, and they were married within a few months.[116]

The marriage did not end their relationship, however, and convincing themselves that they would continue to relate as brother and sister, they kept up a relationship quite as intimate as before her marriage. In the fall of 1726 some months after her wedding she told John:

> I would certainly tell you if my husband should ever
> resent our freedom, which I am satisfied he never
> will; such an accident as this would make it neces-
> sary to restrain in some measure the appearance of
> the esteem I have to you, but the esteem as it is
> grounded on reason and virtue and entirely agreeable
> to us both, no circumstances of life will ever make
> me alter.[117]

If Wesley was pained at having lost Sally as a potential bride, he rationalized that the continuing relationship was an important aid to religious commitment and virtue. He continued to reaffirm his commitment to their relationship:

> ...you make me a little uncomfortable and I think it
> is almost sinful to use the expressions of tenderness
> which I use in relation to you in relation to other
> people. It isn't expedient or right to break off our
> friendship. It is one of my main incentives to vir-
> tue.[118]

One of Wesley's sisters, however, was wise to the source of the intensification of Wesley's religious zeal:

> Had you not lost your dear Mrs. C----n, where had
> your love been fixed? On heaven, I hope, princi-
> pally: but a large share, too, had been hers: you
> would not have been so spiritualized, but something
> of this lower world would have had its part in your
> heart, wise as you are; but being deprived of her
> there went all hope of worldly happiness: and now
> the mind, which is an active principle, losing its
> aim here, has fixed on its Maker for happiness.[119]

Wesley was to continue his relationships with the Cotswold circle for some time, and we will discuss another important feminine companion from that same group below. Yet another important relationship must be noticed which developed in Epworth.

In the summer of 1726 Wesley spent several months with his family at Epworth. Recently named Fellow of Oxford, he had been

granted a leave of absence before assuming his duties again in
September. The summer was an enjoyable one for the young Wesley
and he found a number of diverse activities which interested him
and provided a pleasant contrast to the Oxford academic life.
At Epworth he found time to help with the family's chores, including transcribing on his father's *Job*. He read, hunted, com-
posed poetry, and even participated in an archeological expedi-
tion.[120] For our purposes, however, the summer is of focal
significance for its manifestation of Wesley's conflict with
both maternal and paternal authority. The conflict with maternal
authority is evident in his relationship with a young woman of
the parish, and that with paternal authority in what we shall
denote below the "Hetty Incident."

Apparently Wesley's disappointment in his relationship with
Sally Kirkham had not caused him to lose interest in attractive
young women. During the summer Wesley began to see a great deal
of a local girl, Kitty Hargreaves, and from all accounts was
becoming quite fond of her. His diary for the summer contains
many references to her, some quite revealing of both his attraction to her and his conflict over that attraction. Green has
suggested that the course of the relationship with Kitty parallels that with Sally Kirkham the year before.[121] First Wesley
is attracted to a young woman, then he becomes hesitant as he
experiences the relationship as a conflict between attraction
and conscience. On the third of July, Wesley wrote:

> As we would willingly suffer a little pain, or forgo
> some pleasure for others we really love, so if we
> sincerely love God we should readily do this for him.
> For this reason one act of self-denial is more grate-
> ful to our Master than the performance of many lesser
> duties....Begin in small things first.[122]

And then he writes in his personal shorthand code, "Never
touch Kitty's hand again."[123] Evidently conscience was having
a real struggle, for on a Saturday night in August he made a
resolution that he would never touch any woman's breasts again.[124]
Nevertheless, though Wesley continued to see Kitty for the rest
of his stay, the relationship was not to deepen or become more
intense.

Yet in spite of his disappointment with Sally Kirkham and
his stillborn relationship with Kitty Hargreaves, on his return

to Oxford Wesley had not lost his interest in intimate relationships with attractive young women. As we have noted above, he
continued seeing Sally Chapone (Kirkham) who was now not a threat
to his conscience but rather simply a beloved "religious friend."
Now, however, another member of the Cotswold circle, the young
widow Mary Pendarves (Aspasia), began to occupy more and more
of his attentions. She, too, was regarded as a fellow religious
pilgrim, and his correspondence is marked by expressions of his
admiration of her traits of holiness and virtue. In this relationship we see no evidence of the threatening physical intimacy. Yet in spite of the predominantly religious subject matter
of the correspondence, Schmidt has noted that:

> ...The letters which Wesley exchanged with her are a
> peculiar mixture of pastoral pronouncements and re-
> pressed eroticism. His words are prompted by senti-
> ment in a way quite unusual for him, yet the result
> is not an unconstrained artlessness but a style which
> is affected and fanciful. Exaggerated declarations
> of gratitude and protestations of his devotion are
> repeatedly shown.[125]

That Wesley had more invested in this relationship than simply
the role of religious tutor is clear. He rationalized his continued intense relationships with the young women of Cotswold,
and especially with Aspasia, by putting them on a pedestal of
holiness and viewing them as necessary inspiration for his own
struggle with the world.[126] As the relationship with Mary
Pendarves deepened he expressed both the depths of his feeling
and the fear that he is opening himself to be hurt again:

> ...I perceive that I am making another avenue for
> grief, that I am laying open another part of my
> soul, at which the arrows of fortune may enter....
> Tell me,...if it be a fault that my heart burns
> within me when I reflect on the many marks of re-
> gard you have already shown.[127]

His fears proved well-founded. By 1734 the press of social
life in higher circles had dampened the young widow's interest
in maintaining her correspondence with Wesley, and she became
increasingly lax in answering his letters. Wesley read between
the lines of her apology and terminated the relationship with his
reply: "...Doubtless you acted upon cool reflection; you de-
clined the trouble of writing, not because it was a trouble, but
because it was a needless one...I sincerely thank you for what
is past."[128]

In closing his discussion of these relationships, Green concludes that:

> It is perhaps fanciful to assume that unrequited love helped to create the mental state which made him ready to leave England and Oxford for what he fondly if inaccurately believed to be the primitive innocence of America. There, as he told Dr. Burton, he might be able to 'attain such a purity of thought as suits a candidate for that state wherein they neither marry nor are given in marriage, but are as the angels of God in heaven.'[129]

There is little doubt that the leaving for Georgia marked, among other things, an attempt on Wesley's part to solve the problem of intimacy by evading it. Schmidt has noted that Wesley hoped that Georgia would give him an opportunity to be free of all ties with the female sex, since in his fantasy of the colony there would be no women of his own race.[130] We shall soon turn to an examination of other factors which were involved in the decision to go to Georgia, and then to an analysis of the significant Georgia experience itself.

It is appropriate at this point, however, to call attention to the structuring of Wesley's movements in attempting to come to terms with an important life task, that of achieving sexual intimacy. We have seen that Wesley's childhood was one of continual interaction with a small group of sensitive and religious female companions. He learned to prefer the company of women and to thrive on it. There was no conflict in the childhood home between religious purity and commitment and intimate relationships with the opposite sex. With the onset of adolescence, however, the bliss of a conflict-free relationship with female peers was to come to an end. His mother had taught him to equate sinful willfulness with bodily passion and to associate both with a hellous conflagration from which, if one is to fulfill his religious vocation, he must be "plucked as a brand from the burning." In spite of his mother's careful, and for the most part successful, attempts to bridle his passions and channel them into religious expressions and commitments, we have seen that the creative and imaginative John found ways at least to approach intimacy with young women. Given the warning to beware of "Delilahs" and the sirens of the carnal, he chose to associate with young women who had such traits that he could rationalize

the pleasure of their company as either necessary inspiration
for his own religious pilgrimage or as a natural outgrowth of
his responsibility to serve as a spiritual guide to others.

In Wesley's attempt to meet the life task of finding psychosexual intimacy, then, we see that a major part of his life-long
adaptive strategy has already been formulated. In order to make
a legitimate place for natural passion, its threads are woven
carefully into the fabric of the unquestioned passion of his
religious commitments. A psychological "Trojan horse" tactic
is manifest here, with the sexual smuggled within the vehicle
of the spiritual in order to deceive both himself and others.
We will have occasion to discuss this adaptive stratagem at length
in our discussion of his relationship with Sophy Hopkey. At this
point, however, it should be noted that Wesley's attempts to
deceive others were less successful than those at self-deception,
and even his self-deception often proved unequal to his assaults
of conscience. A recurrent fear is summarized by the question
Wesley put to himself, "Have I loved women or company more than
God?"[131]

If we interpret the precocious conscience evident alongside
his attempts to achieve psychosexual intimacy as an internalized
expression of the maternal authority, then the reason for the
choice of a subtitle for this section will become evident. The
only front in which John Wesley tested the boundaries established
by his mother during his development was that involving intimacy
with women. Despite his employment of evasive and functionally
compensatory strategies in order to avoid the painful confronta-
tions with conscience, Wesley returned to direct assaults on the
barriers between him and psychosexual fulfillment in his adult,
and later, middle-aged life. In this writer's opinion he came
closest to a successful resolution of the psychosexual task in
his engagement to Grace Murray. With this promising relationship
aborted through the manifestation of Wesley's long-operative
tendency toward hesitation and indecision in such matters, coupled
with the machinations of his brother Charles, he lost the opportunity for conjugal fulfillment which had long been a frustrating
preoccupation. Finally, throwing all caution to the winds, Wesley
married a woman uniquely ill-suited to allow him integration of
his need for psychosexual fulfillment with his commitment to his
chosen professional identity.

Wesley, then, in fact never won his struggle on the one front in which he felt compelled to resist the internalized maternal authority. We shall see how this same protracted struggle manifested itself in Georgia through his relationship with Sophy Hopkey, and how it figured in the attractiveness of the revival as Wesley finalized his formulation of personal and professional identity.

Wesley and Conflict with Paternal Authority

If the summer of 1726 provides a poignant glimpse of the struggle between conscience and the carnal in Wesley's ill-fated resistance to maternal authority, it also provides us with a veritable scenario with which to grasp the basic structure of his successful resistance to the paternal authority. The event which provides us with such a helpful insight into John Wesley's tactics in dealing with his father we have denoted the "Hetty Incident."

Though the lives of all of Wesley's sisters were marked by tragedy and acute unhappiness, the story of Hetty Wesley has been viewed as the saddest. While Hetty was from all accounts a quite intelligent and attractive young lady, she seemed to chafe under the restrictions of parental authority and particularly that of her father.[132] She fell in love with a young lawyer who was apparently intensely disliked by her father. Forbidden to see him, she met him secretly and soon spent a night with him. The family was scandalized, but none so explosively as the father. His disgust at her behavior was monumental, and he subsequently forced her to marry a drunken and insensitive man that she hardly knew. As if this were not punishment enough, Samuel and most of the rest of the household continued to withhold their forgiveness and affection months after the marriage.

When John arrived at Epworth for his visit during the summer of 1726 he was shocked to find that his sister Mary was the only family member who had forgiven Hetty and re-established an open and constructive relationship with her. He began to try to reason with his father and the others, but even as the summer drew to a close Samuel was still unrelenting in his condemnation of Hetty. On Sunday, August 28th, John took the case to the pulpit, taking as his topic, "Universal Charity or the Charity

Due to Wicked Persons." He had consulted his mother on the sermon, and after she read it she commented, "You writ this sermon
for Hetty; the rest was brought in for the sake of the last paragraph."[133] John seemed to believe that his appeal to reason and
conscience would change his father's mind. He was gravely mistaken. His father was so angry that he would not speak to John
concerning the matter, but confided his anger and hurt with John
to Charles, lamenting John's disrespect and deliberate defiance:
"Every day, you hear how he contradicts me, and takes your sister's part before my face. Nay, he disputes with me, preach--."[134]
Though the account has him not finishing his sentence, he clearly
was communicating his shock that John had had the audacity to
preach a sermon calling *him* to repentance.

Charles communicated his father's hurt and anger to John
and, strangely enough, John was surprised at the intensity of
his father's response. He had obviously believed that his sermon
had already softened his father's stance not only toward Hetty,
but toward the offending young lawyer as well: "I had the same
day the pleasure of observing that my father the same day, when
one Will Attkins was mentioned, did not speak so warmly nor
largely against him as usual."[135] He now found that his father
was "speaking warmly and largely" against the would-be agent of
reconciliation.

John's response at this point is of focal interest to the
psychohistorian. Instead of standing pat upon realizing the
alienating effects of his assertiveness toward his father, John
went immediately to him and apologized for his "offense." He
promised that he would never contradict his father again and
offered to do penance to demonstrate his sincerity by transcribing
for his father as often as he wished. The apology brought about
a tearful reconciliation, sealed with a filial kiss and with a
transcribing assignment for the next day. Samuel's statement
that he had always known that "John was good at bottom" was certainly faint enough praise, but indicated that he thought John's
rebellion against his authority was terminated.

However, in spite of the fact that John did diligently
transcribe for his father during the remainder of his stay at
Epworth, he chose as his final sermon topic "Rash Judging."[136]
This parting blow angered Samuel so much that he protested to

Samuel Jr. indicating that John's rebellion against his authority had gone so far as to break a canon of the law of the Church of England. He invoked the 53rd Canon which stipulated that no preacher shall "...of purpose, impugn, confute any doctrine delivered by any other preacher in the same church."[137]

It was clear that John had not been successful in subjugating his reason and conscience to what he felt to be the irresponsible and abusive authority of his father. Yet it was equally clear that open conflict with his father, even when John was sure that Samuel was misusing his parental and ecclesiastical authority, continued to be extremely painful for him and required a price of penance to be paid for his challenge to that authority. The determination to resist all capricious and uncharitable authority was to continue throughout his life. We shall see, however, that the need to do penance for his resistance continues only through the Georgia experience and terminates at Aldersgate.

The Hetty incident has in effect provided us with an understanding of the continuing struggle of John Wesley to master the challenge presented by the potent but unpredictable person of his father. We have seen that John early became adept at the use of reason and argument from a coherent religious perspective in making his way through his experienced life-space. We have also seen that Susanna consistently, and with varying degrees of success, used this tactic in order to limit the effects of Samuel's caprice. We may conclude at this point that Wesley chose very early in life to cast his lot with the moral order which Susanna had created in the nursery and that he had, in formulating his unique style of ego-synthesis and adaptation, committed himself to carrying the principles of that microcosmic moral order to their logical conclusions in the world beyond.

We shall see the ramifications of his chosen adaptive style as they figure in his mature self-image as a religious leader and in his fully-formed understanding of the soteriological economy. At this point, however, we are still contemplating a young John Wesley who has not yet laid the potency of the paternal authority to rest. We now turn to the last real internal conflict with that authority. In this decisive sequence of events the stakes for the formation of Wesley's personal and professional identity were far higher than those in the Hetty incident.

By 1733 the health of Samuel Wesley was failing, and, concerned about the continuing welfare of his family in the event
of his death, he began to seek a successor from his sons to take
over the Epworth living. He first asked Samuel Jr., but he de-
clined since he had just taken a position as headmaster of a
school. Charles was not yet ordained, and therefore an attempt
was made to enlist John to become the successor.[138] With this
request a struggle was engaged between Wesley and his father
which was to extend until his father's death in 1735, and which
had ramifications extending to the Aldersgate experience and beyond. John was at first not totally resistant to the idea, and
seemed to be considering it. Nevertheless, in correspondence
with his mother he expressed some doubt regarding his ability
to handle the assignment and communicated some of his grounds
for not readily wanting to leave Oxford: "I knew if I could
stand my ground here and approve myself a faithful minister of
our blessed Jesus...then there was not a place under heaven like
this for improvement in every good work."[139] Samuel, of course,
was not one who would take a weak refusal as final. He wrote
to John pointing out that his recalcitrance was jeopardizing all
of the accomplishments of his forty years of ministry.[140] The
implicit appeal to consider the welfare of Susanna and the sisters who remained at home was understood by the whole family,
and, given John's unquestioned affection for the women of his
family, must have tugged heavily at his resolve to stay at Oxford.

If seen in the context of the Hetty incident, this struggle
was undoubtedly the source of extreme pressures of conscience
and guilt for the sensitive son and brother. He had criticized
his father during the earlier conflict for lack of charity and
failure to live up to the responsibilities of a loving and just
father. And even then, when he was sure he was in the right,
he was beset by waves of guilt for angering his father and made
amends by working on one of his father's literary projects. Now,
however, it was *he* who seemed uncharitable and irresponsible
toward the family, and, instead of being asked to assist in a
literary project, he was being called upon to recant and to sal-
vage the most important project of his father's life--his ministry
--and to secure the livelihood of his beloved mother and the
sisters who remained at home.

Nevertheless, this time Wesley stood fast under the pressure which continued month after month. In December of 1734 he wrote a letter to his father which was an all-out attempt to put the issue to rest.[141] It was his purpose in the letter to offer a comprehensive and carefully reasoned justification on religious grounds of his decision not to leave Oxford. Here we see the mature flowering of Wesley's lifelong tactic of using reasoned argument to limit the effectiveness of his father's authority. Under twenty-five points he presented the reasons why he could not in good conscience accept the living at Epworth.

He began by claiming that the glory of God was in fact his only real consideration. This end of glorifying God demanded first of all that he cultivate holiness in himself so that he might better foster it in others. At Oxford, he points out, he has an ideal setting for his own spiritual pilgrimage. He has a regular income and is free from the more mundane cares of the world. Free from "trifling acquaintance" he always has inspirational company:

> I know no other place under heaven where I can have
> always at hand half a dozen persons nearly of my
> own judgment and engaged in the same studies: per-
> sons who are awakened into a full and lively con-
> viction that they have only one work to do upon
> earth...who...have according to their power re-
> nounced themselves, and wholly and absolutely de-
> voted themselves to God.[142]

In addition to such inspiring company, opportunities for cultivating his coveted personal holiness abounded. Not only did he have myriad opportunities for corporate worship, but also for engaging in good works:

> There is scarce any way of doing good which here is
> not daily occasion...here are poor families to be
> relieved; here are children to be educated; here are
> workhouses wherein both young and old want, and gladly
> receive, the word of exhortation; here are persons to
> be visited, wherein alone is a complication of all
> human wants; and lastly, here are the schools of the
> prophets--here are tender minds to be formed and
> strengthened, and babes in Christ to be instructed
> and perfected in all useful learning.[143]

John had earlier pled to his father the spiritual signifi-cance of the opposition to which the Holy Club member was sub-ject at Oxford. For John this represented the persecution which

he believed to be inevitable in the life of a Christian. Samuel
Wesley's reply was a telling one, and necessitated a quite involved evasion in John's response. The father had noted that
while most of the parishioners were eager for John to succeed
him, in a parish of two thousand souls there would certainly be
plenty persecution. In his circuitous reply, John questioned
both his ability to minister to such a large group of people
and their sincerity in wanting him as their pastor. In support
of this apprehension he reminded his father of the persecution
that Samuel had received at their hands. Yet he continued to
affirm the spiritual importance of persecution, and concluded
that while Epworth did promise opposition, at Oxford he had it
already. In a subsequent letter to his mother he went on to
argue that he could be replaced more easily at Epworth than at
Oxford, that in working with students he could "sweeten the
fountain" rather than try to purify the myriad "streams."[144]

Despite all his apparent resolve and commitment to staying
at Oxford, Wesley apparently had some reservations with regard
to his position on the matter. When his brother Samuel took
his father's side and questioned the sincerity of John's stated
reasons for his refusal, the increased pressure evidently raised
doubts in John's own mind. In the end Wesley recanted his "irrevocable" commitment to the Oxford life and indicated his willingness to reconsider his father's request. In this case, however, as in many others, Wesley had allowed his own hesitance
and indecision to decide the matter for him. By the time he had
decided to open himself to submitting to his father's wishes,
the living had already been promised to another candidate.

The question of the basis for Wesley's refusal to succeed
his father is an important one, and we must consider what the
request must have meant to him at this important juncture in
his personal and professional development. For the psychohistorian two factors stand out here as important contributing factors: Wesley's own sense of a special destiny and the shared
family assumption that their father had abilities and potential
which were frustrated by the effectual exile of Epworth.

With regard to Wesley's prodiguous sense of a special destiny
we must agree with Wesley that the analysis should begin prior
to his birth. First of all, most biographers have missed the

reason that Wesley, contrary to all of the other children, was given a middle name. That middle name, Benjamin, was the name of the infant boy who immediately preceded John and who died in infancy.[145] The psychological significance of this naming has been lost even on those who have noted it. Specialists in the psychodynamic significance of birth order have noted that a child born immediately after the death of a preceding sibling often is treated in a manner which indicates the heightened significance of the child for his parent. Living, in effect, for two persons (in this case John *and* Benjamin), the child is early predisposed toward having an exaggerated sense of uniqueness and corresponding "destiny."[146]

When this fact of Wesley's position at birth is combined with the circumstances related above which led to his conception, we see that the beginnings of Wesley's sense of destiny probably has roots antedating the "miraculous rescue" of 1709. We have already noted the primary significance of John's experience of being a "brand plucked from the burning," both for his mother and for their relationship. This experience and the continual later reference to it indicate clearly that John early came to have a sense of a special religious destiny captured in his image of having been saved by God and set aside for a most providential role.

Having grasped the high expectations Wesley had for himself we are led to ask why the prospect of succeeding his father at Epworth seemed so inappropriate to him. In order to understand Wesley's rejection of the living we must look not simply at his lengthy statements regarding his motives, but rather at the meaning Epworth had for Wesley given his search for that providential special role. We ask, therefore, if the family circle shared any particular viewpoint regarding the appropriateness of the Epworth appointment for Samuel Sr.? Upon examination it is clear that there did exist an agreement in the family that the parish ministry at Epworth did not facilitate the fulfillment of the potential of the father. For all of Susanna's awareness of her husband's faults, she thought it a great waste that he had had to spend his life in the parish ministry at Epworth:

> And did I not know that Almighty Wisdom hath views and
> ends, in fixing the bounds of our habitation, which
> are out of our ken. I should think it a thousand

> pities that a man of his brightness, and rare endow-
> ments of learning and useful knowledge, in relation
> to the church of God, should be confined to an ob-
> scure corner of the country, where his talents are
> buried, and he determined to a way of life for which
> he is not so well qualified as I could wish;...[147]

The Rector himself had long had fantasies of an escape from
Epworth. At the time of the acute marital conflict related above,
Samuel was thinking of returning to the naval chaplaincy.[148]
Early in his career he had been disappointed in his hopes of becoming a bishop.[149] And for a large part of his career he had
entertained elaborate fantasies of leaving Epworth for the mission field. He had proposed several schemes to the Society for
Propagating the Gospel in Foreign Parts, including missions to
India, China, or Abyssinia.[150] In his old age he was an enthusiastic supporter of Oglethorpe's plans for a Georgia colony and
lamented his frustrated hopes of becoming a missionary in such
a promising field. In a letter to Oglethorpe in 1734 he re-
vealed his continuing excitement about the challenge of a mission
to the "heathen":

> I had always so dear a love of your colony that if it
> had been but ten years ago, I would gladly have de-
> voted the remainder of my life and labours to that
> place and think I might before this time have con-
> quered the language without which little can be done
> among the natives.[151]

Samuel sought unsuccessfully to have his son-in-law, John White-
lamb, chosen to go with Oglethorpe that he might at least have
a vicarious participation in a project which had all the marks
of his own frustrated fantasy.

We now have a vantage point from which we can understand
not only John Wesley's reluctance to accept the Epworth living,
but also an important, and heretofore neglected, ingredient in
his decision to undertake the Georgia mission. It is clear that
Wesley had developed a sense of personal destiny that required
a role which would have the marks of being special or extraordinary. And it is equally clear that the general conclusion
of the family was that being rector of Epworth was not a role
which facilitated the fulfillment of the potential of its occu-
pant. Seen in this perspective, Wesley's decision to reject the
living is quite understandable: Epworth had frustrated the
dreams of his father, but he was determined that it was not to
frustrate his own.

The decision to reject the living, however, was a costly one for Wesley. We have seen in our discussion of the Hetty incident that John did not take overt conflict with his father lightly. Even when his father was guilty of irresponsible conduct toward a family member John's conduct necessitated doing penance through working on one of his father's pet projects. Now Wesley had, in rejecting the living, not only effectually raised a question regarding the worth of his father's life-long labor at Epworth, but also in so doing he had cast himself in the role of the insensitive and irresponsible family member. Such a transgression of the will of his father would no doubt require an act of penance that no amount of transcribing on *Job* could ever satisfy.

Opportunities for such attempts at a satisfactory reconciliation were to be cut short by the death of Samuel on April 25, 1735. After his father's funeral John transcribed on the *Dissertationes in Librum Jobi* until it was finished and ready for publishing. While visiting in Westminster making arrangements for its publication, Wesley was contacted by Dr. John Burton on behalf of the trustees of the colony of Georgia and asked to accompany Oglethorpe to Georgia as missionary to the Indians and pastor to Savannah. After ten days of consultations with his mother and a number of friends Wesley accepted the offer of the Georgia trustees. On October 14, 1735, John and Charles Wesley were among the passengers of the *Simmonds* as it began its journey to Georgia.[152]

The question of why Wesley chose to leave Oxford so soon after having declared his irrevocable commitment to stay there has long figured as a primary puzzle for Wesley scholars. No doubt there had been some internal difficulties within the ranks of the Holy Club, but it would be stretching the evidence too far to suggest that such difficulties alone would have led John to abandon the club in the midst of a challenge to his leadership ability. We have noted above that Wesley's frustrated relationships with the opposite sex had undoubtedly rendered an opportunity to get away from women of "his own kind" an attractive option. But his most lengthy protestations of intent to remain at Oxford were written after the relationship with Asphasia had drawn to a close. While affirming the role of these previously

noted ingredients in the decision, I propose an additional interpretation: in deciding to undertake a mission to the Indians
Wesley was also engaging in an act of penance on a grand scale.
Taking on the challenge of a mission to the Indians enabled Wesley
to work on a pet project of his father's fantasies. It can be
seen as an attempt by Wesley to do for his father that which
Samuel himself was never able to do, but which he considered an
extraordinary ministry of highest priority.

Wesley's rejection of the Epworth living and his subsequent
acceptance of the Georgia mission, then, was a complex but understandable unfolding of his struggle with the difficult task of
finding an acceptable personal and vocational identity. The call
to Epworth offered little to Wesley in the task of ego-synthesis
and identity formation. First, it offered a role that Wesley
knew had proven to be the bane of his father's ambitions for
greatness. Given his own need to find a special or extraordinary
role for himself, this alone would probably have been sufficient
cause for him to reject the living. Second, the Oxford experience
functioned as an extended psychosocial moratorium for Wesley and
he was reluctant to take on an unpromising assignment which would
entail resigning his fellowship and the security and flexibility
which it provided. He could accept the Georgia mission while
simply on a leave-of-absence from Oxford. If it did not prove
to be a successful experiment, he could always return to Oxford.
Third, Epworth had been the scene of some of his most guilt-ridden
encounters with young women. In his fantasies Georgia offered
him an opportunity to lay aside the immensely frustrating task
of coming to terms with psychosexual intimacy. This attempted
avoidance of his sexuality combined in the same movement with
a choice of an extraordinary mode of ministry enthusiastically
sanctioned by his mother indicates that the decision to go to
Georgia was fully in accord with the dictates of the maternal
authority. And lastly, the decision for the Georgia mission
marked an attempt to do penance for his blatant transgression
of paternal authority.

CHAPTER III

THE RESIGNED SELF: FROM RESIGNATION TO EXALTATION

If John Wesley had hopes of working out his own salvation
in Georgia he was soon to find himself frustrated on every front.
The fantasy which had led him to undertake the mission soon became a nightmare. At the beginning, however, there was little
warning of the oncoming debacle. On February 5, 1736, Wesley's
ship arrived in Savannah harbor. Since his predecessor had not
yet left Savannah, Wesley and his companions lodged for a few
weeks on board the *Simmonds* and later with the Moravian community.
He found the opportunity to continue his associations with the
Moravians, begun on shipboard, quite stimulating and was enthusiastic about the promise of an ongoing dialogue with the community
and its leaders. As quickly as possible, however, he began to
settle into the routine of duties required of him as chaplain
to the colony and to investigate the requirements of an effective
ministry to the Indians.

In his first encounters with the Indians Wesley was sobered
by the dimensions of the task but not discouraged by it. When
he viewed the mission to the "heathen" along with his pastoral
responsibilities to the settlement, he began to think of trans-
planting the Holy Club to Georgia in order to provide an adequate
staff for the work at hand. Soon, however, the very conflicts
which the Georgia experiment was to have put to rest began to
manifest themselves again--almost simultaneously. We have discussed at some length above the rejection by Wesley of any role
which smacked of the ordinary, and we have characterized his
basic understanding of the Georgia excursion as one of an extraordinary mission to the Indians. Oglethorpe, on the other hand,
had conceived Wesley's role quite differently. The General's
main interests were that his colony not only survive, but thrive.
In his view this success necessitated an active pastoral and
priestly ministry by his clergymen which would serve as an integrating force among the residents of the colony. Any mission to
the natives would have to take a very secondary place in the
hierarchy of priorities.

63

As the press of the duties as chaplain to the colony began
to mount, Wesley did not reject the claims made upon him by
Oglethorpe. For a while he attempted to fulfill both his pastoral
and missionary responsibilities. As he learned more about the
native morals and mores his earlier images of the "noble savage"
seemed increasingly ridiculous and he began to be discouraged
with the prospects of his work among the Indians. While he did
not give up his hopes of a ministry to the natives, his routine
as recorded in the *Journal* began to focus on his pastoral responsibility to the settlers at Savannah and Frederica. Though
he had manifested a "methodist" strictness in his early pastoral
work in the colony, the increasing anger of his parishioners at
his heavy-handedness in application of ecclesiastical discipline
seems to indicate that he was now performing his role with a
vengeance.

Given our perspectives on his goals in assuming the Georgia
appointment, it seems appropriate for us to reflect upon what
meaning this increasing strictness in pastoral work had for John
Wesley. Certainly Wesley believed himself simply to be doing
his duty. But we know that the nature of this duty--the parish
ministry--was that which he believed he had rejected in choosing
the Georgia assignment. Now we see him assuming the role his
father had wanted him to choose, but for all practical purposes
under the coercion of Oglethorpe and the realities of the situation with regard to the natives. If Wesley found himself coerced
into a role not really of his choosing, why then did he not rebel
and reject the ministry to the settlers? Wesley seemed instead
to be actually embracing the style of ministry which his father
pursued at Epworth, both as to the role and the manner of enacting
it.

We must remember, however, that Wesley considered his father
to be a failure, and that he believed insensitivity and overly
strict discipline to be among his father's cardinal weaknesses.
From this perspective, then, Wesley can be said to be manifesting
a quite subtle rebellion, one in a passive-aggressive mode. His
eventual miserable failure as a parish minister to the colony
can be seen as a defiant proclamation in itself, and a rough
translation might read: "See, I *told* you I was not cut out for
the ordinary role of a parish priest!" We can best document this

"ministry with a vengeance" and its consequences by relating the developments which led up to Wesley's humiliated flight from Georgia. These events offer us in a striking way a microcosm of the significance of the Georgia experiment. In them we see manifest the struggles with both maternal and paternal authority.

Temptation: The Sophy Hopkey Affair

If John Wesley had fantasies of being freed of sexual temptations in Georgia, he was soon to be shocked back into reality. In a note written to his brother in Frederica John included a cryptic message in code: "I stand in jeopardy every hour. Two or three women are here, young, pretty, God-fearing. Pray for me, that I know none of them after the flesh."[1] On March 13, 1736 Wesley had met Sophia Christiana Hopkey at the home of her uncle, Thomas Causton, the director of supplies and chief magistrate of Savannah.

We have already noted above that the conflict between sexual passion and religious commitment engendered by his mother led Wesley to take his libidinally "loaded" relationships with women and force himself to think of them as "spiritual relationships" only. As long as women were mothers, sisters, or counselees it seemed alright for him to be in intimate relationship with them. Wesley's women, however, seemed to be able to "read between the lines," and the mixed signals which they received often led them to expect more on the earthly side from John. When nothing more was forthcoming, the typical outcome was for the ladies to become impatient and to seek other relationships. Therefore, although the decision against further psychosexual intimacy is in effect made for him by the female involved, he in reality, because of the rein of maternal authority, rejected further sexual involvements through his decisive indecision. The Sophy affair manifests this pattern in all of its elements.

From the very first John was impressed with the purity and spiritual promise of the young woman and took every opportunity to tutor her in the basics of the spiritual life. She was a regular visitor at the rectory and was the most attentive of students. Though she had been engaged to one of the outlaws of the colony, Thomas Mellichamp, and had thereby scandalized her magistrate uncle, she now seemed bent on nothing more than the

salvation of her soul and the imitation of Christ. In his journal
Wesley expressed his admiration for the young woman:

> She was eighteen years old. And from the beginning
> of our intimate acquaintance till this day, I verily
> believe she used no guile: not only because even
> now I know no instance to the contrary, nor only be-
> cause the simplicity of her behavior was a constant
> voucher for her sincerity; but because of the entire
> openness of all her conversation, answering whatever
> questions I proposed, without either hesitation or
> reserve, immediately and directly.[2]

She was humble and put on no pretense of sophistication.
She seemed very patient and satisfied even in the absence of the
niceties of life which the primitive conditions in Georgia made
necessary. Her simplicity of taste extended to her dress:

> Little of a gentlewoman in delicacy and niceness, she
> was still less so, if possible, in love of dress. No
> philosopher would have despised her love of adornment.
> Though always neat, she was always plain. And she
> was equally careless of finery in other things. It
> was use she considered, not show; nor novelty either,
> being as little concerned for new as for fine or
> pretty things.[3]

Not only that, but she showed little interest in the typical
diversions of young ladies of her age such as balls or dancing.
But her simplicity of taste did not mean that she manifested a
dullness of mind or personality:

> Her constant, even seriousness was very far from
> stupidity. Indeed, her understanding was not of a
> piece with her years. Though unimproved, it was
> deep and strong. It reached the highest things and
> the lowest. It rose to the greatest, yet stooped to
> the least. With fine sense she had a large share of
> common sense, and particularly of prudence, suiting
> herself readily to all persons and occasions, nature
> in her supplying the place of experience. Her appre-
> hension was so quick that there was scarce ever need
> to repeat a thing twice to her, and so clear as to
> conceive things the most remote from common life with-
> out any mistake or confusion.[4]

After continuing to wax eloquent regarding the virtues he
could discern in the attractive young lady, he added a few lines
which serve as a summary of her spiritual condition:

> The temper of her heart towards God is best known by
> Him 'who seeth in secret.' What appeared of it was
> a deep, even reverence, ripening into love, and a
> resignation unshaken in one of the severest trials

which human nature is exposed to. The utmost anguish
never wrung from her a murmuring word. She saw the
hand of God, and was still. She said indeed, 'If it
be possible, Father!' But added, 'Not as I will, but
as Thou wilt.'[5]

Whether Miss Sophy in fact manifested the strong faith and
resignation Wesley perceived in her, or whether he was projecting
upon her an emotional and spiritual state which he himself was
avidly seeking cannot be ascertained. The comments here are
nevertheless quite revealing. The resignation which Wesley believed that he discerned and clearly admired was a resignation
in the face of a troublesome love affair. The gravity with
which Wesley assessed such a condition is evident in his characterization of it as "one of the severest trials which human
nature is exposed to."[6] That Wesley was beginning to perceive
himself to be a fellow-sufferer in this condition, if not sharing
the resignation, is evident in the following statement which
closed his account of Sophy's character:

Such was the woman, according to my close observation,
of whom I now began to be much afraid. My desire and
design was still to live single; but how long it would
continue I knew not. I therefore consulted my friends
whether it was not best to break off all intercourse
with her immediately. They expressed themselves so
ambiguously that I understood them to mean that I ought
not to break it off. And accordingly she came to me
(as had been agreed) every morning and evening.[7]

The threat to his own resolution "to live single" had been
building for some time. He had been particularly interested in
this "pupil" since the inception of their relationship. He had
undoubtedly felt that one of his appropriate tasks as her spiritual director was to help her bring her involvement with and
investment in the petty criminal Mellichamp to an end. He had
tried to turn her mind to spiritual things and believed that he
was making some progress toward that end. Her uncle, believing
that a stay away from Savannah would help her to forget Mellichamp
had sent her away to Frederica. John was troubled that he could
no longer minister to her as carefully as previously and his
fears concerning her spiritual and emotional state proved to be
well-founded. After a short time in Frederica Sophy's depression
became much more pronounced, and the concerned Causton asked
Wesley to do what he could to help her. Causton's plea had

undertones which suggest that he believed Wesley could be helpful
in a way that the young clergyman would find very problematic:

> Some of his words were as follows: 'The girl will
> never be easy till she is married.' I answered,
> 'Sir, she is too much afflicted to have a thought
> of it.' He replied, 'I'll trust a woman for that.
> There is no other way.' I said, 'But there are
> few here who you would think fit for her.' He
> answered, 'Let him be but an honest man--an honest,
> good man; I don't care whether he has a groat. I
> can give them a maintenance.' I asked, 'Sir, what
> directions do you give me with regard to her?' He
> said, 'I give her up to you. Do what you will with
> her. Take her into your own hands. Promise her
> what you will. I will make it good.'[8]

If Wesley had been concerned about Sophy's condition when
he left Savannah, on arriving in Frederica he found it even worse
than he had feared. She had decided that there was no reason
for her to stay in Georgia and she had now resolved to return to
England at the first opportunity. His immediate response to this
proposal was that such an action would "complete her destruction."
This response on his part is an indication of his increasing
investment in the young woman. On the face of it, Sophy's return to England would remove a major source of temptation which
he perceived to be a threat to his mission in the colony. But
instead of supporting her resolve to leave Georgia he brought
every religious argument which he could muster into play against
this new design of hers. For more than a week he sought to per-
suade her that her soul would be greatly endangered if she left
the colony and, more particularly, his spiritual tutelage. Her
lack of response to his arguments forced him to change his approach:

> In the evening I asked Miss Sophy if she was still
> determined to go to England. On her answering 'Yes,'
> I offered several arguments drawn from the topics
> of religion against it. But they did not appear to
> make any impression. Then I pressed her upon the
> head of friendship. Upon which she burst into tears,
> and said, 'Now my resolution begins to stagger'; as
> it did more and more every day.[9]

It was, however, an unpleasant encounter which Wesley had
with General Oglethorpe which led to her decision to remain in
the colony. The exploits of the Wesley brothers had increasingly
come to be viewed by Oglethorpe as a divisive force in the colony.

He had been surprised and disappointed at Charles Wesley's seemingly incompetent and irresponsible behavior, and, after several conflicts which were embarrassing to both of them, the younger brother had found an excuse to return to England. Now, it seemed, John's own somewhat problematic relationship with the General was deteriorating. Oglethorpe had just returned to the colony from a diplomatic mission and John now found him more cold and withdrawn than before. Disconcerted by this negative turn in his relationship to the General and believing his own position in the colony to be threatened, he shared his fears with Sophy:

> When I mentioned it to Miss Sophy, and added, 'Now,
> Miss Sophy, you may go to England, for I can assist
> you no longer; my interest is gone'; she answered,
> 'No, now I will not stir a foot.' 'If Mr. Oglethorpe,'
> I said, 'advised you to go, he may be displeased.'
> She replied, 'Let him be pleased or displeased. I
> care not'; and then, turning to me with the utmost
> earnestness, she said, 'Sir, you encouraged me in
> my greatest trials. Be not discouraged in your own.
> Fear nothing. If Mr. Oglethorpe will not, God will
> help you.'10

Sophy had now decided to remain in the colony, and it was soon decided that for her own good she should return to Savannah. Wesley's growing emotional investment in this relationship was to come to a head during the subsequent boat trip. It had been decided that John and Sophy were to share passage on one of the small boats during the difficult journey of several days. The conditions thrust them together in a situation which enabled them to talk incessantly and to renew their spiritual discussions in a context of physical hardship. That Wesley had been aware of the temptation involved before leaving Frederica is evident in the following journal entry:

> I asked Mr. Oglethorpe in what boat she should go.
> He said, 'She can go in none but yours, and indeed
> there is none so proper.' I saw the danger to my-
> self, but yet had a good hope I should be delivered
> out of it, (1) because it was not my choice which
> brought me into it; (2) because I still felt in my-
> self the same desire and design to live a single
> life; and (3) because I was persuaded should my
> desire and design be changed, yet her resolution
> to live single would continue.11

This was the first mention in the journal of Sophy's intention not to marry. Evidently in an earlier discussion of the

Mellichamp relationship she had told him of her decision and, since his involvement with her had not yet developed to this alarming degree, he had failed to enter the comment. Now, however, *her* resolve had taken on a new importance since his was beginning to weaken.

The trip was even more difficult than usual and a violent storm forced them to camp on St. Katherine's Island and wait for suitable weather and winds. Sophy's courage and patience during a journey under such adverse conditions combined with her openness to religious instruction seem to have warmed his heart and softened his resolution. The close proximity to her in the boat was one thing, but the intimacy of soft conversation with her at night by a campfire was quite another. John Wesley's resolution was indeed endangered:

> Observing in the night, the fire we lay by burning bright, that Miss Sophy was broad awake, I asked her, 'Miss Sophy, how far are you engaged to Mr. Mellichamp?' She answered, 'I have promised him either to marry him or to marry no one at all.' I said (which indeed was the expression of a sudden wish, not of any formed design), 'Miss Sophy, I should think myself happy if I was to spend my life with you.' She burst out into tears and said, 'I am every way unhappy. I won't have Tommy; for he is a bad man. And I can have none else.' She added, 'Sir, you don't know the danger you are in. I beg you would speak no more on this head.' And after a while, 'When others have spoken to me on the subject, I felt an aversion to them. But I don't feel any to you. We may converse on other subjects as freely as ever.' Both my judgment and will acquiesced in what she said, and we ended our conversation with a psalm.[12]

John had said what he meant rather than what he meant to say. Given his fantasies of resolution to "live single" he must have been shaken by what he heard himself saying. Neither was her weak rejoinder to settle the matter for either of them. She continued to protest her unwillingness to live with her uncle, and Wesley proposed, among other alternatives, that she could move into one of the rooms in his house. Though she did not accept this *very* generous offer on his part, on arriving in Savannah he arranged the next best alternative. She would lodge with her uncle and would spend most of her time with John at his residence.

The time she was at my house was spent thus. Immediately after breakfast we all joined in Hickes'
Devotions. She was then alone till eight. I taught
her French between eight and nine, and at nine we
joined in prayer again. She then read or wrote
French till ten. In the evening I read to her and
some others select parts of Ephrem Syrus, and afterwards Dean Young's and Mr. Reeve's *Sermons*. We
always concluded with a psalm.[13]

Wesley was not altogether unaware of the temptation involved
in the new arrangement with Miss Sophy. In a reference to the
schedule noted above he concluded:

This I began with a single eye. But it was not long
before I found it a task too hard for me to preserve
the same intention with which I began, in such intimacy of conversation as ours was.[14]

It was indeed the question of intimacy which was central in
Wesley's ambivalence with regard to Sophy. Earlier in his life
he had learned to bridle his desire for psychosexual intimacy
by staging an opposition between such a desire and his commitment to hard work in matters relating to his religious vocation.
This occasion was to be no exception. He began to entertain
seriously again the mission to the Indians. He raised the matter
again with Oglethorpe who was in Savannah preparing for another
trip to England. The General's response was brief and to the
point: "You cannot leave Savannah without a minister."[15] John's
response to Oglethorpe and his reflections on that response are
of central importance to our analysis of the significance of
the Georgia experience. The following journal entry reflects
not only his growing frustrations at not having made progress on
his "extraordinary" mission to the heathen but also the use of
evasion as a tactic to deal with the problem of psychosexual
intimacy.

To this indeed my plain answer was, 'I know not that
I am under any obligation to the contrary. I never
promised to stay here one month. I openly declared
both before, at, and ever since my coming hither
that I neither would nor could take charge of the
English any longer than till I could go among the
Indians.' If it was said, 'But did not the Trustees
of Georgia appoint you to be minister of Savannah?'
I replied, 'They did; but it was not done by my
solicitation: it was done without either my desire
or knowledge. Therefore I cannot conceive that appointment to lay me under any obligation of continuing
there any longer than till a door is opened to the

> heathen; and this I expressly declared at the time
> I consented to accept of that appointment.'16

Wesley was obviously feeling caught up in an ordinary role
which he believed he had escaped by undertaking the Georgia mission. His attempt, if our analysis is correct, to do penance
for the transgression of paternal authority had been, up to now,
sidetracked. But here again we see the urge to go "among the
Indians" manifesting itself as an attempt to obey the dictates
of the internalized maternal authority.

> But though I had no other obligation not to leave
> Savannah now, yet that of love I could not break
> through; I could not resist the importunate re-
> quest of the more serious parishioners 'to watch
> over their souls yet a little longer till some one
> came who might supply my place.'17

He did not press the question of his ministry to the Indians
at this point, primarily because he had managed to interweave his
involvement with a "love I could not break through" with his duty
as a spiritual guide to the residents of Savannah. Again his old
tactic of disguising his role as suitor within the trappings of
that of a spiritual guide enabled him to maintain his quest for
psychosexual intimacy without having to admit honestly to himself the degree of his interest in the "fleshly" and "carnal"
aspect of life.

His other old tactic, that of hard, obsessive work was also
pressed into service at this point. He threw himself into his
almost ruthless work schedule. He compiled a French grammar for
Sophy, continued his study of Spanish, continued his work on a
German grammar, learned Byrom's shorthand, transcribed hymns and
prepared them for publication, all while continuing his heavy
load of pastoral duties.

A new element entered the situation at this time in the
person of William Williamson, a young man who was serving as
Causton's clerk and who was boarding in the magistrate's residence. Sophy had invited him to attend the meeting of the society which was meeting in John's home. Wesley later apparently
felt that he had been partially responsible for the beginning
of her relationship with Williamson and made a note of the irony
of his own contribution to the beginning of the end of their
relationship.

> In the beginning of December I advised Miss Sophy
> to sup earlier, and not immediately before she
> went to bed. She did so; and on this little cir-
> cumstance (for by this she began her intercourse
> with Mr. Williamson) what an inconceivable train
> of consequences depend! Not only 'All the colour
> of remaining life' for her; but perhaps all my
> happiness too, in time and eternity![18]

But even his obsessive work load and his armor provided by his role as spiritual advisor did not alleviate his belief that his resolution was in a great deal of danger. To bolster his commitment to his resolution, he wrote down a list of his best intentions:

> Dec. 19, 1736.
> In the name of God.
> 1--To be more watchful, before and in prayer,
> 2--To strive to be thankful in eating.
> 3--Not to touch even her clothes by choice; think
>   not of her.
> 4--Every hour, Have I prayed quite sincerely? Pray
>   that you may watch, strive.
> 5--Look into no book but the Bible till Christmas.
> 6--From 12 to 4 o'clock, meditation or parish, no
>   writing or reading.
> 7--At Miss Bovey's start up the moment you end the
>   paragraph. No word afterward.
> 8--Speak no untended or unintended word.[19]

Wesley's methods, however, did not save him from the effect of his rapidly weakening resolution. Up to this point he had managed to minimize the intensity of his own feelings and to deny the very real possibility that he was approaching the point of an irrevocable commitment in the relationship. Indeed, his capacity for denial had been and continued to be formidable. Nevertheless, the realities of his relationship with Sophy began to strain even his over-developed defense mechanisms to the breaking point. Three weeks after the solemnly recorded reso- lutions noted above he again began to feel the weakness of his position.

> I was now in a great strait. I still thought it
> best for me to live single. And this was still
> my design; but I felt the foundations of it
> shaken more and more every day. Insomuch that
> I again hinted at a desire of marriage, though
> I made no direct proposal. For indeed it was
> only a sudden thought, which had not the con-
> sent of my own mind. Yet I firmly believe, had
> she (Miss Sophy) closed with me at that time, my
> judgment would have made but a faint resistance.[20]

Sophy had coyly responded that she believed it was best for clergymen not to marry and that she thought herself also resolved never to marry. Later in the relationship Wesley began to reflect upon the possibility that some of her responses were designed to "quicken" him and induce him to declare himself more forthrightly. If he had any such insights at this time, however, there is no indication of it. Still, he was very concerned about this narrow escape and sought out the pastor of the Moravians to ask his advice as to whether or not he should break off the relationship.

> He asked, 'What do you think would be the conse-
> quence if you should?' I said, 'I fear her soul
> would be lost, being surrounded with dangers, and
> having no other person to warn her of and arm her
> against them.' He added, 'And what do you think
> would be the consequence if you should not break
> it off?' I said, 'I fear I should marry her.'
> He replied short, 'I don't see why you should not.'[21]

Wesley was amazed. The Moravian obviously did not share his fear of and distaste for the institution of matrimony. He now began to question for the first time the necessity of re-maining unmarried. When he told his friends and co-workers Ingham and Dellamotte of Pastor Toltschig's comments they im-mediately took the opposite point of view, suggesting that her apparent sincerity and character were really a facade designed to interest him in marrying her. At any rate, they counselled him, he should avoid seeing her for a while so that he could think the matter over with more detachment. He was never one to neglect an advisor recommending detachment, and he decided to go to the little settlement of Irene to ponder the question. Before leaving he wrote Sophy a short note.

> I find, Miss Sophy, I can't take fire into by bosom,
> and not be burnt. I am therefore retiring for a
> while to desire the direction of God. Join with me,
> my friend, in fervent prayer, that He would show me
> what is best to be done.[22]

After arriving in the little village he began to weigh the pros and cons endemic to the relationship with Sophy. His spirits fluctuated between cheerfulness and depression and he seemed to make little or no progress in his deliberations. The next morn-ing it was necessary for him to make a trip back into Savannah to attend to some pastoral responsibilities. There he found the proximity to Sophy without being able to see her almost unbearable.

> There I stayed about an hour; and there again I
> felt, and groaned under the weight of, an unholy
> desire. My heart was with Miss Sophy all the time.
> I longed to see her, were it but for a moment. And
> when I was called to take boat, it was as the sen-
> tence of death; but believing it was the call of
> God, I obeyed.23

If at this point Wesley had indulged his "unholy desire"
to be with Sophy the affair might well have turned out differently. The Moravian had given him at least some support in his
struggle against the prohibitions of the maternal authority and
he realized that to return to Irene at this critical juncture
might mean the death not only of the relationship with Sophy but
also of a very precious, though neglected, part of himself.

Resignation

Wesley had come to the end of his leash and was unable or
unwilling to break it. Sophy had proved to be far more tempting
than he had ever thought possible, and he had begun to entertain
thoughts which he had previously believed unthinkable. The attitude of the Moravians had lent support to his own desire for
psychosexual intimacy by denying that a conjugal relationship
necessarily had to be harmful to one's religious vocation.
Ingham and Delamotte, however, jealously gave their support to
his earlier resolve to remain celibate. His statement to Sophy
that he could not take "fire" into his bosom and not be burned
probably indicates that even before retiring to meditate on the
issue the outcome was little in doubt. If the passion he was
feeling had become identified in his mind with the fires of the
Epworth parsonage and of hell, then there was little doubt but
that it was something to escape from. Before taking boat back
to Irene he experienced a fantasy or daydream which marks clearly
the beginning of the end of their relationship and which offers
an important insight into the "resigned self" of John Wesley.

> I walked awhile to and fro on the edge of the water,
> heavy laden and pierced through with many sorrows.
> There One came to me and said, 'You are still in
> doubt what is best to be done. First, then, cry to
> God, that you may be wholly resigned, whatever shall
> appear to be His will.' I instantly cried to God for
> resignation. And I found that and peace together.
> I said, 'Sure it is a dream.' I was in a new world.
> The change was as from death to life. I went back

> to Irene wondering and rejoicing; but withal exceed-
> ing fearful, lest my want of thankfulness for this
> blessing, or of care to improve it, might occasion
> its being taken away.[24]

Wesley's ambivalence with regard to this "blessing" of
resignation merits some careful reflection. At one moment he
is experiencing the call to return to Irene as a "sentence of
death" and shortly afterward he experiences his new-found resignation to be a change "from death to life." On one level to
turn away from the promise of psychosexual intimacy with Sophy
he felt to be equivalent to writing a death warrant for an important part of his developing self. On another, much more
familiar, level the consummation of that relationship threatened
an outbreak of the dangerous "fires" which his mother had taught
him would consume his commitment to his special religious vocation. The "fire" which could be admitted into his bosom would
have to be of a very special kind, and certainly not overtly
sexual in nature.

Though not particularly thankful for this "blessing" of
resignation, through it he had managed to dampen to a significant degree his ardour for intensifying the relationship with
Sophy. His battle with the internalized maternal authority had
been lost, and his commitment to seek his religious vocation in
a state of celibacy began to gain in strength.

> I was now more clear in my judgment every day. Be-
> side that I believed her resolve, never to marry, I
> was convinced it was not expedient for me, for two
> weighty reasons: (1) because it would probably ob-
> struct the design of my coming into America, the
> going among the Indians; and (2) because I was not
> strong enough to bear the complicated temptations
> of a married state.[25]

Wesley obviously thought that he had settled the issue once
and for all. On returning to Savannah he informed Ingham,
Delamotte, and his Moravian friends of his decision. That he
was hesitant to face Sophy with the results of his sojourn in
the wilderness is evident in the fact that he delayed two days
after returning before he confronted her.

> About seven in the morning, I told her in my own
> garden, 'I am resolved, Miss Sophy, if I marry
> at all, not to do it till I have been among the
> Indians.'[26]

From Wesley's previous experiences with women we can conclude that he fully intended to continue his relationship to
her as a spiritual advisor. He had managed to handle intense
and intimate relationships with others in this way and he undoubtedly saw no reason why this should not be the case in this
situation. Sophy, however, was not to be flanked so easily by
his over-rationalized tactics and began to make a few strategic
moves on her own. Her response was a surprising one to him.
She told him that others in the colony were wondering why she
spent so much time at his house, that she would stop having
breakfast with him, and that she would cease coming to the parsonage alone.

Here we have a hint as to Sophy's attitude toward John at
this time. One less blind to the intricacies of courtship rituals
would no doubt interpret this move on Sophy's part as an attempt
to shake John's resolve by denying him her company in lieu of a
more acceptable commitment on his part. When no change of mind
was forthcoming, the next morning she escalated her attack on
his recalcitrance.

> She said, 'I don't think it signifies for me to learn
> French any longer.' But she added, 'My uncle and aunt,
> as well as I, will be glad of your coming to our house
> as often as you please.' I answered, 'You know, Miss
> Sophy, I don't love a crowd, and there is always one
> there.' She said, 'But we needn't be in it.'27

She seems to have hoped that these warnings would be enough,
for she continued to come to the parsonage for devotional meetings
and prayer services. She even continued her French lessons,
though at her uncle's house. In spite of her seemingly purpose-
ful moves to force John into a proposal, she allowed their close
association to continue, apparently still hoping that his resolve
would weaken without further moves on her part. Her frustration,
nevertheless, soon became evident. Three days later, he noticed
a distinct change in her behavior.

> I called upon her at Mr. Causton's, and we walked to-
> gether in the garden. She did not seem to be affected
> with anything I said, but was in such a temper as I
> never saw her before, sharp, fretful, and disputatious.
> Yet in an hour she awaked as out of sleep, told me she
> had been very ill all day, and indeed scarce in her
> senses, and feared she had given a sufficient proof
> of it in her behavior, which she begged I would not
> impute to her, but solely to her disorder.28

At this time a dispute had broken out between Causton and
the Moravians as to whether the latter could be pressed into
military service against their will. John took the side of the
Moravians, and, thinking that he could use a trip to England to
recruit additional help for his ministry in Georgia, decided that
either he or Ingham should make a trip to London to consult with
the Trustees and other friends of their mission. Perhaps John
now saw leaving Georgia as an escape from temptation. He raised
the question with Sophy, and her intense response was puzzling
to him. She had stated that if he left America then she had no
other ties to the colony. That evening he asked her what she
had meant, and with tears she responded that he was "the best
friend" she had ever had "in the world." He tested the degree
of her commitment to him by raising the spectre of his losing
his position in the colony. Would she then remain loyal to him?
Her response left no question as she declared that he would never
want while she had anything.[29]

Such a protestation must have weakened his capacity for dis-
tancing himself from her, since in the following few days he
felt himself to be acutely threatened in his resolve once again.

> (Calling at Mrs. Causton's Saturday 26th), she was
> there alone. This was indeed an hour of trial.
> Her words, her eyes, her air, her every motion and
> gesture, were full of such a softness and sweet-
> ness! I know not what might have been the conse-
> quence had I then but touched her hand. And how I
> avoided it I know not. Surely God is over all![30]

At least his maternally-inspired resignation was still intact in spite of the buffeting it was receiving at the hands of
this tempting young lady. The next day he found himself alone
again with Sophy, and this time he made the "mistake" of taking
her by the hand. He felt himself "utterly disarmed" when she
was not displeased by his action.

> ...I should have engaged myself for life, had it
> not been for the full persuasion I had of her en-
> tire sincerity, and in consequence of which I
> doubted not but she was resolved (as she had said)
> 'never to marry while she lived.'[31]

Here again Wesley betrays either a lack of understanding
or a lack of willingness to understand the meaning of behavior
which seemed so clear to others. We see here a repeat of Wesley's

tendency to force others to take responsibility for decisions
that are rightfully his. If his behavior leads to a rejection
by others, then the separation is their responsibility, not his.

Still, he was aware that he had had a close call. He re-
affirmed his resolution, made several months earlier, "Not to
touch even her clothes by choice," and also resolved with the
help of God to be more wary in the future.[32]

Delamotte, however, was not aware of the degree of Wesley's
aversion to marriage. He was extremely fearful that Wesley was
about to marry Sophy, and in tears announced his decision to
move out of the parsonage since he could not remain after John's
marriage. After consultation with both Ingham and Delamotte lots
were cast to gain insight into God's will on the subject. On
the three lots were written: "Marry....Think not of it this
year....Think of it no more."[33] Delamotte drew the third. Lots
were cast again to determine whether John should converse with
Sophy any more. The answer came, "Only in the presence of Mr.
Delamotte."[34] Wesley was surprised to find that he could say
cheerfully, "Thy will be done." Delamotte had suggested that
Wesley did not "know his own heart" with respect to Sophy. There
is little doubt that he was still greatly tempted, and the positive aspects of a marriage to Sophy were clearly on his mind.

> I saw and adored the goodness of God, though what he
> required of me was a costly sacrifice. It was indeed
> the giving up at once whatever this world affords of
> agreeable--not only honour, fortune, power (which in-
> deed were nothing to me, who despised them as the clay
> in the streets), but all the truly desirable conven-
> iences of life--a pleasant house, a delightful garden,
> on the brow of a hill at a small distance from the
> town; another house and garden in the town; and a third
> a few miles off, with a large tract of fruitful land
> adjoining to it.[35]

For someone to whom such things were as "the clay of the
streets," the young man had certainly done a very thorough ac-
counting of the things which would accrue to him through a marriage to Sophy. Yet the costliest part of the sacrifice was
Sophy herself.

> And above all, what to me made all things else vile
> and utterly beneath a thought, such a companion as
> I never expected to find again, should I live one
> thousand years twice told. So that I could not but
> cry out: 'O Lord God, Thou God of my fathers, plen-
> teous in mercy and truth, behold I give Thee, not

> thousands of rams or ten thousands of rivers of oil,
> but the desire of my eyes, the joy of my heart, the
> one thing upon earth which I longed for! O give me
> Wisdom, which sitteth by Thy throne, and reject me
> not from among Thy children![36]

The increasing dominance of this "temptation in the wilderness" theme calls for some reflection on the changing role the Georgia experiment was coming to have in Wesley's experience. At the outset the Georgia excursion had been seen as an escape from the temptations of the ordinary--the parish priesthood and psychosexual intimacy--and certainly not as the locus of his severest test in this area. With the onslaught of Sophy and the real possibility of becoming a prosperous but quite ordinary planter-priest, the role of Georgia in his spiritual economy underwent a quite radical transformation. The script now called for dramatic suffering in the arena of sexuality and for a self-righteously flamboyant failure (on principle of course) in the arena of his ordinary and altogether unsatisfactory role as a parish priest. The dramatic suffering was to begin first and to modulate at various levels of intensity throughout the rest of his life. The flamboyant failure was to terminate with this his last and unplanned engagement in an ordinary parish ministry. And both manifested a submission before the maternal authority and a resignation to Susanna's early-inculcated master plan for his life.

A drama of temptation would not be too impressive if one found complete resignation too early, and John was not one to make this error. John reflected on the magnificance of God's intervention in bolstering his faltering will:

> From the directions I received from God this day
> touching an affair of the greatest importance, I
> could not but observe, as I had done many times
> before, the entire mistake of those who assert,
> 'God will not answer your prayer, unless your
> heart be wholly resigned to His will.' My heart
> was not wholly resigned to His will. Therefore,
> not daring to depend on my own judgment, I cried
> the more earnestly to Him to supply what was want-
> ing in me. And I know, and am assured, He heard
> my voice, and did send forth His light and His
> truth.[37]

John found opportunities still abounded for temptation. He went riding with Causton over the latter's plantation and found that the pleasantness of the experience "shot a softness" into his soul. Returning to the home of the magistrate he found Sophy still very much the temptress and the dark side of his soul still much too receptive.

> Soon after I came in, Miss Sophy went out, and walked
> to and fro between the door and the garden. I saw
> she wanted to speak to me, but remembered my resolu-
> tions, especially that to converse with her only in
> Mr. Delamotte's presence. Yet after a short struggle,
> the evil soul prevailed in me, and I went.[38]

Apparently Sophy had received a letter from her old lover Mellichamp and had refused to take it from the messenger. Though John had apparently already heard about this from Causton, Sophy's apparent purpose was to ask him not to question the messenger about the letter. A more likely conclusion is that Sophy wanted to emphasize to him that she had in fact refused the letter. Evidently John had already begun to see William Williamson as a potential rival for Sophy's affections, since he used this opportunity to tell Sophy that Williamson had been the one who had informed her uncle of her receipt of the letter. He empha-sized that he would not have been guilty of such a breach of confidence. In these shared moments of intimacy he again felt the sweet threat.

> I looked upon her, and should have said too much had
> we had a moment longer. But in the instant Mr. Causton
> called us in. So I was once more 'snatched as a brand
> out of the fire.'[39]

Wesley must have felt that God had great plans in store for this "brand" to be continually snatching it from the "fire." Still, he showed a reluctance to see the situation resolved in such a way that would remove the "flames" to a more comfortable distance. He questioned Sophy at some length regarding her feelings for both Mellichamp and her new suitor Williamson, and she assured him that she had no inclinations for either. Con-veniently ignoring the deceptive quality of the message he was communicating to Sophy at this point, he extracted assurances from her that she would never deceive him and that she would take no steps of importance without first consulting him. He had insured the continuing presence of his conflict regarding what to do about the relationship with Sophy.

> She went, and I saw myself in the toils. But how to
> escape I saw not. If I continued to converse with
> her, though not alone, I found I should love her
> more and more. And the time to break it off was
> past. I felt it was now beyond my strength. My
> resolutions indeed remained. But how long? Yet a
> little longer, till another shock of temptation, and
> then I well knew they would break in sunder as a
> thread of tow that has touched the fire. I had
> many times prayed that if it was best our inter-
> course should break off, and that if I could not
> do it she might. But this too I saw less and less
> reason to expect. So that all these things were
> against me, and I lay struggling in the net; nay,
> scarcely struggling, as even fearing to be delivered.[40]

That night another letter from Mellichamp to Sophy was inter-
cepted by her aunt and Sophy came under an angry attack by the
Caustons. Sophy pleaded with John to intercede for her and he
found the aunt enraged, threatening to throw Sophy out of the
household and asking John to take her away with him. There is
little doubt that this solution would have satisfied Sophy, but
John offered only lodgings in his house and any of his belongings
but no proposal of marriage. He left Sophy while she was still
weeping over her situation and found himself extremely depressed.

It had become far too costly for Sophy to continue playing
the role of temptress with no resolution of the situation in
sight. Williamson had none of John's conflicts and reticence,
and, seeing his opportunity, proposed to her that evening. From
her point of view it must have seemed that Wesley had had his
opportunity to rescue her from her distress and, when no move
on his part was forthcoming, she had to accept the only alternative that the situation offered. If, as John later suspected,
there was "artifice" on her part and she hoped to force an intervention from him, there is little doubt that she was resolved
to get out of the Causton household one way or the other.

The next morning Wesley received the news of Sophy's be-
trothal from Mrs. Causton. She told him first that they were
all appreciative of the many things he had done for Sophy and
then announced in quick succession that Williamson had proposed
to their niece the night before, that he had asked for their
consent and had received it. His shock must have been obvious:

> She added, 'Sir, you don't seem to be well pleased.
> Have you any objection to it?' I answered, 'Madam,
> I don't seem to be awake. Surely I am in a dream.'

> She said, 'They agreed on it last night between
> themselves after you was gone. And afterwards Mr.
> Williamson asked Mr. Causton's and my consent,
> which we gave him; but if you have any objection
> to it, pray speak. Speak to her. She is at the
> Lot. Go to her.[41]

She continued to press him and to suggest that he go to
Sophy and talk to her about the decision. He resisted her at
this point since he had long known of the Causton's interest
in him as a potential match for Sophy and was now suspicious
that he was being manipulated in some way.

> I doubted whether all this were not artifice, merely
> designed to quicken me. But though I was uneasy at
> the very thought of her marrying one who, I believed,
> would make her very unhappy, yet I could not resolve
> to save her from him by marrying her myself.[42]

That Sophy had little chance to force an intervention on
Wesley's part is evident by the reasoning which he employed at
that time to justify avoiding any precipitate acts on his part.

> Besides, I reasoned thus, 'Either she is engaged or
> not; if she is, I would not have her if I might:
> if not, there is nothing in this show which ought
> to alter my preceding resolution.[43]

In the following section of his account Wesley pleads ignorance with regard to the real nature of what was going on.
The question, however, arises as to whether his own feigned
ignorance was not an "artifice" designed, not to quicken him,
but to support his resolution not to marry.

> Thus was I saved purely by my ignorance; for though
> I did doubt, I would not believe. I thought it un-
> kind and unjust to believe an artifice of which I had
> not full proof. Oh, let no one ever fear the being
> lost by thinking no evil! Had I known the snare, I
> had perished thereby. All the world could not have
> saved me. Had I then seen the real case to be this
> --'She is engaged, but conditionally only. Mr.
> Williamson shall marry her, if you will not'--I could
> not have stood that shock. I should have incurred
> any loss rather than she should have run that hazard,
> of losing both her body and soul in hell.[44]

That afternoon he did confront Sophy and Williamson.
Williamson initiated the tedious conversation on the subject
after an initial exchange of pleasantries by inquiring as to
whether Wesley had heard the news. Wesley responded that he
wanted to hear it from Sophy directly. Their interchange is
significant:

> She replied, 'Sir, I have given Mr. Williamson my
> consent--unless you have anything to object.' It
> started into my mind, 'What if she means, unless
> you will marry me?' But I checked the thought with
> 'Miss Sophy is so sincere: if she meant so, she
> would say so'; and replied, 'If you have given your
> consent, the time is past; I have nothing to object.'[45]

Wesley was indeed getting the message, but was refusing to
let himself hear it. His plans had no real place for marriage,
and, despite the intense pain during and following this episode,
Sophy was viewed not as a potential mate for life, but as a siren
playing the role of chief temptress in the American wilderness.
That he was relieved at her taking the decision out of his hands
is evident by the scriptural "oracles" which he then regarded
as "answers" to his situation. One read, "Blessed be thou of
the Lord, my daughter; for thou hast showed more kindness at the
latter end than at the beginning."[46] Sophy's decision was a
relief.

After their initial conversation, Williamson felt secure
enough of his position to leave John and Sophy alone together.
John describes his state of mind at this moment:

> 'Tis hard to describe the complication of passions
> and tumult of thought which I then felt: fear of
> her approaching misery, and tender pity; grief for
> my own loss; love shooting through all the recesses
> of my soul, and sharpening every thought and passion.
> Underneath there was a faint desire to do and suffer
> the will of God, which, joined to a doubt whether
> that proposal would be accepted, was just strong
> enough to prevent my saying plainly (what I wonder
> to this hour I did not say), 'Miss Sophy, will you
> marry me?'[47]

Wesley pressed her regarding her resolution not to marry
a man who was not clearly religious. She replied that she had
no proof that Williamson was not, but Wesley insisted that she
should have been unsatisfied with anything less than a positive
proof. Under a great strain, Sophy protested weakly that she
had given her consent on the condition that he would not object
to the union. John did not accept this clear plea and respond
to it. Instead they both spent the rest of their time alone in
tears as about an hour passed. When Williamson returned she
told him that she hoped they could always be friends. His response indicated that as his ties to Sophy were severed, so also
were those to America. His realization that the relationship
was finally at an end cast him into a deep depression.

I came home and went into my garden. I walked up and
down, seeking rest but finding none. From the beginning of my life to this hour I had not known one such
as this. God let loose my inordinate affection upon
me, and the poison thereof drank up my spirit. I was
as stupid as if half awake, and yet in the sharpest
pain I ever felt. To see her no more: that thought
was as the piercings of a sword; it was not to be
borne, nor shaken off. I was weary of the world, of
light, of life. Yet one way remained, to seek to
God--a very present help in time of trouble. And I
did seek after God, but I found Him not. I forsook
Him before: now He forsook me. I could not pray.
Then indeed the snares of death were about me; the
pains of hell overtook me. Yet I struggled for life;
and though I had neither words nor thoughts, I lifted
up my eyes to the Prince that is highly exalted, and
supplied the place of them as I could: and about
four o'clock He so far took the cup from me that I
drank so deeply of it no more.[48]

Still, Wesley was unable to back out of the situation grace-
fully. He sent a note initiating a session with Causton. Sophy's
uncle lost no time in making clear that he believed John to be
a far better match for Sophy and scolded John for not having
intervened. He suggested that he would reopen the question with
Sophy, and that John could also do so.

John continued to profess a lack of understanding of the
messages he was receiving from Sophy and her relatives. The
decision had been taken out of his hands, and he wanted it to
stay that way. After his conversation with Causton he did seek
conversation with Sophy after evening prayers.

Had he then said plainly, 'If you please, you may have
her still; but if you won't, another will,' I know not
what might have been the event; or had Mr. Delamotte
left us alone, when she came to my house after evening
prayers.[49]

Wesley's continued dramatics regarding this seemingly end-
less series of close calls now seem quite forced, and the question arises as to the meaning of these continued involvements
with Sophy. Upon reflection Wesley's exaggerated conviction as
to the degree of Sophy's commitment to remaining single and to
being totally and vulnerably open and frank with him raises
another perspective on his unwillingness to accept responsibility
for what had occurred. If he was unwilling to see how much se-
ductive behavior he had engaged in and the degree to which he
had promised far more than he ever intended to produce in the

way of concrete commitment, he was also unwilling to see that he
was now casting Sophy as the chief culprit in the relationship
in another sense. Before he had cast her as temptress and himself
as the tempted. Now he was building a case that he had been
wronged and that Sophy was indeed the chief master of deceit.
After the company had left that evening he began to challenge
her on these grounds.

> Mr. Williamson begged her not to stay after the rest
> of the company. But she did very readily. He walked
> to and fro on the outside of the house, with all the
> signs of strong uneasiness. I told her, 'Miss Sophy,
> you said yesterday you would take no steps in any-
> thing of importance without first consulting me.'
> She answered earnestly and many times over, 'Why,
> what could I do? I can't live in that house. I can't
> bear these shocks. This is quite a sudden thing. I
> have no particular inclination for Mr. Williamson. I
> only promised if no objection appeared. But what can
> I do?' Mr. Williamson, coming in abruptly, took her
> away, and put a short end to our conversation.[50]

Williamson obviously sensed how shallow Sophy's commitment
to him was, but in reality he had little to fear. Sophy was
determined to get out of the Causton household, and Wesley, again
faced with obvious openings even at this late stage, had no intention of marrying her. He was rapidly becoming the stern,
wronged, and disappointed spiritual director who, on high principle of course, was soon to retaliate against Sophy in a manner
reminiscent of his father's heavy-handed treatment of Hetty.
The next day he sought her out again to see if she had changed
her mind, and by this time she had finally realized that Wesley
did not intend to intervene. He questioned her motivation for
her decision, heard her declare her determination to go through
with the marriage, advised them to publish the banns properly,
and assured them of his continuing friendship and counsel.
Wesley was comfortable and satisfied with himself after the conversation. It seemed that he was going to be able to retain
his intimacy with Sophy after the wedding, though in a spiritual
vein. Such an arrangement had been a common one in Wesley's
earlier relationships with women. To his surprise, the very next
morning the couple were on their way to Purrysburg and were married the following day, Saturday, March 12, 1738. To John, the
irregularity of not having waited until the banns were properly
published added insult to injury and on Friday and Saturday he
suffered intense emotional torment.[51]

It is significant that on the day of the marriage Wesley wrote his will.[52] As we have noted above, he associated the termination of the courtship with a death of a sort, and the marriage concretized his passage. What was dying was his own exertion of will, not only that which seemed to be testing the boundaries of the maternal authority, but also that which was expressed in his own striving for a kind of independence or autonomy through his attempt to work out his own salvation. All that remained was for him to compound his sense of failure by acting out in a style reminiscent of his father the role of a harsh disciplinarian whose motives were questioned by almost the entire colony.

When Sophy returned to Savannah Wesley attempted to continue his role as her pastor and spiritual advisor. For a short time she came to services and engaged in conversation with him afterward. Apparently this continued contact was resented by Williamson, and he pressured her to stay away from Wesley altogether. Wesley, however, became more and more convinced that Sophy had been guilty of lying to him on a number of points, mostly because of the intense gossip which was centering on the entire affair in the colony. He seemed to want to extract a full confession from her that he had been the one who was wronged in the situation, probably in order that he could in good conscience forgive her. But such a confession was not to be forthcoming. Exasperated, Wesley penned the following note on July 5th outlining his case against her:

> If the sincerity of friendship is best to be known from the painful offices, then there could not be a stronger proof of mine than that I gave you on Sunday: except that which I am going to give you now, and which you may perhaps equally misinterpret.
> Would you know what I dislike in your past or present behavior? You have always heard my thoughts as freely as you asked them. Nay, much more freely; you know it well, and so you shall do, as long as I can speak or write.
> In your present behavior I dislike (1) your neglect of half the public service, which no man living can compel you to; (2) your neglect of fasting, which you once knew to be a help to the mind, without any prejudice to the body; (3) your neglect of almost half the opportunity of communicating which you have lately had.
> But these things are small in comparison of what I dislike in your past behavior. For, (1) you told me

over and over you had entirely conquered your inclina-
tion for Mr. Mellichamp. Yet at that very time you
had not conquered it. (2) You told me frequently, you
had no design to marry Mr. Williamson. Yet at the very
time you spoke you had the design. (3) In order to
conceal both these things from me, you went through a
course of deliberate dissimulation. Oh how fallen!
How changed! Surely there was a time when in Miss
Sophy's life there was no guile.
  Own these facts, and own your fault, and you will
be in my thoughts as if they had never been. If you
are otherwise minded, I shall still be your friend,
though I cannot expect you should be mine.
  To Mrs. Williamson, July 5.[53]

The letter clearly casts Wesley in the role of the wronged
suitor rather more than in that of concerned spiritual counselor.
Two things are evident in this letter. First, Wesley seems to
believe that he was totally innocent of dissimulation in the
relationship. This is a relatively clear instance which illustrates the probable degree to which projection figured in his
relationship to Sophy, with him dealing with his own deceptive-
ness by ascribing it to her. The second point to be noticed is
his idea of the requirements for reconciliation in a relationship
which is estranged. Repenting openly of wrongs done wipes the
slate clean and the relationship is restored. Also clearly implicit in the requirement is a swallowing of one's pride by the
transgressor. This soteriology is congruent with that of
Susanna's nursery, that implicit in the Aldersgate experience,
and that made explicit in Wesley's later theology and preaching.
We shall have occasion to discuss this further at some length
later.

We have little indication of Sophy's response to the letter.
Little response, that is, except the fact that she miscarried
less than a week after receiving it. There is little doubt that
Wesley's continued aggressive and intrusive behavior was very
disturbing to her. In his note in the *Journal* concerning the
event Wesley himself expresses his awareness that at least some
others had made a connection between his treatment of her and
the loss of her baby!

  Mon. 11.--Mrs. Williamson miscarried, as Mrs. Causton
  told one, because of my chiding her eight days before;
  as she told another, because of my unkind letter; as
  she herself said, because of the hurry and concern
  which Mr. Williamson's illness threw her into.[54]

Two things are evident in this entry. The different stories told by her concerning the event seem to back up his conviction regarding her tendency to misrepresent and dissimulate. He had apparently confronted her with the story and expected her to admit to his face that which she had confided to others. Related to this questioning of her is his apparent disavowal of any connection between his continuing pressure and the loss of the child. Again Wesley simply did not feel responsible for what had happened to Sophy.

John was still not satisfied that Sophy was properly penitent. After an absence from Holy Communion which seemed to Wesley to be altogether too long, on August 7, 1737 Sophy appeared for the service but was repelled. His account of the incident follows:

> Sun. 7.--I repelled Mrs. Williamson from the Holy Communion (for the reasons specified in my letter of July 5, as well as for not giving me notice of her design to communicate after having intermitted it for some time). I foresaw the consequences well, but remembered the promise in the Epistle for the day, 'God is faithful, who will not suffer you to be tempted above that ye are able; but will with the temptation also make a way to escape, that ye may be able to bear it.'[55]

Whether John really understood the violent response which his action was to receive cannot be established. But if Georgia was now seen as the locus of his temptation, and if, as he had told Sophy and Williamson, he was thinking of leaving the colony, his actions can certainly be seen as preparing the way for an escape.

Sophy was angry, and her uncle and husband were more so. Two days later a warrant was served on John by one of the constables of the colony. It read:

> Georgia, Savannah Ss
> To all Constables, Tithingmen, and others, whom these
>   may concern:
> You, and each of you, are hereby required to take the body of John Wesley, Clerk:
> And bring him before one of the bailiffs of the said town, to answer the complaint of William Williamson and Sophia his wife, for defaming the said Sophia, and refusing to administer to her the Sacrament of the Lord's Supper, in a public congregation, without cause; by which the said William Williamson is damaged one thousand pounds sterling: And for so

doing, this is your warrant, certifying what you are
to do in the premises. Given under my hand and seal
the 8th day of August, *Anno Dom*. 1737.
                    Tho. Christie[56]

Causton set out immediately to discredit Wesley. He went
through John's letters to Sophy selecting the most embarrassing
and indiscrete segments to read to anyone who would listen. At
the same time Williamson formed an alliance with a disgruntled
medical doctor of the colony, one Patrick Tailfer, and participated in writing the angry account which was later published
under the title *A True and Historical Narrative of the Colony
of Georgia in America*. Wesley had never been very popular in
the colony, and his actions that summer unleashed a shrill caco-
phony of attacks upon his character and ministry.

> And now to make our subjection the more complete, a
> new kind of tyranny was this summer (1737) begun to
> be imposed upon us, for Mr. John Wesly (Wesley), who
> had come over, and was received by us as a clergyman
> of the Church of England, soon discovered that his
> aim was to enslave our minds, as a necessary prepara-
> tive for enslaving our bodies. The attendances upon
> prayers, meetings and sermons inculcated by him, so
> frequently, and at improper hours, inconsistent with
> necessary labour, especially in an infant colony,
> tended to propagate a spirit of indolence, and of
> hypocrisy, amongst the most abandoned; it being much
> easier for such persons, by an affected shew of re-
> ligion, and adherence to Mr. Wesly's (Wesley) novel-
> ties, to be provided, by his procurement from the
> public Stores, than to use that industry which *true*
> religion recommends....[57]

But worse than this, they felt they had reason to suspect
that Wesley was a Papist in disguise. He mistreated the dissenters of the colony and doted over those suspected of leaning
towards Roman Catholicism. They sensed that his real plan was
to depress their minds and spirits, to break their spirit of
liberty, and to humble them, probably in preparation for a civil
or ecclesiastical tyranny. To this end, they believed that he
engaged spies in the various homes of the colony to report on
the behavior of their inhabitants, and those colonists, especially
women, who placed themselves in his spiritual care *were* required
to tell him everything about their most secret actions including
their dreams and personal thoughts. They disliked Causton as
much or more than Wesley, but saw the providence of God in the
split between the magistrate and the minister.

Mr. Wesly (Wesley) at this time repulsed Mrs. Sophia
Williamson, niece to Mr. Causton, from the sacrament.
This young lady was by her friends put under the
ghostly care of Mr. Wesly, who was pleased to make
proposals of marriage to her: these she always rejected; and in some time married Mr. William Williamson, of Savannah, much contrary to Mr. Wesly's inclinations: After the said marriage, Mr. Wesly used all
means to create a misunderstanding betwixt Mrs. Williamson and her husband, by persuading her, that Mr.
Williamson had no right to regulate her behaviour as
to conversing with him, or attending meetings as formerly; but at last finding he could gain nothing upon
her, and that Mr. Williamson had forbad him any conversation with his wife out of his presence; he took
the aforesaid means, by repelling her from the Holy
Communion, of shewing his resentment. Mr. Williamson
thought himself well founded in an action of damages;
and Mr. Wesly (being no longer supported by Mr. Causton,
who was highly nettled at the affront put upon his
niece, and could now declaim as fluently against spiritual tyranny as any person) was indicted before a Grand
Jury of forty-four freeholders, and thirteen indict-
ments were found against him; one concerned Mr. Williamson and his spouse; the others concerning the grievances
we felt by his measures, and the exercise of his ecclesiastical functions, as above related....[58]

Wesley wanted the court to begin its deliberations immediately, but the dislike of Causton in the colony expressed itself among the jurors and their hesitation led to the continued
postponement of the hearings. A minority of the jury drew up
an account more favorable to Wesley, and both the accusation and
defense were forwarded to the Trustees of the colony in England.
The deliberations were at a standstill, but the controversy still
raged. John began to be more and more convinced that he should
return to England and present his case directly to the Trustees.
He was informed on November 22nd that he had been branded by the
court as a disturber of the public peace.[59] He told Causton that
day of his intent to leave immediately for England, and posted
a notice that he was leaving. When the magistrates got word of
this they ordered him not to leave and warned all of the officers
and sentinels of the colony to prevent him from leaving if he
tried to do so. He was now resolute in his decision to escape.

Being now only a prisoner at large, in a place where
I knew by experience every day would give fresh opportunity to procure evidence of words I never said,
and actions I never did, I saw clearly the hour was
come for me to fly for my life, leaving this place;
and as soon as evening prayers were over, about eight

> o'clock, the tide then serving, I shook off the dust
> of my feet, and left Georgia, after having preached
> the gospel there (with much weakness indeed and many
> infirmities), not as I ought, but as I was able, one
> year and nearly nine months. ('Oh that thou hadst
> known, at least in this thy day, the things which
> make for thy peace!')[60]

That night, December 2nd, he left quietly by boat for
Purrysburg, then treked overland to Port Royal.[61] He soon made
his way to Charleston and from there, on December 22, 1737, he
embarked for England on board the *Samuel*.[62]

The Georgia experiment had proved to be a disastrous failure
on all fronts. First of all, the mission to the natives which
had promised to serve so well as a grand act of penance had never
materialized. Secondly, this left him in a role which he had
already rejected actively and which he now rejected passively.
If he failed as a parish priest, he did so in the style of his
heavy-handed father and could appeal to his "good intentions"
in the face of that failure. And finally, the failure of his
relationship to Sophy indicates his inability to reject dominant
maternal images and the control of the internalized maternal
authority. He had not expected to be tempted by women in Georgia,
and his discovery of attractive young women there was experienced
as a "sweet threat" to his religious mission. In Sophy his temptations had been concretized and he experienced his attraction
to her as frightening and almost overwhelming. Yet the maternal
prohibitions proved too powerful for him to break and he suc-
cumbed to obedience.

The Georgia excursion had, of course, been an experiment,
and, as with many experiments, an unexpected outcome can prove
as useful as one that had been anticipated. Georgia gradually
came to mean, not a locus for a special ministry isolated from
the temptations of the world, but the wilderness of temptation
itself, a trial by fire during which he was purified of his illusions about his own righteousness and his tendencies toward
self will.

It is appropriate at this point to analyze briefly the ways
in which the Georgia fiasco seemed to turn on the issue of will.
At the outset, of course, we should remember that it was the
aftermath of a mighty struggle of wills between himself and his
father that eventually led Wesley to undertake the Georgia

mission. Indeed, in Eriksonian terminology the unifying theme
for the Georgia experience might well be understood as initiative
vs. guilt.[63] It was, in a way, a kind of precocious *spiritual
initiative* which formed one of his main reasons for wanting to
stay at Oxford, and which formed the basis for his stated reason
for undertaking the mission to the Indians. At the outset of
the journey he had little sense of the self-will and pride which
he later came to believe lay at the root of his desire to save
his own soul. On board the *Samuel*, as we shall see below, things
looked quite different. The most glaring expression of initiative and accompanying guilt was, of course, his passion for and
involvement with Sophy. During the sojourn in Georgia he came
to view his will, even when it manifested itself in the form of
spiritual initiative, as hopelessly flawed. Increasingly it
began to dawn on him that his own initiative had to die, that
it could not be trusted, that his only hope lay in resignation
to the will and initiative of God.

He had sought to work out his own salvation in fear and
trembling, and it was that very fear which made him begin to
question the adequacy of his faith. Even as early as the voyage
to Georgia on board the *Simmonds* he had been impressed with the
fearlessness of the Moravians. The uneasy feeling that he lacked
something that the Germans had led him to become very close to
them throughout the time of his stay in the colony. His conversation with Spangenberg on his arrival in Georgia has posed the
questions which occupied him during his ministry there and which
now, on leaving it, obsessed him.

> I asked Mr. Spangenberg's advice with regard to my-
> self--to my own conduct. He told me he could say
> nothing till he had asked me two or three questions.
> 'Do you know yourself? Have you the witness within
> yourself? Does the Spirit of God bear witness with
> your spirit that you are a child of God?' I was sur-
> prised, and knew not what to answer. He observed it,
> and asked, 'Do you know Jesus Christ?' I paused, and
> said, 'I know he is the Saviour of the world.' 'True,'
> replied he; 'but do you know He has saved you?' I
> answered, 'I hope He has died to save me.' He only
> added, 'Do you know yourself?' I said, 'I do.' But
> I fear they were vain words.[64]

Now, on leaving the colony in disgrace and despair, the
same issues were on his mind. Though he busied himself in min-
istering to the ship's company, he was engaged in a ruthless
self-analysis.

Sun. 8.--In the fullness of my heart, I wrote the following words:
By the most infallible proofs, inward feeling, I am
convinced,
1. Of unbelief; having no such faith in Christ as will
prevent my heart from being troubled; which it could
not be, if I believed in God, and rightly believed
also in Him:
2. Of pride, throughout my life past; inasmuch as I
thought I had what I find I have not:
3. Of gross irrecollection; inasmuch as in a storm I
cry to God every moment; in a calm, not:
4. Of levity and luxuriancy of spirit, recurring whenever the pressure is taken off, and appearing by my
speaking words not tending to edify; but most by my
manner of speaking of my enemies.
Lord, save, or I perish! Save me,
1. By such a faith as implies peace in life and in
death:
2. By such humility as may fill my heart from this
hour for every, with a piercing sense, *Nihil est quod
hactenus feci*; having evidently built without a found-
dation:
3. By such a recollection as may cry to Thee every moment, especially when all is calm: Give me faith, or I
die; give me a lowly spirit; otherwise, *mihi non sit
suave vivere*:
4. By steadiness, seriousness...sobriety of spirit;
avoiding, as fire, every word that tendeth not to
edifying; and never speaking of any who oppose me, or
sin against God, without all my own sins set in array
before my face.[65]

He continued his soul-searching, and was not at all happy
about what he found there. His lament was perhaps best expressed
in his sorrowful realization, "I went to America, to convert the
Indians; but oh, who shall convert me?"[66]

On February 1, 1738, Wesley landed again on English soil.[67]
At this point, though he later questioned these thoughts, he was
convinced that he had never been converted. In an account of
his reasoning on the matter he takes note of his scholarly accomplishments in the area of divinity, his good works, his sac-
rifices and concludes that he is still a child of wrath. He was
convinced that his whole heart was "altogether corrupt and abomi-
nable" and that he had no hope except that of being justified,
not by any claim of righteousness on his own part, but "that
which is through the faith of Christ, the righteousness which
is God by faith."[68]

Wesley went on to describe the kind of faith which he longed
for and which he lacked:

> The faith I want (the faith of a son) is 'a sure trust
> and confidence in God, that, through the merits of
> Christ, my sins are forgiven, and I reconciled to the
> favour of God.' I want that faith which St. Paul
> recommends to all the world, especially in his Epistle
> to the Romans: that faith which enables every one
> that hath it to cry out, 'I live not; but Christ liveth
> in me; and the life which I now live, I live by faith
> in the Son of God, who loved me, and gave Himself for
> me.' I want that faith which none can have without
> knowing that he hath it (though many imagine they have
> it, who have it not); for whosoever hath it, is 'freed
> from sin, the' whole 'body of sin is destroyed' in him:
> he is freed from fear, 'having peace with God through
> Christ, and rejoicing in hope of the glory of God.'
> And he is freed from doubt, 'having the love of God
> shed abroad in his heart, through the Holy Ghost which
> is given unto him'; which 'Spirit itself beareth wit-
> ness with his spirit, that he is a child of God.'[69]

The trials of Georgia had finalized the process which
Susanna Wesley had initiated and facilitated in the Epworth parsonage, the breaking down of John's self-will. The fires of
passion and even of spiritual initiative had burned him out,
and he now felt himself to be a cold, dead cinder, a resigned
self waiting for the Spirit of God to move in him and to warm
his heart.[70]

Vindication

On his arrival back in England Wesley did not allow his
intensive self-analysis to interfere with his continued work as
a minister. He read prayers and counseled with travelers in
the inns where he stayed during his journey to London. A hint
that his supposed intentions of returning to Georgia to attempt
once again the ministry to the natives were soon to be supplanted
may be found in his response to the first Englishmen he encoun-
tered in providing religious leadership again in his homeland:

> I here read prayers, and explained the Second Lesson
> to a few of those who were called Christians, but
> were indeed more savage in their behavior than the
> wildest Indians I have yet met with.[71]

Wesley was soon to become convinced that England provided
"heathen" enough without returning to Georgia, and that an extraordinary ministry did not have to focus entirely on foreign
missions. At this point, however, Wesley was too depressed and
disoriented by the events in Georgia and his realizations about
himself to be much concerned with any grand designs.

By the third of February he was back in London renewing his relationships with family and friends. He met with Charles and soon visited with his mother. After discussions with a number of his old acquaintances and, after telling them the circumstances surrounding his unexpected arrival, he realized that he could no longer postpone his encounter with the Trustees of the colony. He met with them several times and defended himself as best he could against the accusations which had been made against him. Nevertheless, in spite of his best efforts and some supporting letters which he had with him, the Trustees saw fit to remove him from his appointment to the colony.[72]

After these no doubt embarrassing and humiliating sessions with the Trustees, he was able to continue with his preaching and discussions with friends. Since he had just returned from a colony which was of great interest to many people at that time he received many invitations to preach in various London churches. The following journal notation was to be repeated in almost identical form many times in the ensuing months:

> ...In the afternoon I was desired to preach at St.
> John the Evangelist's. I did so on those strong
> words, 'If any man be in Christ, he is a new crea-
> ture.' I was afterwards informed, many of the best
> in the parish were so offended, that I was not to
> preach there any more.[73]

Much of the "old creature" in John had already passed away, although he was not at all sure whether there was going to be a new one. Still, a substantial residue of the old merit-hoarding self remained, and when myriad listeners were repelled by his attacks on works-righteousness he counted the points in the plus column as being part of that persecution which true followers of Christ are bound to endure.[74]

He was gratified to find a warm welcome from numerous old friends, but it was the making of a new friend in the person of the Moravian Peter Bohler which was to prove most important in his continuing personal and theological development. Bohler and several of his friends had just arrived in London from Germany and, since they knew no one in England, Wesley assisted them in finding lodging for their stay. The young German had formerly been a Lutheran, but had more recently been ordained into the ministry of the Moravian Brethren.[75] What Spangenberg had been

to Wesley in Georgia, Bohler was to pick up and carry much further in England.

It was quite natural that Bohler and Wesley immediately
seemed to have an affinity for each other, since Bohler was on
his way to a ministry in Georgia. The attraction on Wesley's
part, however, went much deeper than that. He had continued to
ruminate on the rocklike trust and assurance which appeared to
be available to the Moravians he had met previously and which
seemed to elude his grasp. Now he had an opportunity to continue
his inquiries under the leadership of this young man with whom
he seemed to be able to relate so easily. He told Bohler of his
experiences with the Moravians in Georgia and of his intention
to visit Herrnhut the following summer. Bohler liked Wesley immediately and, though he believed John's understanding of the
faith left something to be desired, he hoped that through his
own influence and that of the visit to the Moravian homeland
Wesley might become a full-fledged member of the Brethren.[76]

Wesley lost no time in engaging Bohler in extensive discussions of the nature of the soteriological economy at every
opportunity. Bohler, after having had time to locate Wesley's
particular stage of spiritual and theological development, proved
himself to be fully as direct and confrontive as Spangenberg had
been.

> All this time I conversed much with Peter Bohler;
> but I understood him not, and least of all when he
> said, *Mi frater, mi frater, excoquenda est ista tua
> philosophia.* 'My brother, my brother, that philo-
> sophy of yours must be purged away.'[77]

Bohler, among other things, was probably referring to the
way in which Wesley continued to intellectualize at an abstract
level regarding the nature of grace and faith. The Moravian
intended to show Wesley and the other young Englishmen with whom
he was involved that faith was indeed central, but that its
presence or absence could not be established by abstract reasoning or logic applied to the presence or absence of good works.

Wesley was becoming more open to Bohler's position, but
still on the level of the abstract. With regard to his own practice, he seemed to be still convinced that when his preaching or
spiritual counseling proved less than effective it was due to his
own lack of discipline, rather than anything more basic.

> With regard to my own behaviour, I now renewed and
> wrote down my former resolutions:
> 1. To use absolute openness and unreserve with all
> I should converse with.
> 2. To labour after continual seriousness, not will-
> ingly indulging myself in any the least levity of
> behavior, or in laughter,--no, not for a moment.
> 3. To speak no word which does not tend to the glory
> of God; in particular, not to talk of worldly things.
> Others may, nay, must. But what is that to thee?
> And,
> 4. To take no pleasure which does not tend to the
> glory of God; thanking God every moment for all I
> do take, and therefore rejecting every sort and
> degree of it which I feel I cannot so thank Him *in*
> and *for*.[78]

Wesley's punitive conscience was still very much at work
and the screws of repression remained as tight as ever. Nevertheless, Bohler's continual hammering at the necessity of saving
faith, a present personal relationship with Christ through which
one would *know* pardon and assurance and not merely speculate about
it, had taken its toll on Wesley. On Sunday, March 5, 1738, John
was finally totally and irrevocably convinced that he did not
have the faith which was necessary for salvation. He had already
realized this intellectually, but now it struck him with renewed
force.

> Immediately it struck into my mind, 'Leave off preach-
> ing. How can you preach to others, who have not faith
> yourself?' I asked Bohler whether he thought I should
> leave it off or not. He answered, 'By no means.' I
> asked, 'But what can I preach?' He said, 'Preach faith
> *till* you have it; and then, *because* you have it, you
> will preach faith.'[79]

Here again Bohler was striking at the heart of Wesley's religious egoism. For the Moravian the power of God's word of
grace had an objective reality and efficacious power that did
not depend on the subjective condition of the preacher no matter
how petty and self-centered that subjective condition might be.
Wesley was experiencing a great deal of resistance to this idea
that God might indeed use him without his own spiritual house
being in obsessive and compulsive order. Nevertheless, he continued preaching in spite of his feelings of unworthiness.

Bohler's next task was to renew his frontal attacks on the
Wesley brothers' tendency to be preoccupied with what they could
do to fight sin. Both John and Charles were present at this

meeting which took place on March 23rd.[80] For years their mas-
ters had been, among other proponents of a rigorous, ascetic
bridling of the will, Thomas à Kempis and William Law. But
Bohler constantly countered their image of Christ as the ideal
with his of Christ as saviour. Wesley finally concluded that
Bohler's view would bear testing as to whether it was scripturally
sound. He was amazed at what he could understand of what the
Moravian was saying: both holiness and happiness could issue
forth in his life *if* he had a living faith.[81]

Within a month Wesley had been convinced that Bohler's
understanding of faith was fundamentally correct.

> I met Peter Bohler once more. I had now no objection
> to what he said of the nature of faith; namely, that
> it is (to use the words of our Church) 'a sure trust
> and confidence which a man hath in God, that through
> the merits of Christ his sins are forgiven and he
> reconciled to the favor of God.' Neither could I
> deny either the happiness or holiness which he de-
> scribed as fruits of this living faith. 'The Spirit
> itself beareth witness with our spirit that we are
> the children of God,' and 'He that believeth hath
> the witness in himself' fully convinced me of the
> former; as 'Whatsoever is born of God doth not com-
> mit sin,' and 'Whosoever believeth is born of God'
> did of the latter.[82]

Wesley had now tested Bohler's position by delving deeply
into his own Greek New Testament and had found that it had stood
the test. Bohler was directing him toward that kind of faith
which he had said that he wanted, the faith of a *son*, and his
objections were becoming fewer in number with each passing day.
Yet he still had one principal problem with Bohler's point of
view. He simply could not stomach the German's espousal of
"instantaneous" conversion.[83] Again he searched the scriptures
and, to his amazement, he found a great deal of evidence for
the existence of such conversions in the early Church. Bohler
had backed him into a corner.

> I had but one retreat left; namely, 'Thus, I grant,
> God wrought in the *first* ages of Christianity; but
> the times are changed. What reason have I to be-
> lieve He works in the same manner now?'
>   But on Sunday the 23rd, I was beat out of this
> retreat too, by the concurring evidence of several
> living witnesses; who testified God had thus wrought
> in themselves, giving them in a moment such a faith
> in the blood of His Son as translated them out of
> darkness into light, out of sin and fear into holiness

and happiness. Here ended my disputing. I could
now only cry out, 'Lord, help thou my unbelief!'[84]

Bohler had marshalled his heaviest spiritual artillery at
the critical moment and John found that he had no defense left.
He was now clear about what he lacked and very depressed about
his condition as he now understood it. He told his brother
Charles about his newest insights and found him still very resistant to the Moravian's point of view. Bohler, on the other
hand, had not given up on the younger brother, and took his
advocacy into combat with Charles' doubts. Again, the German
was not to be resisted and on May 3rd the reluctant Charles had
capitulated.[85]

Bohler now felt that he had done all that was humanly possible to prepare the way for God's action in the life of the
Wesleys. He had stripped away their defenses with all the skill
of a tender surgeon, and, from his point of view, they now stood
naked awaiting a move only God could make. He then left London
to depart for his work in the new world. He summed up his case
as God's advocate in a letter mailed to John before embarking:

> I love you greatly, and think much of you in my
> journey, wishing and praying that the tender mer-
> cies of Jesus Christ the Crucified, whose bowels
> were moved towards you more than six thousand years
> ago, may be manifested to your soul: that you may
> taste, and then see, how exceedingly the Son of God
> has loved you, and loves you still; and that you may
> continually trust in Him, and feel His life in your-
> self. Beware of the sin of unbelief; and if you have
> not conquered it yet, see that you conquer it this
> very day, through the blood of Jesus Christ. Delay
> not, I beseech you, to believe in *your* Jesus Christ;
> but so put Him in mind of His promises to poor sin-
> ners that He may not be able to refrain from doing
> for you what He hath done for so many others. Oh
> how great, how inexpressible, how unexhausted is His
> love! Surely He is now ready to help; and nothing
> can offend Him but our unbelief.
>   Believe, therefore. Greet in my name your
> brother Charles and Hall; and admonish one another
> to believe, and then to walk *circumspectly* in the
> sight of God, to fight *lawfully* against the devil
> and the world, and to crucify and to tread all sin
> under your feet, as far as you are permitted through
> the grace of the second Adam, whose life exceeds the
> death of the first Adam, and whose grace far surpasses
> the corruption and damnation of the first Adam.[86]

The Moravian had done his work well, and Charles was the
first to experience the results of his long and tedious teaching. The younger Wesley had been having periodic bouts of ill
health, and was still bedfast from one of his attacks when he
experienced his conversion to a saving faith.[87] John, however,
was still without such an experience. His depression continued
without any relief. He continued his preaching, and continued
to find that wherever he preached from his new understanding
the pulpits were closed to him.

In a state of deep dejection Wesley wrote a lengthy letter
describing his spiritual state. The letter is written with such
intensity that it seems to be an outpouring of bitterness concerning his own unworthiness and lack of faith, using the friend
for a sounding board. He begins by acknowledging the strange
and incomprehensible character of a God who would use someone
like him to forward divine purposes, but he does not question
the fact that God continues to use him. He believes the law of
God is just, but is convinced that he deserves nothing from him.
All of those things which he had previously considered to be
good works he now believes to be simply further evidence of his
corruption. God is a fire which has every right and reason to
consume him.

But he does have some hope in the promise of God that who-
ever believes will be saved. The last part of the letter is a
prayer which calls upon Jesus for help in emptying himself and
in coming to a state of trusting faith.[88]

The next entry in Wesley's journal is presented by him as
a narrative which can put the events of Wednesday, May 24th, in
context.[89] The narrative is a summary of his spiritual pilgrimage from his childhood to this critical moment. In it the
central theme is his continual dependence upon his own works
and his own righteousness for his hope of salvation. He narrates
the influences which gradually changed his mind concerning his
goal and what was required of him. This was a "justifying,
saving faith, a full reliance on the blood of Christ shed for
me; a trust in Him, as *my* Christ, as *my* sole justification,
sanctification, and redemption."[90] He notes that prior to
Bohler's influence he had desired a true and living faith, but
that he had still failed to fix his hope on the "right object."

Previously, he had "meant only faith in God, not faith in or through Christ."[91] Bohler's tutelage had corrected this, and he now looked to Christ for the help which he needed.

On May 24th, he found that experience which he had been seeking. In the evening of that day he went without enthusiasm to a small group meeting which was located on Aldersgate Street. One of the members of the group was reading from Luther's preface to the *Epistle to the Romans*.

> About a quarter before nine, while he was describing the change which God works in the heart through faith in Christ, I felt my heart strangely warmed. I felt I did trust in Christ, Christ alone for salvation; and an assurance was given me that He had taken away my sins, even *mine*, and saved *me* from the law of sin and death.[92]

His temptations had not ended, however, and almost immediately he wondered why he was not experiencing joy.[93] He was taught at that time that though joy usually accompanies the beginning of faith, it does not always do so. This eased his concerns somewhat, but after returning home his fears continued. Now, rather than allowing himself to sink into a deep depression, he prayed for grace to assist him and found some solace.

> And herein I found the difference between this and my former state chiefly consisted. I was striving, yea, fighting with all my might under the law, as well as under grace. But then I was sometimes, if not often, conquered; now, I was always conqueror.[94]

A close reading of the journal, as we shall see below, raises some doubts as to whether Wesley was now "always conqueror." Still, there is little doubt that the experience was in fact an important one for Wesley. Popular Wesley biography has taken this event and interpreted it as *the* decisive event in Wesley's personal and spiritual development.[95] Wesley himself evidently wanted to present the experience as the occasion of a most significant upturn in his psychic and spiritual condition. We must inquire, however, into the nature of the change which had occurred.

This intense experience of the grace of God following so closely upon the failure of an important experiment and "grand act of penance" raises the question of the possible relationship between the failure and the forgiveness. Two failures of real magnitude to John occurred in Georgia. He had failed to carry out his extraordinary ministry to the heathen, thus aborting his project of penance to the paternal authority. Maternal expectations of an extraordinary role for him had also been thwarted by this contingency, and, in addition, his unexpected struggle with the carnal was a head-on conflict with maternal prohibitions. We have noted above that Susanna was satisfied with a child's obedience of her rules, and granted approval even of a failure when good intentions were manifest. Samuel, on the other hand, was mysteriously ambivalent and often made fun of John precisely *because* he kept the rules and obeyed so well. And Samuel took no note whatever of "good intentions." Even a successful carrying out of an act of penance could not be depended upon to effect a reconciliation with the capricious father. Samuel simply did not have the charity, as John had put it, which was due even to "wicked persons."

It is significant that the qualities which Samuel lacked were precisely those which Wesley had come to attribute to the heavenly father. Wesley at a quite early age had formulated an understanding, through the counsel of his parents, that justification is made possible solely through the merits of Christ. He knew, too, that the work of Christ had to be appropriated by man. The important part, however, of his early understanding was that the conditions of salvation were faith and a sincere, though imperfect obedience to the law of God. Faith here was conceived of more as an intellectual assent than as a personal relationship of trust. Yet equally as important was the emphasis on the fundamental necessity of the subjugation of the will, purity of intention, and fulfilling the law. The latter was, of course, much more difficult to deal with than the requirement of assent. But Wesley committed himself to seek total devotion and obedience. The training of his parents was supplemented and not contradicted by Wesley's reading of Jeremy Taylor, Thomas à Kempis, and William Law.[96] He had set out to prove himself worthy of receiving the benefits of the sacrifice of Christ, but he was to find this struggle very problematic. Just as he had trouble knowing where he stood with his father, even when he had done his very best, he feared that he had not yet pleased his heavenly father either.

Georgia had intensified his feelings of inadequacy and his fear that all of his works and feigned righteousness would meet only with God's wrath. He had found his will far more infected with carnality than he had previously believed, and now his hope that he might find favor with God was greatly weakened. It was not until he had continued his learning from the Moravians, begun in Georgia, under Peter Bohler that his image of God began to change. Now a different kind of faith seemed to become a possibility, that of a *son* rather than a servant. We should remember in this context that reconciliation with Samuel had always required John's serving him as a scribe, or working on some other task which the father assigned. The new image of God, facilitated by Bohler and actualized in the Aldersgate experience, was of a heavenly father who was not only trustworthy, but whose love reached out to man, even in his imperfection, and made man *want* to obey him. After Aldersgate Wesley was no longer inhibited by a capricious, unloving, unreasonable father. He now had a heavenly father who was not only just, but loving and gracious. The demand of the drudgeries of constantly proving oneself, and doing penance after having failed, seemed to have been replaced by an opportunity for joyous obedience.

It is clear that one can discern in the superstructures of the new soteriological economy elements of the moral order of Susanna's nursery. For if the potency of the capricious paternal authority had finally been laid to rest, that of the maternal authority not only continued in the form of a search for a providential role, but also was transformed and elevated into the demanding, yet gracious, image of the heavenly father.

Wesley's theological development and the psychosocial infrastructures of his mature thought will be analyzed in some depth in the next chapter. It should suffice at this point to note two other points of interest in reflecting on the significance of the conversion experience. First, Wesley's obsessive-compulsive over-controlling style with regard to what he considers as being permissible expressions of self-will, including feelings, remains intact. He continues to be suspicious of taking pleasure in anything which is not completely innocuous.[97] For him the adjudication of what qualifies under this rubric is determined by the question of whether the enjoyment is directly

related to his religious mission. In this sense, then, the law,
both psychological and theological, is still functional and
rigorous obedience is seen as a natural out-growth of an experience of justification by grace through faith. Second, and closely
related to the above, the issue of initiative vs. guilt is resolved finally not through rebellion against authority, but in
submission to it and identification with it. The "face" or image
of authority is altered so that it *deserves* obedience. There is
now no *good* reason to resist it. The intrusive authority is now
welcomed into his being to replace his perverted will. Whereas
before good works were a burden which might or might not elicit
an expression of approval and favor from the divine authority,
now the expression of encouragement and favor precedes the works
and his initiative is now far less inhibited by feelings of fear
and acute uncertainty. His self-will and perverted initiative
had led to failure in Georgia. Yet in a manner reminiscent of
the Epworth nursery, when his good intentions and repentance
were presented to the relevant authority he found pardon, and
in that pardon he had concrete evidence that he was a son and
not a servant.

Confirmation and Exaltation

While reflecting on the assurance of the availability of
pardon, we should also be aware of the cost which that same
pardon elicited prior to its being granted. As a child Wesley's
expressions of will brought punishment not pardon and this dynamic continued in his emerging soteriological economy. Levity or
pleasures which could even remotely be construed to be "worldly"
in nature continued to be forbidden. It is not surprising, then,
that Wesley had little room in his heart for the joy which he
wanted so much to experience. For him real religious commitment
issued in a radical seriousness, and Wesley continued to be suspicious of anyone who manifested the least lightheartedness.
Now he felt he had "peace with God," but "the enemy injected a
fear, 'If thou dost believe, why is there not a more sensible
change?'"[98] As the days passed he became more and more concerned
about his lack of a continuing experience of joy. Bohler had
taught him that justification would bring with it a full experience of assurance and accompanying joy. He finally decided that

he would embark on his planned trip to Herrnhut to see if he could find some answers there.[99]

On his way to Herrnhut he stopped for a brief visit with Count Zinzendorf at Marienborn. There he was to find the first of several confirmations by Moravians that his partial assurance and seeming lack of joy did not nullify the reality of his experience of justification. His first reassurance came from the Count himself. Wesley has summarized the teaching he heard at that time regarding justification under eight points:

(1) Justification is the forgiveness of sins.
(2) The moment a man flies to Christ he is justified;
(3) And has peace with God; but not always joy.
(4) Nor perhaps may he know he is justified, till long after;
(5) For the assurance of it is distinct from justification itself.
(6) But others may know he is justified by his power over sin, by his seriousness, his love of the brethren, and his 'hunger and thirst after righteousness,' which alone prove the spiritual life to be begun.'
(7) To be justified is the same thing as to be born of God.
(8) When a man is awakened, he is begotten of God, and his fear and sorrow, and sense of the wrath of God, are the pangs of the new birth.[100]

In the Count's teaching he found a rationale under which he could accept his continuing lack of joy without questioning his experience of justification. Zinzendorf was contradicting the words of Bohler which had made his experience up to now seem inadequate. After arriving at Herrnhut he was to find further confirmation of the validity of his Aldersgate experience. This came in a series of talks with eleven of the members of the Moravian community. The most intense impact on Wesley was made by the carpenter Christian David. In listening to his sermons and discussing privately with him, Wesley again heard the encouraging word that even a weak faith is still faith and that the experience of the full fruits of that new trust in God may take a while to develop. Now he was confident that he had an adequate theological explanation for what he experienced during the doldrums which followed Aldersgate.[101]

The entire experience was proving a heady one for Wesley. He had for years tried to learn as much as possible about "primitive Christianity" and to exemplify its spirit in his own life.

Here, it seemed, he was in the presence of a community that had
a sense of its oneness with the early church. Wesley's identification with the early Christian community and its leaders is
manifest in two letters written on August 4, 1738, one to his
brother Charles and another to James Hutton.[102] In a sensitive
analysis of these letters Martin Schmidt has noted the affected
imitation of the style and organization of a Pauline epistle.[103]
An ironic aspect of these letters is his pompously-worded exhortation to his colleagues that they use "great plainness of
speech." Schmidt also notes Wesley's use of phrasing which was
very typical of Zinzendorf.[104] That he engaged in such posturing
at this critical time is of great interest from a psychological
perspective. It is evident that he had not given up his goal
of a *very* extraordinary ministry. Here he is identifying with
the Apostle Paul and with a corresponding figure, Zinzendorf,
in this contemporary recapitulation of the early church. His
evaluation of the experience at Herrnhut is evident in the following journal entry.

> I would gladly have spent my life here; but my Master
> calling me to labour in another part of His vineyard,
> on *Monday* the 14th I was constrained to take my leave
> of this happy place; Martin Dober and a few others
> of the brethren walking with us about an hour. Oh
> when shall THIS Christianity cover the earth, as the
> 'waters cover the sea'?[105]

The accounts written before leaving Herrnhut both in journal
entries and in letters had been almost, if not completely, un-
equivocal in their praise of the Moravian community. After his
return to London, however, he began to have some questions regarding the way of life which he had observed. At that time he
wrote a letter which was never mailed and which was published
only after his open break with the Moravians. In it he intended
to confront his German friends with some questions which were
highly critical of their leader's dominance in their lives and
which raised the issue of the relative depth of their religious
commitment. Among them were these queries:

> Is not the Count all in all? Are not the rest
> mere shadows, calling him Rabbi, almost implicitly
> both believing and obeying him?
> Is there not something of levity in your be-
> havior? Are you in general serious enough?
> Are you not straitened in your love? Do you
> love your enemies and wicked men as yourselves?

> Do you not mix human wisdom with divine, joining
> worldly prudence to heavenly?
> Do you not use cunning, guile, or dissimulation
> in many cases?
> Are you not of a close, dark, reserved temper and
> behavior?[106]

If his criticisms were accurate it may well have been because he had become used to finding these same faults in himself
and could easily transfer the focus of his discerning eye to
others. That he did not mail the letter, nevertheless, may indicate that he had some doubt as to the accuracy of his percep-
tions. At any rate these comments suggest not only that he was
continuing to identify with the Count, but that he was projecting
his doubts about his own motives and behavior onto the Brethren.
In a largely discredited bit of lore concerning his days at
Charterhouse Wesley is said to have remarked: "Better to rule
in hell than to serve in heaven."[107] Even if this anecdote is
apocryphal it expresses a characteristic of Wesley that is clearly
evident both before and after the Aldersgate experience, the drive
to dominate and control not only himself but other people. It
should be clear from this that Wesley's identification with
Zinzendorf was multifaceted and included at least an envy of his
position of dominance and leadership of a group which was quite
extraordinary in his mind. The issues of dominance, control, and
purity of motivation are central to his criticisms. and Wesley
himself was struggling with each of these.

The Moravians could not be faulted on one point, however;
they had joy. Wesley continued to be troubled by his lack of
joy and a sensible love for God. Although on his return to
England he had continued preaching the "glad tidings of salvation," he was agonizing in private.[108] He still felt that he
had been truly pardoned and saw evidence that in spite of what
he lacked on the experiential level, the grace of God was present
and seemed to use him more than ever. On September 30th he had
had the surprising and encouraging experience of helping a man
to face the depths of his wickedness and to receive pardon.[109]
The man had shown evidence of a total change in the orientation
of his life, and, probably more important to John, had begun to
experience the joy of his newfound trust in God. A little more
than a week later Wesley read a book which probably magnified in
his mind the significance of the conversion which he had helped

to bring about. As Wesley put it in the journal entry, "In walking I read the truly surprising narrative of the conversions lately wrought in and about the town of Northampton, in New England. Surely 'this is the Lord's doing, and it is marvellous in our eyes.'"[110] He took an abstract from this account by Jonathan Edwards and included it in a letter to a friend. The friend's response initiated another crisis of self-doubt in Wesley that rivaled any that he had had before in severity. Following St. Paul's directive to "Examine yourselves, whether ye be in the faith," Wesley asked himself once more the ways in which he was "a new creature" and found himself lacking.[111] Although he had some of the "fruit of the Spirit," he could not find the presence of other important qualities.

> I cannot find in myself the love of God, or of Christ. Hence my deadness and wanderings in public prayer; hence it is that even in the Holy Communion I have frequently no more than a cold attention....Again: I have not that joy in the Holy Ghost; no settled, lasting joy.[112]

The lack of these important aspects of the assurance of faith led Wesley to conclude that he was not yet, in the full sense of the words, "in Christ a new creature." He took some comfort in the fact that he still believed that his sins had been forgiven and that he was reconciled to God in a real way. Wesley may have been considering whether one with a faith as weak as his might expect to lead a revival in England which was similar to that in New England. He had already had one man converted under his ministry but he needed assurance that his work too was really "of God." During the following days he continued his self-analysis and found nothing to change the judgments he had made on previous days. He found that he still desired "creature-happiness."

> My soul is almost continually running out after one creature or another, and imagining 'How happy should I be in such or such a condition!' I have more pleasure in eating and drinking, and in the company of those I love, than I have in God. I have a relish for earthly happiness. I have not a relish for heavenly.[113]

He was convinced that, though his ultimate purposes were directed toward the proper object, in many ways conflicting purposes seemed to smuggle themselves into his motivations in devious ways.

> This is my *ultimate* design--but *intermediate* designs
> are continually creeping in upon me: designs (though
> often disguised) of pleasing myself, of doing my own
> will; designs wherein I do not eye God--at least, not
> Him singly.[114]

Were his desires those of a "new creature?" He could not
honestly conclude that they were. They seemed to be very much
like his "designs" or purposes: very mixed.

> My great desire is to have 'Christ formed in my heart
> by faith.' But little desires are daily stealing in-
> to my soul. And so my great hopes and fears have re-
> spect to God. But a thousand little ones creep in
> between them.[115]

In the conclusion of this searching and ruthlessly honest
letter he summarized his bitter awareness of his conflicts and
ambivalence as they expressed themselves in his lack of purity
of intention:

> Again, my desires, passions, and inclinations in gen-
> eral are mixed; having something of Christ and some-
> thing of earth. I love you, for instance. But my
> love is only partly spiritual and partly natural.
> Something of my own cleaves to that which is of God.
> Nor can I divide the earthly part from the heavenly.[116]

It should be evident from this candid account that we do
not have to justify speaking in terms of sublimation or displace-
ment in discussing Wesley's penchant for gratifying his needs
for love, intimacy, and the expression of self-will and initiative
through religious channels. Here Wesley himself has given us a
good phenomenological description of these processes as they are
present in his experience. He was under tremendous conflict and
though he continued to actively "preach faith" he did not experience the change in himself and the assurance which he sought. Two
weeks after the above account his self-scrutiny was equally ruthless. His friends had considered him mad a year before when he
had said that he was not a Christian. He still believed that he
did not have in his life the true marks of a converted Christian.
The real Christian manifested love, peace, and joy.

> But these I have not. I have not any love of God. I
> do not love either the Father or the Son. Do you ask
> how do I know whether I love God? I answer by another
> question, 'How do you know whether you love me?' Why,
> as you know whether you are hot or cold. You *feel* this
> moment that you do or do not love me. And I *feel* this
> moment I do not love God; which therefore I *know* be-
> cause I *feel* it.[117]

His desire to love and be loved, to have real intimacy with other human beings, to enjoy the pleasures of human life were a continuing drive which again he acknowledged honestly.

> For I love the world. I desire the things of the world, some or other of them, and have done all my life. I have always placed some part of my happiness in some or other of the things that are seen. Particularly in meat and drink, and in the company of those I loved. For many years I have been, yea, and still am, hankering after a happiness in loving and being loved by one or another. And in these I have from time to time taken more pleasure than in God.[118]

He was stuck in a spiritual rut. Bohler's formula had not worked. Assurance and confirmation that his ministry was truly of God would have to come from some other source than his internal state. At this point we should remember that, according to Erikson, it is not enough for a young man to find an integrating ideology. He must find an institution, a role through which his embryonic identity can find social sanction and support.[119] We have seen above that for Wesley the providential role had long been an object of first priority in his search for selfhood. The account of the exciting events in New England suggested a possible role for him, but his continuing spiritual crisis raised a serious question as to whether or not one with his shortcomings could be used by God in such a wondrous way. It was not until George Whitefield's return from America that the opportunity to test his role as the leader of a revival would present itself.

Whitefield was convinced that the time had come for the revival to begin in England, and had initiated a series of services among the Bristol colliers. When it became necessary for him to leave the Bristol area, he pressed Wesley to take his place in the field-preaching.[120] Wesley was highly resistant to the idea. The practice was very irregular, and particularly repugnant to the more conservative principles regarding Anglican church order which his brother Charles adhered to even more closely than John. It is perhaps significant that at this time death re-enters the picture. His colleagues seemed to feel that going to Bristol would prove fatal to John. Wesley's response is a revealing one. He enters into his journal at this point the letter which he had previously written to his father to reject the Epworth living.[121] In it, we should remember, he

contrasts the relative claims of the authority of a parent, in
this case his father, with those of a call of Providence. The
entry is a clear indication that the opportunity for an extraordinary role would take precedence over any authority which was
of man. In one of his letters written from Herrnhut he had affirmed that he would call no man master in faith, practice, or
discipline.[122] This affirmation in truth covered his father,
Count Zinzendorf, his brothers, and later, the bishops of the
Anglican church. He had had, in fact, only one earthly master--
Susanna--and he had by now so thoroughly internalized the structures, values, and intentions of her authority that he was soon
to become her spiritual parent, and, more important, that of
thousands of his fellow Englishmen.

Finally, after having convinced his colleagues in London
that he should accept Whitefield's invitation, he departed for
Bristol. Arriving there on March 31, 1739, he found himself
still a little troubled at the prospect of field-preaching.[123]
In the evening of the following day he led a society in an ex-
position of the Sermon on the Mount. In a revealing comment he
noted that these passages could serve as a "remarkable precedent"
for field-preaching.[124] We have noted above his identification
with Paul the Apostle. Now we see him identifying with the person and ministry of Jesus. The beginning of the following important entry indicates with little room for doubt that in his
resignation and submission he had been clearing the way for his
exaltation into a most extraordinary ministry:

> Mon. 2--At four in the afternoon I submitted to be
> more vile, and proclaimed in the highways the glad
> tidings of salvation, speaking from a little eminence
> in a ground adjoining to the city, to about three
> thousand people. The scripture on which I spoke was
> this (is it possible any one should be ignorant that
> it is fulfilled in every true minister of Christ?),
> 'The Spirit of the Lord is upon Me, because He hath
> anointed Me to preach the gospel to the poor. He
> hath sent Me to heal the broken-hearted; to preach
> deliverance to the captives, and recovery of sight
> to the blind; to set at liberty them that are bruised,
> to proclaim the acceptable year of the Lord.'[125]

He had had his temptation in the wilderness, had been
claimed as a son, and now preached his own sermon on a mount.
His need to enter the comment regarding the fulfillment of the
scripture in the life of every true minister probably indicates

that he had an uneasy awareness of the degree of his identification. When John's followers had asked Jesus if he were the one
that they had been led to expect, the scriptural account in
Matthew 11:2-5 portrays Jesus as pointing to the concrete manifestations of his ministry as indication that it had been confirmed by God. In the following month Wesley too was to have
his evidence. Great crowds were coming to hear him preach. He
was treated like a saint and even acknowledged as a prophet.
But more than that, many persons were convicted of their sins,
repented, and found peace and joy through their new faith.[126]
In a letter to his brother Samuel written on May 10th his new
conviction that his work has been found favorable in God's sight
is evident.

> I am one of many witnesses of this matter of fact,
> that God does now make good His promise daily, very
> frequently during a representation (how made I know
> not, but not to the outward eye) of Christ either
> hanging on the cross or standing on the right hand
> of God. And this I know to be of God, because from
> that hour the person so affected is a new creature
> both as to his inward tempers and outward life.[127]

He goes on to relate the conversion of John Haydon, who,
like many others, had found both joy and love through his ministry.[128] The reviving impact of these events upon Wesley himself is evident in the closing paragraph of the letter. John
states that his health, which had bothered him a good deal in
earlier years, was now as good as it had been at any time in
his memory.[129] The revival had begun, and Wesley himself had
been revived in a remarkable way. Bohler had told him that he
should preach faith until he had it, but he had failed in this.
Now he had preached faith until *others* had it, and the assurance
which he could not gain through a sensible change in himself he
now gleaned from that which his ministry was facilitating in
the lives of others.

It is evident that here at Bristol Wesley had found the
long-sought "providential role" and the necessary confirmation
of the extraordinary personal and professional identity which
had been his life-long goal. Let us examine some of the factors
which made this role seem so acceptable to him. If Aldersgate
had marked the end of the inhibiting effects of the paternal
authority, it did not do away with the necessity of dealing with

parental identifications. It is perhaps significant to note
that his father had also engaged in fantasies of becoming a
traveling evangelist in the British Isles. His paternal grandfather had in fact been an itinerant preacher who engaged in an
irregular ministry and came into conflict with ecclesiastical
authority. By engaging in field-preaching, Wesley was able to
claim a role which represented a positive identification with
his father and which, in its "irregular" style, reenacted the
life and style of religious leadership of his paternal grandfather. The role, given its similarity to traditional dissent,
was, in effect, an affirmation not only of the negative identity
of the father (who converted from dissent), but also of those
tendencies of Susanna toward irregular behavior in the dissenting mode.

Therefore Wesley had found a role which enabled him to
integrate identifications gleaned from two generations of his
family, which manifested his sense of being different and
"special," and which challenged him to use the skills of leadership which had long been cultivated by him.

The enthusiastic responses of the masses had convinced him
that he had finally found God's will for him, and, in Eriksonian
terms, had *confirmed* him in this social role. Not only had *he*
come to view himself as an evangelist, but the fact that others
responded to his leadership provided concrete evidence that he
was correct in viewing himself in this way. His resignation
and submission to the internalized maternal authority had enabled
him to be exalted, and his initiative, self-will, and desire for
love and intimacy were so sublimated into his religious work
that he could find at least partial gratification of these previously conflict-inducing needs. If he still could not "take
fire into his bosom and not be burnt," at least he could kindle
it in the hearts of others and warm his hands and heart vicarious-
ly through proximity to and participation in their newfound love
and joy.

CHAPTER IV

WESLEY'S THEOLOGY AND THE PROBLEM OF INITIATIVE

The problem of initiative vs. guilt took precedence over other potential areas of conflict to become the focal issue in John Wesley's movement toward an adult ego-identity. This chapter will discuss the manner in which this issue is manifest in his theology in the form of his position on the nature and dynamics of divine initiative and human response. Before proceeding, however, we must present some of the basic parameters of ego-activity and passivity which I believe underlie the question of psychoanalytic perspectives on the problem of initiative.[1]

The question of the relative autonomy of the ego has occupied a great deal of the efforts of the major theorists of psychoanalytic ego psychology.[2] Perhaps the most fruitful discussion on this topic was initiated by the late David Rapaport and subsequently developed and extended by Erika Fromm and Donald Stolar. Rapaport focused primarily on the question of the relative autonomy of the ego from id demands.[3] For him, an active ego either channels an impinging demand into an acceptable outlet or defends against it. A passive ego, on the other hand, proceeds under duress to execute unacceptable or dystonic demands or is rendered totally helpless in the face of id pressures. Fromm and Stolar extended this paradigm to include the relationship of ego and superego, and it is their typology which can enable us to think more systematically about the question of initiative in Wesley's life and thought.[4]

For Fromm and Stolar, ego activity can be manifest in two ways. Either the ego can reconcile superego demands to ego interests and ideals, or it can defy the demands of the superego and act more directly in favor of ego interests and ideals. Either type of ego activity may be subjectively conscious or unconscious.

Passivity of the ego, on the other hand, they define as "a state in which ego functioning is wholly or partially controlled by superego demand."[5] Passivity is manifest in three ways. First, compliance with superego demands is so total that

ego interests and ideals receive little or no attention. In the
second form the ego is helpless in the face of persecution by
the harsh superego to the extent that severe depression occurs.
Lastly, defiance of the superego demand is attempted, but is
sufficient only to prevent compliance and not to fulfill alternative ego interests and ideals.[6]

The fundamental issue underlying this entire area of inquiry
into the question of initiative turns on the question of the
relative degree to which an individual's behavior is either
"driven" by id demands or superego dictates or marked by purposive movements toward fulfillment of chosen ego ideals. I
emphasize "relative degree" since from the point of view of
psychoanalytic ego psychology the behavior of an individual must
be envisioned on a continuum from helplessness in the face of
pressures from the id to total domination by a severe superego.
A complicating factor is that in any given individual the struggle for adaptation may lead to a complex configuration of "lay-
ering" in the psychic economy in which the ego "surrenders" in
a given area of conflict in order to make definite progress in
another.[7] In this event the psychic maneuver in question is a
manifestation of what has been aptly called "regression in service of the ego."[8] We shall have occasion to refer to these
complex dynamic considerations in context at a later stage of
our discussion. At this point, however, we can conclude that
if we are to understand the manner in which Wesley's cognitive
behavior reflects his strategic adaptive patterns we must be
alert to the nuances of movement which may be discerned as his
struggle unfolds. Only then will we be able to assess Wesley's
attempt to achieve activity or initiative. Our method in the
following discussion will be to embark on an analytical reconnaissance of Wesley's cognitive formulations with an eye toward
determining their role in his struggle to attain initiative.

The Early Theology of Activity: Conflictual Dimensions

A superficial reading of Wesley's dynamics could easily
lead one to the conclusion that he was a stereotypical obsessive-
compulsive neurotic whose dominant ego state was that of passivity in the face of a harsh superego. Such a simplistic conclusion would have been almost inevitable prior to the development

within ego psychology of the distinction between ego ideals and superego standards or demands.[9] This distinction, along with the increasing awareness of the rich variety of subtle ego-grounded tactics available to the person in search of adaptation and mastery make possible--indeed necessary--a more complicated and sensitive understanding of Wesley's unique style of ego synthesis and the role of his theology in that synthesis.

Let us review the way in which Wesley's particular task of ego synthesis was rendered especially problematic. His highly ambitious set of ego ideals, later to issue in his taking the "world as his parish," were formulated quite early in his personal development. His acceptance in childhood of the mantle of a special destiny--one which was to issue in an extraordinary ministry--proved to be one of the main motifs underlying the myriad activities of his life. Though his mother certainly influenced him in this choice of ego ideals and subsequently supported him in it, it would be quite incorrect to ascribe this striving for competence and mastery to the realm of ego-dystonic superego dictates. Susanna was indeed responsible for the fundamental conflict with regard to initiative, but the double-bind in question issued from her strictures against self-will and not from her role in his formulation of ego ideals. Wesley's dynamic adaptive problem was roughly as follows: *how can one find and fulfill an extraordinary role without willing it*? Wesley's ambitions, in short, were ego-syntonic and non-conflictual in themselves. His task was to find a way to fulfill his ambitions without incurring the wrath of a superego for which initiative itself seemed to be anathema.

In this perspective it is rather easy to understand why the Anglican Arminianism of his early struggle was to prove to be a dead-end for him. Nevertheless, it took much bitter conflict and punishment at the hands of his harsh superego before he would try another more successful tactic in dealing with his severe censor. At Oxford he seemed oblivious to the willfulness which was manifest in his attempt to work out his own salvation. His guilt over the intense conflict with his father regarding the Epworth appointment led him to no significant insights regarding the maladaptive results of spiritual initiative, but instead to a rather stereotyped response pattern involving an

act of penance for his transgression. His ego state at this
point would have to be characterized as one of relative activity
in that he sought a way in which he could both comply with superego dictates and still strive to fulfill his ego ideals. As we
have seen above, Wesley's decision to go to Georgia pacified his
conscience not only for his resistance to his father's demands
but also for his increasing psychosexual interests while, in
addition, offering a movement toward the fulfillment of his ambitions.

Circumstances in Georgia, however, led to the dismal failure
of this experiment. The sudden change in his understanding of
the opportunities for him in the colony erased the possibility
that this involvement would provide him with the extraordinary
role he coveted. But perhaps more threatening was the failure
of his defenses against a conscious awareness of the extent of
his "willfulness." While he had been capable of a degree of
defiance of superego dictates with regard to Sophy--with the
aid of massive denial and other defense mechanisms--in the end
this conflict resulted in functional ego passivity in the form
of a stalemate. Neither ego nor superego standards had been
met. As the miserable episode came to an end and as the magnitude of not only his failure but also of the degree of his active
willfulness began to emerge into his awareness, his ego state
became even more markedly passive and issued in the onset of
feelings of helplessness and severe depression. At this point
Wesley was finally becoming aware of the seriousness of his
spiritual plight. The difficulty did not lie, it seemed, in
the areas that he had previously believed. Not only had his
striving to bridle his will and merit salvation failed to lead
him to his goals, but he now began to realize that his vaunted
spiritual initiative was as problematic as his sexual temptations.
His theology had been a theology of activity and it had served
only to bring him to his knees. Let us examine the structure of
this problematic theology with regard to the question of the
role of human initiative.

The roots of Wesley's early theology of activity are grounded
solidly in the Anglican Arminianism which had become dominant in
England prior to Wesley's formative years. To be sure, the
Anglican communion had earlier emphasized the fundamental primacy

of the divine agency in the soteriological economy. Richard
Hooker, for example, emphasized not only the importance of man's
response to the divine initiative, but also the primacy and objective character of God's grace. Though not a Calvinist, he
respected the Genevan emphasis on the fundamental helplessness
of man in his sinful state and was careful to avoid highlighting
the role of human agency.[10]

With William Laud, however, human initiative had become
much more important. Faith began to be conceived much more as
man's own act made in cooperation with divine grace. Man's own
reason had taken on the primary role, and grace served to cleanse
the vision of man's rational nature--to help it function more
effectively.[11] Lancelot Andrewes made it very clear that in
his view faith itself was dependent on man's rational decision,
on his own will and initiative.[12] At the beginning of the eighteenth century this emphasis on man's cooperation with God in
effecting his own salvation had gained a widespread acceptance.
Morality and good works had become the basis on which men were
to be judged as worthy or unworthy of the benefits of the atonement of Christ. Of course, it was Christ who had made satis-
faction to God for man's fall and redemption was a universal
possibility for all men. The universality of this proffered
redemption lay in God's intention, but it was conditional. As
one Anglican divine put it, "Christ died for all if all will
take care to perform the condition required by Him."[13]

In his *Harmonia Apostolica* Bishop Bull focused attention
on the centrality of good works in the salvific process.[14] For
him the teachings of St. Paul and St. James formed a harmony in
God's plan of salvation. Faith involved not only an assent to
the truth of the teachings of the church, but also a firm resolve to perform works of repentance through which the person
thereby appropriated the merits of Christ.[15] Though the Bishop
sought to balance faith and works, the overall effect was to
place a great emphasis on the role man was to play in meeting
the requirements necessary for salvation. Given the available
options, Bull's stance was clearly a "theology of activity,"
and, more importantly, it was representative of the dominant
emphases in the Anglican communion at the turn of the century.

A question of greater importance, however, is that of the
view of justification held by Wesley's parents. As we have seen
above, both had roots in the English Puritan tradition but in
later life prided themselves on their adherence to Anglican
"orthodoxy." Though at an early age Susanna's rational bent
had led her to a deep interest in Socinianism, the young Samuel
had steeped her in the writings of Bishop Bull and induced her
to share his enthusiasm for the rational--but orthodox--tenets
of the mainstream currents of Anglican thought.[16] As we shall
see below, both parents rejected the Calvinist decrees and later
supported John in his antagonism toward predestination. Though
they too sought to preserve the sovereignty of God and emphasized
the fundamental necessity of Christ's atonement in the drama of
redemption, the practical thrust of their position was to emphasize the requirement of man's active appropriation of the
work of Christ.[17] Through God's action man's salvation had been
made possible, but the realization of this redemptive potential
was conditional upon an individual's willing assent to the truth
of the faith and his active obedience, imperfect though it might
be, to the law of God.

We have already seen above the manner in which Susanna's
theology issued in her own moral psychology of human development. John Wesley was tutored in the psychology of Anglican
Arminianism from infancy, and it is not at all surprising that
the young Wesley's years prior to his fiasco in Georgia were
dominated not only by a desire for greatness, but by an unabashed
assault on destiny in the form of an energetic and enthusiastic
spiritual athleticism.

Wesley would have thrown himself into any vocation which
promised greatness, but the greatest identity models that he
found attractive both inside his family tradition and out of it
were religious figures. When in the latter part of 1724 John
announced his decision to enter the ministry, his parents both
seemed somewhat surprised. Samuel seemed to intimate that John's
motives for entering the ministry lacked something in the manner
in which they had been presented to him.

> As to what you mention of entering into Holy Orders,
> it is indeed a great work, and I am pleased to find
> you think it so. As to the motives you take notice
> of, my thoughts are; if it is no harm to desire get-
> ting into that office, even as Eli's sons, to eat a

> piece of bread; yet certainly a desire and intention
> to lead a stricter life and a belief that one should
> do so, is a better reason: though this should, by
> all means, be begun before, or ten to one it will
> deceive us much afterwards....But the principal spring
> and motive, to which all the former should be only
> secondary, must certainly be the glory of God, and the
> service of his Church in the edification of our neigh-
> bor.[18]

Samuel Wesley had never been very impressed with John's
attitudes toward his father's authority, and now he seemed to
have reservations regarding the acceptability of his son's rever-
ence for the divine authority. Susanna, on the other hand,
seemed quite enthusiastic. She seemed less concerned about his
motivation for the role than about his possibilities for success
in it:

> I think the sooner you are a deacon the better, be-
> cause it may be an inducement to greater application
> in the study of practical divinity, which of all
> other studies I humbly conceive to be the best for
> Candidates of Orders.[19]

By all means she did not want John to end as a failure because of impracticality mirroring that of her husband. John's
decision to be ordained had seemingly led to an increase in
seriousness, and Susanna's response indicates reservations of
her own with regard to the character of John's motivations:

> ...the alteration of your temper has occasioned me
> much speculation. I, who am apt to be sanguine, hope
> it may proceed from the operations of God's Holy
> Spirit, that, by taking off your relish for earthly
> enjoyments, he may prepare and dispose your mind for
> a more serious and close application to things of a
> more sublime and spiritual nature...now, in good
> earnest, resolve to make religion the business of
> your life....I heartily wish you would now enter upon
> a strict examination of yourself, that you may know
> whether you have reasonable hope of salvation by
> Jesus Christ.[20]

John had already resolved to make religion the "business"
of his life, and he already intended to be very good at it--
although at this point he was still gathering materials to put
together his picture of what being "spiritually outstanding"
would look like. The night before his ordination he had been
reading Bishop Bull's views on the subject. Before retiring
he jotted down what he believed to be his major faults, the most

prominent being boasting and greed of praise.[21] His mother's
words had expressed the conflict well. She had encouraged him
to set high goals while raising the dilemma of how one can be
ambitious without conscious subjective manifestations of impure
intention or willfulness being involved.

In Jeremy Taylor's *Rules and Exercises of Holy Living and
Holy Dying* he had found what seemed to be a good guidebook for
one seeking spiritual superiority. The goal of Taylor's book
was to portray a style of life which promised great religious
rewards including great opportunities to serve God in this life
and an assurance of eternal life to those who could manifest
rigorous obedience to divine demands and purity of intention in
carrying out the myriad tasks. The central problem Wesley had
with Taylor is indicative of the depth of his conflict in what
amounted to a "double-bind" situation. He noted the troubling
parts of Taylor's injunctions in a letter to his mother:

> In his fourth section of the second chapter, where
> he treats of humility, these, among others, he makes
> necessary parts of that virtue:
> Love to be little esteemed, and be content to be
> slighted or undervalued.
> Take no content in praise when it is offered thee.
> Please not thyself when disgraced by supposing thou
> didst deserve praise though they understood thee not
> or enviously detracted from thee.
> We must be sure in some sense or other to think
> ourselves the worst in every company where we come....
> A true penitent must all the days of his life
> pray for pardon and never think the work completed
> until he dies. Whether God has forgiven us or no we
> know not, therefore still be sorrowful for ever hav-
> ing sinned.[22]

Wesley was somewhat taken aback by Taylor's view of the uncertainty of the reward of the spiritual athlete, and particularly
of the radical definition of humility. He concluded his letter
with the query, "...if all these things are essential to humility,
who can be humble, who can be saved?"[23] The point which seemed
even more unacceptable to John than the others was Taylor's in-
sistence that he think himself the "worst in every company."
This appeared to him to be almost incredible. In a subsequent
letter to his mother he argued that such a requirement went
against the plain evidence of reason, and therefore could not
be a just requirement, since faith is "a species of belief and
belief is defined as 'an assent to a proposition upon rational

grounds.' Without rational grounds there is therefore no belief, and consequently no faith."[24] Plainly, if he accepted this teaching on humility he would have to stop seeing himself as spiritually superior to others, and this in itself would undercut his chosen mode of being "successful" in his spiritual vocation. Thus he was enabled through an appeal to reason to ease his mind in the face of this troubling question. Still, the issue of the purity of his intentions and of whether he had truly bridled his unruly will continued to occupy his self-evaluations.

He had taken on other guides in his spiritual training, one being Thomas à Kempis. Wesley used Kempis' *The Christian Pattern* to suggest further guidelines in ordering his internal life and his outward actions. He had every intention of reforming himself in every area, yet as with Taylor there seemed to him to be a problem with regard to the rewards of a spiritually successful life:

> I was lately advised to read Thomas à Kempis over, which I had frequently seen, but never much looked into before. I think he must have been a person of great piety and devotion, but it is my misfortune to differ from him in some of his main points. I can't think that when God sent us into the world He had irreversibly decreed that we should be perpetually miserable in it. If it be so, the very endeavour after happiness in this life is a sin; as it is acting in direct contradiction to the very design of our creation. What are become of the innocent comforts and pleasures of life, if it is the intent of our Creator that we should never taste them? If our taking up the cross implies our bidding adieu to all joy and satisfaction, how is it reconcilable with what Solomon so expressly affirms of religion--that her ways are ways of pleasantness and all her paths peace? A fair patrimony, indeed, which Adam has left his sons, if they are destined to be continually wretched! And though heaven is undoubtedly a sufficient recompense for all the afflictions we may or can suffer here, yet I am afraid that argument would make few converts to Christianity, if the yoke were not easy even in this life, and such as one as gives rest, at least as much as trouble.[25]

It is clear that young John fully expects that spiritual success should bring with it at least some tangible worldly rewards. Here we see a very early expression of Wesley's life-long assumption that holiness should result in happiness. He

was never to abandon the values expressed here, but the struggle
with a punitive superego would force him to screen his motivations for worldly pleasure and success from subjective awareness.
The letter continues with his criticism of the way in which Kempis
seems to contradict the obedience-reward system which he had
internalized at Epworth:

> Another of his tenets, which is indeed a natural
> consequence of this, is that all mirth is vain and use-
> less, if not sinful. But why, then, does the Psalmist
> so often exhort us to rejoice in the Lord and tell us
> that it becomes the just to be joyful? I think one
> could hardly desire a more express text than that in
> the 68th Psalm, 'Let the righteous rejoice and be glad
> in the Lord. Let them also be merry and joyful.' And
> he seems to carry the matter as much too far on the
> other side afterwards, where he asserts that nothing
> is an affliction to a good man, and that he ought to
> thank God even for sending him misery. This, in my
> opinion, is contrary to God's design in afflicting us;
> for though He chasteneth those whom He loveth, yet it
> is in order to humble them: and surely the method Job
> took in his adversity was very different from this,
> and yet in all that he sinned not.[26]

John intended to be one of the "righteous" and he intended
to insist upon his just desserts and be "merry" as well. His
father had identified with Job in quite another way, feeling
superior through the magnitude of his miseries in the Epworth
exile. Susanna's response to her son's letter indicates her
approval of the ambition and strength manifest in his query:

> I have Kempis by me; but have not read him lately.
> I cannot recollect the passages you mention; but,
> believing you do him justice, I do positively aver
> that he is extremely in the wrong in that impious,
> I was about to say blasphemous, suggestion, that
> God, by an irreversible decree, has determined any
> man to be miserable even in this world. His inten-
> tions, as Himself, are holy, just, and good; and
> all the miseries incident to men here or hereafter
> proceed from themselves. I take Kempis to have been
> an honest weak man, that had more zeal than knowledge.[27]

Susanna clearly did not view John as an "honest weak man"
like her husband and Kempis. Success, even in the world, was
really a possibility. John would never give up the view that
God was "holy" and "just" or that "all the miseries incident to
men...proceed from themselves." He had yet to learn that his
success, both worldly and spiritual, would depend upon his cultivating a state of "honest weakness" in his subjective awareness.

His later introduction to the works of William Law, especially *Christian Perfection* and *Serious Call to a Devout and Holy
Life*, made a great impact upon him, an impact sufficient to convince him that the rewards of spiritual athleticism were important enough to warrant a total commitment to the effort to attain
them. Wesley commented upon the significance of these treatises
for him:

> These convinced me more than ever, of the absolute
> impossibility of being half a Christian; and I
> determined, through his grace (the absolute neces-
> sity of which I was deeply sensible of), to be all-
> devoted to God, to give him all my soul, my body,
> and my substance.[28]

Indeed, Law's works served to focus Wesley even more on
that lofty goal of perfection. For Law, perfection "does not
consist in any singular state or condition of life, or in any
particular set of duties, but in the holy and religious conduct
in every state of life."[29] Law set a standard for world renunciation that rivaled the most severe monastic disciplines.
Wesley obviously believed that Law could serve him as a spiritual
guide without peer:

> The light flowed in so mightily upon my soul, that
> everything appeared in a new view. I cried to God
> for help, and resolved not to prolong the time of
> obeying Him as I had never done before. And by my
> continued endeavor to keep His whole law, inward
> and outward, to the utmost of my power, I was per-
> suaded that I should be accepted of Him, and that
> I was even then in a state of salvation.[30]

Wesley threw himself into an enthusiastic attempt to answer
Law's "serious call," corresponding with his new mentor and
making a number of pilgrimages to Law's home in Putney.[31] He
consulted with Law before undertaking the Georgia mission and
used his works extensively during the voyage and early work in
the colony. This period represented the high mark of the influence of Law and of the entire adaptive strategy which he and
his works represented.

The structure of Wesley's theology of activity is easily
discernible. The goal is clearly that of becoming a superior
man in the "business" of religion. The nature of the divine
reality is such that it can be trusted to provide man--all men
--with a chance at achieving this spiritual greatness and with

it the grand prize of salvation. In order for this to be true,
a number of accompanying assertions are made. First of all, if
Wesley is to be sure he has a chance to achieve his goals, the
Calvinist decrees on predestination must be in error. In the
same letter in which he complained against Taylor's views on
humility he took his stand on the issue:

> What, then, shall I say of Predestination? An ever-
> lasting purpose of God to deliver some from damnation
> does, I suppose, exclude all from that deliverance
> who are not chosen. And if it was inevitably decreed
> from eternity that such a determinate part of mankind
> should be saved, and none beside them, a vast majority
> of the world were only born to eternal death, without
> so much as a possibility of avoiding it. How is this
> consistent with either the Divine Justice or Mercy?
> Is it merciful to ordain a creature to everlasting
> misery? Is it just to punish man for crimes which he
> could not but commit? How is man, if necessarily
> determined to one way of acting, a free agent? To
> lie under either a physical or a moral necessity is
> entirely repugnant to human liberty. But that God
> should be the author of sin and injustice (which must,
> I think, be the consequence of maintaining this opin-
> ion) is a contradiction to the clearest ideas we have
> of the divine nature and perfections.[32]

Wesley was concerned to insure that the "election" of real
importance lay within the capacities of the individual--that
the power of choice is not illusory, but is the basis for man's
chance at "spiritual success."

In a letter to his father written in 1731 he elaborated on
his view of this fundamental human capacity:

> I propose to show: 1. What is the nature of choice
> or election. 2. That our happiness consists in the
> elections or choices we make. 3. What elections are
> improper to be made. 4. How we come to make such
> elections. And, 5. How our making them is consistent
> with the divine power and goodness.
>   1. By liberty I mean an active, self-determining
> power, which does not choose things because they are
> pleasing, but is pleased with them because it chooses
> them.[33]

He goes on to argue that God manifests this power in the
process of his creation, and that man also has the capacity.
That ability in man is obvious by his experience--he observes
himself the presence of such a power. Wesley then proceeds to
give his thoughts regarding the relation between activity or
self-determination and happiness:

The more of this power any being possesses, the less
subject he is to the impulses of external agents and
the more commodious is his condition. Happiness
rises from a due use of our faculties: if, therefore,
this is the noblest of all our faculties, then our
chief happiness lies in the due use of this--that is,
in our elections. And farther, election is the cause
why things please us: he therefore who has an un-
controlled power of electing may please himself always;
and if things fall out contrary to what he chooses, he
may change his choice and suit it to them, and so still
be happy.[34]

This power of choice, of course, can be disturbed--for
example by one's "natural appetites"--thereby preventing perfect happiness. Still, the very capacity enables an individual
to find some happiness in spite of what the external circumstances might be. Such a self-determining power can, however,
be the cause of acute discomfort:

True it is that this power sometimes gives pain--
namely, when it falls short of what it chooses;
which may come to pass, if we choose either things
impossible to be had, or inconsistent with each
other, or such as are out of our power (perhaps because others chose them before us), or, lastly,
such as necessarily lead us into natural evils....
And into these foolish choices we may be betrayed
either by ignorance, negligence, by indulging the
exercise of liberty too far, by obstinacy or habit,
or, lastly, by the importunity of our natural appetites. Hence it appears how cautious we ought to
be in choosing; for though we may alter our choice,
yet to make that alteration is painful--the more
painful the longer we have persisted in it.[35]

Wesley soon found that his power of "election" did indeed
lead him into painful experiences--and his words on the causes
of such pain seem to be an outline of his "mistakes" during
the Georgia fiasco. He had chosen to join the colony in order
to at the same time enter an extraordinary ministry and do
penance for his transgression against his father. If obstinacy
had led to his conflict with his father and been partially responsible for his choice of the Georgia mission, the whole episode marked an example of his election having fallen short of
what he had chosen. Not only had his "natural appetites" led
him into desiring a relationship he deemed inconsistent with his
destiny, he had persisted in his self-contradictory behavior
until it had brought him the bitter fruit of humiliation and
disgrace.

His discourse on free will, uttered long prior to the
disastrous Georgia experiment, is significant in its revelation
of Wesley's blissful unawareness of the basic conflict posed by
his theology of activity. In fact, his most troublesome choice
of inconsistencies lay in his affirmation of human self-determination and initiative on the one hand and the call for purity
of intention and rejection of self-will on the other. He had
learned very early in life to use the defense mechanisms of
rationalization and denial to avoid total domination by his
parents, and later, parental introjects. The picture of the
young Wesley that emerges here as elsewhere is that of an extremely ambitious young man who manifests ego-activity and yet
whose chosen adaptive stratagems contain a built-in conflict
which will later require substantial alterations.

As we have seen above, Wesley's experiences in Georgia led
to an overloading and failure of his complex defenses against
recognizing the extent of his self-will. The intense depression
manifest in the later phases of the Georgia experience and in
subsequent months serves as clear evidence that his adaptive
strategies had failed, that his theology of activity had made
defense against awareness of the degree of his very human ambition all too difficult. He had regressed into resignation
and felt much in need of a divine initiative to help him out
of his dilemma. His cognitive formulations had proved to be
overwhelmingly dysfunctional and conflict-inducing. The same
young man who had with great flair undertaken the adventure
chiefly to save his own soul now had great doubts. Had he in
electing to work out his own salvation chosen a goal which was
"impossible to be had"?[36]

On his return to England he summarized his new awareness
that his reach had exceeded his grasp:

> This, then, have I learned in the ends of the earth,
> --that I 'am fallen short of the glory of God':
> that my whole heart is 'altogether corrupt and
> abominable'; and consequently my whole life (seeing
> it cannot be that an 'evil tree' should 'bring
> forth good fruit'): that, 'alienated' as I am from
> the life of God, I am 'a child of wrath,' an heir
> of hell: that my own works, my own sufferings, my
> own righteousness, are so far from reconciling me
> to an offended God, so far from making any atonement
> for the least of those sins, which 'are more in num-
> ber than the hairs of my head,' that the most specious

of them need an atonement themselves, or they can not
abide His righteous judgment: that 'having the sentence of death' in my heart, and having nothing in or
of myself to plead, I have no hope, but that of being
justified freely, 'through the redemption that is in
Jesus'; but that if I seek I shall find Christ, and
'be found in Him, not having my own righteousness,
but that which is through the faith of Christ, the
righteousness which is of God by faith.'[37]

His theology of activity had aggravated the conflict between his ego ideals and the dictates of his superego. He now
realized that he had no choice but to alter in a radical way
his entire approach to faith and works.

Salvation by Faith: Wesley's Discovery of a Theology of Passivity

Wesley's words quoted above indicate that the Moravians
had already managed to plant in his mind an approach to theology
which marked a radical break with his past orientation. In a
previous chapter we have related the manner in which Peter Bohler
stepped into Wesley's life as a tutor in a theology of passivity.
On March 6, 1738, Bohler's influence as Wesley's new mentor
issued in his preaching for the first time the "new doctrine"
of salvation by faith alone.[38] Within less than three months
Bohler had led Wesley to the point of a final break with his
old tutor, William Law, and with the view of redemption which
he represented. In two letters written in the latter part of
May, 1738, Wesley attacked Law for having led him in a path which
proved to be a dead-end:

> For two years (more expecially) I have been preach-
> ing after the model of your two practical treatises;
> and all that heard have allowed, that the law is
> great, wonderful, and holy. But no sooner did they
> attempt to fulfill it, but they found that it is too
> high for man, and that by doing 'the works of the
> law shall no flesh living be justified.'[39]

He went on to emphasize how he and his followers had made
every effort to realize the spiritual rewards which Law's point
of view seemed to offer. Yet even after they had extended
themselves to the limit and used every acceptable means of
grace they seemed to remain in a state of captivity to the law
of sin. They had become convinced that they could not live
under such a law:

> Under this heavy yoke I might have groaned till death,
> had not an holy man, to whom God lately directed me,
> upon my complaining thereof, answered at once: 'Be-
> lieve, and thou shalt be saved. Believe in the Lord
> Jesus Christ with all thy heart, and nothing shall be
> impossible to thee. This faith, indeed, as well as
> the salvation it brings, is the free gift of God.
> But seek, and thou shalt find. Strip thyself naked
> of thy own works and thy own righteousness, and fly
> to Him. For whosoever cometh unto Him, He will in no
> wise cast out.'[40]

Wesley was convinced that he had been misguided and led
into misguiding others. He rationalized his attack on Law as
a sincere expression of concern for the state of the man's soul.
In reality, he wanted Law to step up and accept some of the
blame for the humiliation and pain he was suffering. Law was
bewildered and angered by this attack from the young man who
had so persistently solicited his advice and valuable time. His
response to Wesley indicated not only that he would not accept
the blame ascribed to him, but also suggested that the arrogance
of John's letter might have another explanation:

> If you had only this faith till some weeks ago, let
> me advise you not to be too hasty in believing that,
> because you have changed your language or expres-
> sions, you have changed your faith. The head can
> as easily amuse itself with a living and justifying
> faith in the blood of Jesus, as with any other notion;
> and the heart, which you suppose to be a place of
> security, as being the seat of self-love, is more
> deceitful than the head.[41]

While we can appreciate the insightful aspects of Law's
question about the nature of the change which has occurred in
Wesley, the young clergyman could not. He had already shifted
his stance too far and was not prepared to question the motives
behind this new point of view which promised some relief from
his severe self-criticism. Instead, he wrote again enumerating
his charges against the older man:

> 'But how are you chargeable with my not having had this
> faith?' If, as you intimate, you discerned my spirit,
> thus:
> (1) You did not tell me plainly I had it not. (2) You
> never once advised me to seek or pray for it. (3) You
> gave me advices proper only for one who had it already;
> and (4) advices which led me farther from it, the
> closer I adhered to them. (5) You recommended books to
> me which had no tendency to plant this faith, but a
> direct one to destroy good works.[42]

In closing the letter--and with it this painful aspect of the ritual of transition--Wesley proved that his capacities for denial had been somewhat rejuvenated. He ended the letter by saying, "I ask pardon, sir, if I had said anything disrespectful."[43] Law, however, did not intend to let the young man project upon him responsibilities which he could not accept. He answered Wesley's contentions point by point and closed with the following scathing remarks:

> Who made me your teacher? or can make me answerable for any defects in your knowledge? You sought my acquaintance, you came to me as you pleased, and on what occasion you pleased, and to say to me what you pleased. If it was my business to put this question to you, if you have a right to charge me with guilt for the neglect of it, may you not much more reasonably accuse them who are authoritatively charged with you? Did the church in which you are educated put this question to you? Did the Bishop that ordained you either deacon or priest do this for you? Did the Bishop that sent you into Georgia require this of you? Pray, sir, be at peace with me.[44]

Law was not to be troubled further by Wesley, and, whether or not Law had helped him formulate the idea, he was soon proclaiming widely--to Bishops and Oxford professors alike--that the Anglican church was not living up to its responsibilities to preach justification by grace through faith. As we have discussed above, except for a brief period of testing the transition to a theology of passivity was completed the evening of May 24, 1738. Luther's words must have weakened any remaining reservations. The words of Luther spoke of the misapprehension which many have regarding the nature of faith. It was not "something that man fetches up from his own imagination and puts over on himself."[45] His description of faith appeared to be in agreement with Bohler's, and, more important, it seemed to speak to Wesley's own need to give up his own conflicted initiative and welcome a life-giving divine one:

> But faith is God's work in us that changes us all over and makes us like new (John I, 13). It kills the past and reconstitutes us utterly different men in heart, disposition, spirit and in all the faculties and the Holy Spirit is implicitly, dynamically present in all of it. Oh! there is something vital, busy, active, powerful about this (experience of) faith that simply makes it impossible ever to let up in doing good works.[46]

Wesley certainly wanted to be "vital, busy, active, powerful," and here he had a promise that his problematic will could
be by-passed, that the Holy Spirit could effect in him what his
years of conflicted struggle had not. He took the following
admonition of Luther to heart:

> And so look out for your own false notions and for
> the idle theological chatterers about faith and
> good works who appear to be very clever but are
> in fact consummate fools. Pray rather to God that
> he work this faith in you; otherwise you will never,
> never come by it, feign all you will or work all
> you can.[47]

According to his journal entry, Wesley's heart was "strangely
warmed."[48] One element in that warmth was undoubtedly the new
hope that Bohler and Luther were right. He was beginning to be-
lieve--as he already was preaching--that the holy Spirit might do
things in and with his life that his own conscious and conflicted
self-will had found impossible. He lost little time in beginning
to proclaim his new insights to the "clever" but "consummate,
fools" of England. On June 11, 1738, he managed to let the divine
initiative take the lead--and it led him to proclaim his message
to the congregation at St. Mary's church, Oxford University.[49]

His preaching of that sermon, "Salvation by Faith," marked
the beginning of his triumphant utilization of his theology of
passivity. He had chosen as his text Ephesians 2:8, "By grace
are ye saved through faith." Now he declared that man's initiative, even expressed in so-called good works, cannot lead to
salvation. The initiative must be solely divine:

> All the blessings which God hath bestowed upon man,
> are of his mere grace, bounty, or favour; his free,
> undeserved favour; favour altogether undeserved; man
> having no claim to the least of his mercies. For
> there is nothing we are, or have, or do, which can
> deserve the least thing at God's hand. 'All our
> works, thou, O God! hast wrought in us.' These,
> therefore, are so many more instances of free mercy:
> And whatsoever righteousness may be found in man,
> this is also the gift of God.[50]

This faith is a faith in Christ and it is not merely one
of rational assent, but includes also a transformation of heart.
It puts total reliance on the merits of Christ's life, death,
and resurrection. The salvation which issues from this faith
is present and attainable in this life. It frees one from fear

and from both the guilt of sin and its power. When a person has
been truly born of God through this new faith, he does not sin
by habitual sin, by willful sin, by any sinful desire, or by any
infirmities. Christ has been formed in his heart and he can be
said to have been born again. Because of this working of the
spirit of Christ in him he grows in the faith until finally he
manifests Christian perfection.[51] He anticipated the objections
of his audience and answered them point by point. He declared
the timeliness--even necessity--of preaching this doctrine
throughout England. His conclusion was a ringing declaration
of the manner in which even the weakest of men could triumph
if they were armed with this faith. The words of Luther had
given him an empowering hope, and in identifying with the reformer he took his own stand before his own hostile audience:

> For this reason the adversary so rages whenever 'sal-
> vation by faith' is declared to the world: For this
> reason did he stir up earth and hell, to destroy those
> who first preached it. And for the same reason, know-
> ing that faith alone could overturn the foundations of
> his kingdom, did he call forth all his forces, and em-
> ploy all his arts of lies and calumny, to affright
> Martin Luther from reviving it. Nor can we wonder
> thereat; for, as that man of God observes, 'How would
> it enrage a proud strong man armed, to be stopped and
> set at nought by a little child coming against him
> with a reed in his hand!' especially, when he knew
> that little child would surely overthrow him, and
> tread him under foot. Even so, Lord Jesus! Thus hath
> thy strength been ever 'made perfect in weakness! Go
> forth, then, thou little child that believest in him,
> and his 'right hand shall teach thee terrible things!'
> Though thou be as helpless and weak as an infant of
> days, the strong man shall not be able to stand before
> thee. Thou shalt prevail over him, and subdue him,
> and overthrow him, and trample him under thy feet.
> Thou shalt march on, under the great Captain of thy
> salvation, 'conquering and to conquer,' until all
> thine enemies are destroyed, and 'death is swallowed
> up in victory.'[52]

With this sermon Wesley had delivered an important part of
the theological manifesto of the coming revival.[53] Though he
was not to begin to appropriate in full measure the subjective
and adaptive benefits of his new stance for some time, his words
express both an awareness of the magnitude of his future struggles and a willingness--in spite of his current feelings of
weakness--to wait for the initiative and power of his divine
champion to flow through him. This sermon is a fascinating

manifestation of the capacity of human beings to employ cognitive formulation in the difficult task of creative adaptation. Here we see Wesley, who only a short time before was suffering the ravages of immobilizing depression and disorientation, in effect casting a gauntlet in the face of English Christendom--clearly anticipating a victory for himself and his message. We will have occasion in the following to discuss in some detail the dynamic infrastructures of his new theology. At this point, however, the themes publicized so enthusiastically in this sermon must be examined more closely. If Wesley dated his mature view of this process of redemption as beginning at this time, then let us engage in a reconnaissance of the structure of his post-1738 soteriology.

Wesley's Soteriology: Divine Initiative and Human Response

For Wesley, man can exist in either of three states: the *natural*, the *legal*, and the *evangelical*. The natural man he likens to a person in a state of sleep: "For his soul is in a deep sleep: His spiritual senses are not awake: They discern neither spiritual good nor evil. The eyes of his understanding are closed; they are sealed together, and see not."[54] Ignorant of the law of God he experiences a kind of peace. "He *sees* not that he stands on the edge of the pit, therefore he *fears* it not. He cannot tremble at the danger he does not *know*."[55]

"Legal" man, on the other hand, is a man who has been stabbed awake by the law of God, and is thereby stripped of his illusions of peace and well-being. "He at last sees the loving, the merciful God is also 'a consuming fire'; that he is a just God and terrible, rendering to every man according to his works, entering into judgment with the ungodly for every idle word, yea, and for the imaginations of the heart."[56] But worse than his consciousness of sin is his consciousness that he is unable to free himself of it no matter how hard he struggles:

> The more he strives, wishes, labours to be free,
> the more does he feel his chains, the grievous
> chains of sin, wherewith Satan binds and 'leads
> him captive at his will'; his servant he is,
> though he repine ever so much; though he rebel,
> he cannot prevail. He is still in bondage and
> fear, by reason of sin: Generally, of some

outward sin, to which he is peculiarly disposed,
either by nature, custom, or outward circumstances;
but always, of some inward sin, some evil temper or
unholy affection. And the more he frets against it,
the more it prevails; he may bite, but cannot break
his chain. Thus he toils without end, repenting and
sinning, repenting and sinning again, till at length
the poor, sinful, helpless wretch is even at his wit's
end, and can barely groan, 'O wretched man that I am!
who shall deliver me from the body of this death'?[57]

Clearly, Wesley's description of these states is autobiographical in nature. He knew what it meant to live in these
states prior to the "working of grace" in his life. But his
description of these painful memories was only a prologue to
his real message of the promises of the life of the man who has
found grace and has the power of Christ working through him.
For him the bondage has ended:

Here end both the guilt and power of sin. He can now
say, 'I am crucified with Christ: Nevertheless I live;
yet not I, but Christ liveth in me: And the life which
I now live in the flesh' (even in this mortal body),
'I live by faith in the Son of God, who loved me, and
gave himself for me.' Here end remorse, and sorrow
of heart, and the anguish of a wounded spirit....His
labour is not now in vain. The snare is broken and
he is delivered. He not only strives, but likewise
prevails; he not only fights, but conquers also....
He is 'dead unto sin, and alive unto God'; 'sin doth
not now reign,' even 'in his mortal body,' nor doth
he 'obey it in the desires thereof.'[58]

How is one to find and appropriate this experience of grace
in order to become a participant in the "evangelical state"?
In his sermon, "Working Out Our Own Salvation," Wesley has given
a short outline of the salvific process which distinguishes between the different types of grace involved and between justification and sanctification:

Salvation begins with what is usually termed (and very
properly) *preventing grace*; including the first wish
to please God, the first dawn of light concerning his
will, and the first slight transient conviction of
having sinned against him. All these imply some
tendency toward life; some degree of salvation; the
beginning of a deliverance from a blind, unfeeling
heart, quite insensible of God and the things of God.
Salvation is carried on by *convincing grace*, usually
in Scripture called repentance; which brings a larger
measure of self-knowledge, and a farther deliverance
from the heart of stone. Afterwards we experience the
proper Christian salvation; whereby 'through grace,'

> we 'are saved by faith'; consisting of those two
> grand branches, justification and sanctification.
> By justification we are saved from the guilt of sin
> and restored to the favour of God; by sanctification
> we are saved from the power and root of sin, and re-
> stored to the image of God.[59]

Wesley had developed his idea of prevenient grace in order
to offer an alternative to what he believed to be the extremism
of Calvinist teachings on predestination. Rejecting the Calvinist
view of election and its limitation of grace to the few in whom
it would work irresistably, Wesley offered an alternative which
posited a universal salvific will of God. Because of prevenient
grace no man "is wholly void of the grace of God."[60] Every man
has a conscience through this gift:

> Can it be denied that something of this (conscience)
> is found in every man born into the world? And does
> it not appear as soon as the understanding opens, as
> soon as reason begins to dawn? Does not every one
> then begin to know that there is a difference between
> good and evil; how imperfect soever the various cir-
> cumstances of this sense of good and evil may be?...
> This faculty seems to be what is usually meant by
> those who speak of natural conscience; an expression
> frequently found in some of our best authors, but yet
> not strictly just. For though in one sense it may be
> termed natural, because it is found in all men; yet,
> properly speaking, it is not natural, but a super-
> natural gift of God, above all his natural endowments.[61]

Through this doctrine Wesley sought to retain his protestant emphasis on the corrupt nature of natural man while offering
a basis for human freedom of response without unduly limiting
the divine initiative.

In Wesley's understanding, justification is "pardon, the
forgiveness of sins," and this pardon is made possible through
the sacrifice of Christ.[62] This gift has only one condition,
faith, and this in itself is a gift:

> We mean thereby this much, that it is the only thing
> without which none is justified; the only thing that
> is immediately, indispensably, absolutely requisite
> in order to pardon. As, on the one hand, though a
> man should have everything else without faith, yet he
> cannot be justified; so, on the other, though he be
> supposed to want everything else, yet if he hath faith,
> he cannot but be justified.[63]

This faith is twofold: *repentance* faith and *justifying*
faith.[64] The former is the free response of the individual to

God's prevenient grace working in him. This faith is a pre-
liminary faith which brings the individual into a state of sincere desire to please God. In this state the individual engages
in "works meet for repentance." In the 1744 Minutes we find the
following discussion in the ubiquitous question and answer form
of the Methodist conferences:

> Q. 3. But must not repentance, and works meet for re-
> pentance, go before this faith?
> A. Without doubt; if by repentance you mean conviction
> of sin; and by works meet for repentance, obeying God
> as far as we can, forgiving our brother, leaving off
> evil, doing good, and using his ordinances, according
> to the power we have received.[65]

The faith spoken of in the question is justifying faith.
For Wesley the presence of repentance and works meet for repentance indicates the presence of the "faith of a servant."
Justifying faith marks the change in the individual to the "faith
of a son." The 1744 Minutes presented justification as follows:

> Q. 1. What is it to be justified?
> A. To be pardoned and received into God's favour; into
> such a state, that, if we continue therein, we shall
> finally be saved.
> Q. 2. Is faith the condition of justification?
> A. Yes; for everyone who believeth not is condemned;
> and everyone who believes is justified.[66]

Though Wesley expected the responsiveness of the individual
to God's prevenient grace working in him to issue in repentance,
the readiness of the individual for justification did not depend
upon the "repentance works" but upon his willingness to open himself, submitting to the further transforming work of grace in
him. He must be aware that he is saved by grace through faith
alone, and not by works of repentance. Of this justifying grace
Wesley writes:

> It is the free gift of God, which he bestows, not on
> those who are worthy of his favour, not on such as
> are previously holy, and so fit to be crowned with
> all the blessings of his goodness; but on the ungodly
> and unholy; on those who till that hour were fit only
> for everlasting destruction; those in whom there was
> no good thing, and whose only plea was, 'God be mer-
> ciful to me, a sinner!' No merit, no goodness in man
> precedes the forgiving love of God. His pardoning
> mercy supposes nothing in us but a sense of mere sin
> and misery; and to all who see, and feel, and own their
> wants, and their utter inability to remove them, God
> freely gives faith, for the sake of Him in whom he is
> always 'well pleased.'[67]

Justification marks God's forgiveness of the repentant
sinner but it also heightens his sense of how much change needs
to occur in his life. His new openness to the working of the
Holy Spirit in him extends now to a welcome of the total transformation which marks God's continuing work in him. The forgiveness itself certified the adoption of the sinner into the fellowship of the children of God. The second benefit of justification
is this transformation which Wesley calls regeneration or the new
birth. Justification and this new birth cannot be clearly distinguished in point of time, yet they are in principle separable:

> Justification implies only a relative, the new birth
> a real, change. God in justifying us does something
> *for* us; in begetting us again, He does the work *in*
> us. The former changes our outward relation to God,
> so that of enemies we become children; by the latter
> our inmost souls are changed, so that of sinners we
> become saints. The one restores us to the favour, the
> other to the image, of God. The one is the taking
> away of the guilt, the other the taking away of the
> power, of sin: so that, although they are joined
> together in point of time, yet are they of wholly
> distinct natures.[68]

Justification is made possible through the objective work
of Christ. Sanctification, the continuing process of transformation, is effected through the subjective work of the Spirit.
For Wesley this new birth or conversion always was accompanied
by a conscious awareness of a real change in the person's life.
He uses the analogy of natural birth to illustrate the nature
of the change:

> The 'eyes of his understanding are opened'...and,
> He who of old 'commanded light to shine out of darkness shining on his heart, he sees the light of the
> glory of God,' his glorious love, 'in the face of
> Jesus Christ.' His ears being opened, he is now capable of hearing the inward voice of God, saying, 'Be
> of good cheer; thy sins are forgiven thee'; 'Go and
> sin no more.'...He 'feels in his heart,' to use the
> language of our Church, 'the mighty working of the
> Spirit of God.'...And now he may be properly said to
> live: God having quickened him by His Spirit, he is
> alive to God through Jesus Christ....From hence it
> manifestly appears, what is the nature of the new
> birth. It is the great change which God works in the
> soul when He brings it into life; when He raises it
> from the death of sin to the life of righteousness....
> In a word, it is that change whereby the earthly,
> sensual, devilish mind is turned into the 'mind which
> was in Christ Jesus.' This is the nature of the new
> birth: 'so is everyone that is born of the Spirit.'[69]

While it is true that the complete ramifications of this transformation are not instantaneous, Wesley was convinced that the believer could ordinarily be acutely aware of its taking place in him and have a sense of assurance that God was in fact in the process of bringing about a radical change. This sense of assurance could provide a "sure trust and confidence in God" that the person was forgiven, reconciled, and being transformed --was indeed a child of God. Wesley had sought for such a sense of assurance for a long period prior to his own conversion and at Aldersgate believed he had found it. For some time subsequent to the 1738 experience he tended to make this sense of pardon a required accompaniment of justification, but later softened his stand on this, realizing that a feeling of pardon could not be made a condition of it. In fact, it became obvious to him that merely subjective signs could be dangerously misleading:

> How many vain men, not understanding what they spake, neither whereof they affirmed, have wrested this Scripture to the great loss, if not destruction, of their souls! How many have mistaken the voice of their own imagination for this witness of the Spirit of God, and thence idly presumed they were the children of God, while they were doing the works of the devil.[70]

For Wesley there were certain marks of true assurance as opposed to the possible false presumptions of the "natural mind." One such sign is the continued presence of repentance. Another is the manifestation of certain traits such as meekness, patience, gentleness, etc.[71] But even more important is a transformation of outward life:

> Once more: the Scriptures teach, 'This is the love of God,' the sure mark thereof, 'that we keep his commandments' (I John v. 3). And our Lord himself saith, 'He that keepeth my commandments, he it is that loveth me! (John xiv. 21). Love rejoices to obey; to do, in every point, whatever is acceptable to the beloved. A true lover of God hastens to do his will on earth as it is done in heaven.[72]

Wesley has here made it obvious that regeneration or new birth opens out into further radical change--that it must do so or question is raised about the true state of the soul of the believer. An even higher stage awaits the developing Christian. But the regenerate babe in Christ must take great care lest the seed of sin still present in him grow and thwart that development:

> There are in every person, even after he is justified,
> two contrary principles, nature and grace, termed by
> St. Paul, the *flesh* and the *Spirit*....Accordingly, be-
> lievers are continually exhorted to watch against the
> flesh, as well as the world and the devil.[73]

This is the reason for the continued need for repentance in
the believer. The new-born Christian must work out his salvation
by living the life of obedience and constantly using the means
of grace. Note here that God is providing the grace which over-
comes the power of sin, and the initiative remains his. If the
believer persists in his responsiveness to this grace working in
him he will eventually be led to what Wesley calls entire sanctification:

> 'Well, but what more than this (the new birth) can
> be implied in entire sanctification'? It does not
> imply any *new* kind of holiness: Let no man imagine
> this. From the moment we are justified, till we give
> up our spirits to God, love is the fulfilling of the
> law; love is the sum of Christian sanctification; it
> is the one *kind* of holiness, which is found, only in
> various *degrees* in the believers who are distinguished
> by St. John into 'little children, young men, and
> fathers.' The difference between one and the other
> properly lies in the degree of love.[74]

Of this teaching of entire or full sanctification Wesley
noted, "This doctrine is the grand depositum which God has lodged
with the people called Methodists; and for the sake of propagating
this chiefly He appeared to have raised us up."[75] This doctrine,
also called perfection, was both fundamental and controversial
and it caused great difficulties in his attempt to formulate an
adequate statement of it. For him, perfection marked liberation
from original sin and therefore the complete restoration of the
image of God. The difficulty he faced was to present an understanding of perfection which could focus on the promise of power
over sin through Christ without ignoring the limitations which
were endemic to the human nature of even the redeemed man. In
correspondence with his brother Charles he counseled that expectations be kept in a realistic perspective:

> One word more, concerning setting perfection too high.
> *That perfection* which I believe, I can boldly preach,
> because I think I see five hundred witnesses of it.
> Of *that perfection* which you preach, you do not even
> think you see any witness at all. Why, then you must
> have more courage than me, or you could not persist
> in preaching it. I wonder you do not in this article

fall in plumb with Mr. Whitfield. For do you not as
well as he ask, 'Where are the perfect ones'? I
verily believe there are none on earth, none dwelling
in the body. I cordially assent to his opinion that
there is *no such perfection* here as you describe--at
least, I have never met with an instant of it; and I
doubt I never shall. Therefore I still think to set
perfection so *high* is effectually to renounce it.[76]

Wesley sought to clarify his position in his "A Plain Account
of Christian Perfection."[77] From his point of view there were a
number of senses in which even the most faithful Christian could
not be said to be perfect. He begins his treatise by listing
these limitations:

> They are not perfect in knowledge. They are not free
> from ignorance, no, nor from mistake. We are no more
> to expect any living man to be infallible, than to be
> omniscient. They are not free from infirmities, such
> as weakness or slowness of understanding, irregular
> quickness or heaviness of imagination. Such in
> another kind are impropriety of language, ungraceful-
> ness of pronunciation; to which one might add a thou-
> sand nameless defects, either in conversation or
> behavior. From such infirmities as these none are
> perfectly freed till their spirits return to God;
> neither can we expect till then to be wholly freed
> from temptation; for 'the servant is not above his
> master.' But neither in this sense is there any ab-
> solute perfection on earth.[78]

A person in Wesley's state of perfection continues to need
forgiveness and remains dependent on the "alien righteousness"
of Christ for both his justification and his continuing sanctification. Even a "perfect holiness is acceptable to God only
through Jesus Christ."[79] Still, a believer who is perfect in
Wesley's use of the term can be said to commit no sin: "It
remains, then, that Christians are saved in this world from all
sin, from all unrighteousness; that they are now in such a sense
perfect, as not to commit sin, and to be freed from evil thoughts
and evil tempers."[80] In the preface to a volume of hymns published in 1741 Wesley itemized some of the changes underlying
this "sinless" state. God's grace has made possible a renewal
of their minds and a cleansing of their hearts. They feel that
they have been released from bondage--especially a bondage to
pride:

> They feel that all their 'sufficiency is of God,'
> that it is He alone who 'is in all their thoughts,'
> and 'worketh in them both to will and to do his good

> pleasure.' They feel that 'it is not they' that
> 'speak, but the Spirit of' their 'Father who speak-
> eth' in them, and that whatsoever is done by their
> hands, 'the Father who is in them, he doeth the works.'
> So that God is to them all in all, and they are nothing
> in his sight. They are freed from self-will, as de-
> siring nothing but the holy and perfect will of God...
> but continually crying in their inmost soul, 'Father,
> thy will be done.'[81]

We should note here the emphasis which is put by Wesley on
the transformation which occurs in the subjective states of the
"perfect" believer. This subjective change includes but is not
limited to what he called "assurance." For the psychohistorian,
the focus on maintaining a *subjective state of passivity* before
the divine initiative provides the skeleton key to understanding
the character of the theology of passivity--far more important
than the subjective states associated with assurance, though
undoubtedly the two cannot be clearly separated. Note the continued emphasis on subjective transformation in a later, more
positive statement of the doctrine of perfection:

> But whom then do you mean by 'one that is perfect'?
> We mean one in whom is 'the mind which was in Christ,'
> and who so 'walketh as Christ also walked'; a man
> 'that hath clean hands and a pure heart,' or that is
> 'cleansed from all filthiness of flesh and spirit';
> one in whom is 'no occasion of stumbling,' and who
> accordingly, 'does not commit sin.'...We understand
> hereby, one whom God hath 'sanctified throughout in
> body, soul and spirit.'
> This man can now testify to all mankind, 'I am
> crucified with Christ: Nevertheless I live; yet not
> I, but Christ liveth in me.'...He 'loveth the Lord
> his God with all his heart,' and serveth him 'with
> all his strength.' He 'loveth his neighbor,' every
> man, 'as himself'; yea, 'as Christ loveth us.'...
> Indeed his soul is all love, filled with 'bowels of
> mercies, kindness, meekness, gentleness, longsuffer-
> ing.' And his life agreeth thereto, full of 'the
> work of faith, the patience of hope, the labour of
> love.'
> This it is to be a perfect man, to be 'sanctified
> throughout'; even 'to have a heart so all-flaming with
> the love of God,' (to use Archbishop Usher's words,)
> 'as continually to offer up every thought, word, and
> work, as a spiritual sacrifice, acceptable to God
> through Christ.'[82]

A close examination of Wesley's concept of an imperfect
perfection indicates that what appears to be a paradox is rendered more understandable by his differentiation between two

types of sin. The first is the sin which comes from falling short of an absolute conformity to the perfect will of God in every sphere of life. For him, no man, not even those manifesting his concept of perfection, escapes this type of sin--it is always present due to man's limitations. It is this type of omnipresent sin which necessitates repentance in the believer and the constant exhortation to grow in grace.

The second type of sin, more germaine to his concept of perfection, is that of a *conscious*, *willful* separation from God manifest in a subjective rebellion, a refusal to obey when God's command is clear in the mind. A person can be perfect in the sense that it is possible to live in a continual unbroken *conscious* relationship with God in Christ. This relationship is marked by a conscious, constant love of God, obedience to his will to the degree that the individual understands it, and dependence on the grace available through Christ. The perfection which Wesley affirms, therefore, is not one of a perfect adherance to *objective* moral standards, but one of a continuous *subjective* submission to the indwelling spirit of God in Christ. Wesley's theology, then, is clearly a theology of passivity in the sense that the perfected man in his conscious, subjective states must manifest total resignation, a "perfect submission" to the will of God. The old subjectively experienced self cannot be reformed --it must die. One has to be "crucified with Christ" so that a new subjective self can arise in its place.

Controversies in Interpretation: From Wesley as Papist to Wesley as Calvinist

Wesley's attempt to combine a doctrine of justification by grace through faith with a doctrine of realizable holiness or perfection has been extremely controversial since its inception, and has since led to radically divergent interpretations of his thought. We have already noted the influence which Roman Catholic conceptions of piety had on his understandings of the nature of the holy life. Maximin Piette, in his *John Wesley in the Evolution of Protestantism*, sought to date Wesley's most significant religious experience from his decision for ordination rather than from the 1738 "conversion experience," thereby seeking to distance Wesley from Luther and Calvin and to emphasize his roots

in Roman Catholic visions of the religious life.[83] Wesley himself had commented of this early period that he was, "for ten
years fundamentally a Papist and knew it not."[84] Even George
Croft Cell who took a radically different point of view had to
admit the Catholic emphases in Wesley's thought and suggested
that the revivalist's doctrines were "a necessary synthesis of
the Protestant ethic of grace with the Catholic ethic of holiness."[85] Cell went on to quote Wesley on the matter:

> Who has wrote more ably than Martin Luther on justifi-
> cation alone? And who was more ignorant of the doc-
> trine of sanctification or more confused in his concep-
> tions of it? As proof let any one examine his comment
> on the Epistle to the Galatians. On the other hand how
> many writers of the Romish Church (as Francis Sales and
> Juan de Castaniza, in particular) have wrote strongly
> and scripturally on sanctification--who nevertheless
> were entirely unacquainted with the nature of justifica-
> tion. As proof let any one examine the doctrinal guid-
> ance for teaching the people by every parish priest,
> ordained by the whole body of their divines at the
> Council of Trent.[86]

William Cannon in his monograph *The Theology of John Wesley*
argued that Wesley had indeed drastically modified the classical
reformation position on sanctification. For Cannon, the "Wesleyan
system of ethics, therefore, stands in contrast to the systems
of Luther and of Calvin in that it is an ethics of *realization*,
not of *aspiration*."[87] Harald Lindström in his able study of the
doctrine of sanctification has provided us with a competent summary of the matter:

> To Wesley perfection was an attainable and higher
> stage in the Christian life after forgiveness and
> new birth. To Luther on the other hand forgiveness,
> which at the same time meant the transformation of
> man, was in itself the highest expression of the
> Christian life. He saw the ethical change of man's
> will as an incomplete beginning. Morally, that is,
> the believer was never perfect in this life; though
> he could be entirely righteous in the sense that he
> had received forgiveness in faith and been delivered
> from the sentence and punishment of sin. To the Re-
> formers perfection was perfection in faith, but to
> Wesley it was an inherent ethical perfection in love
> and obedience....Both Calvin and Luther thought in-
> herent ethical perfection came only with death,
> Wesley that entire sanctification could be realized
> during life on earth.[88]

This tendency to separate the position of Wesley from that
of the reformers with regard to the dynamics of redemption received a significant challenge in 1935 with the publication of
Cell's monograph, *The Rediscovery of John Wesley*.[89] Cell argued
that too much had been made of theological differences between
Wesley and the reformers. In particular he suggested that the
tendency to interpret Wesley as giving man an active role in
his own salvation was in error. The error was based, he believed,
on the assumption that Wesley's stand against predestination made
him essentially anti-Calvinist in his view of redemption. Cell
pointed to Wesley's 1739 sermon on "free grace" as a basis for
his contention. The sermon had been written by Wesley as a cor-
rective to the Calvinist preaching of some of his opponents.
Noting that Wesley's critique was directed solely against the
predestinarian decrees, Cell argued that Wesley adhered to the
position that, with regard to the redemptive process, "God is
everything, man is nothing."[90] Cell summed up his argument as
follows:

> If then in the most radically anti-Calvinist dis-
> course Wesley ever wrote, wherein he pitched into
> the doctrine of absolute predestination as a doctrine
> 'full of blasphemy,' as a doctrine which cancels the
> first principle of the Christian revelation, namely
> the essential righteousness of God, he has taken the
> precaution and been at considerable pains to reaffirm
> in the most complete and unequivocal manner a mon-
> ergistic and in the same manner to deny a synergistic
> view of faith and repentance, of justification and
> sanctification, it would seem an end of all argument
> about, not the soundness of Wesley's doctrine, but
> what his position actually was. For us, Wesley's
> thesis, which he taught consistently for full fifty
> years, that 'whatsoever good is in man or is done by
> man, God is the author and doer of it,' and the further
> fact that he has crowded into this category every par-
> ticular of Christian experience, carries the conclusion
> with it and is final.[91]

Cell's view was not, however, final for others in the
Wesleyan tradition. Cannon's monograph mentioned above was, at
least in part, an attempt to answer Cell's argument. He argues
that, in Wesley's view, although man does not justify himself,
"he does have an active part in the acquisition of faith, which
is the sole condition of justification."[92] He continued to
elaborate his position in the matter:

> Granting, therefore, man's ability to stifle and kill
> the grace of God within him, have we the right to
> ascribe to him the positive role of a co-operator
> with God? We have. For in the very act of not kill-
> ing grace and of listening to the voice of natural
> conscience, even though at times very inattentively,
> man is actually co-operating with God in God's efforts
> in behalf of his salvation. This must be the case;
> it cannot be otherwise. Once you grant to man a
> power great enough to make itself felt as the decid-
> ing factor in the acceptance or rejection of the means
> necessary for the bestowal of saving faith, you lift
> him, whether you will or not, out of a state of mere
> passivity into one of activity and of co-operation or
> non-co-operation with the grace of God....Wesleyan
> thought, therefore, is decidedly synergistic in its
> description of the operations prior to justification
> and essential to the bestowal of saving faith.[93]

Here we have a Methodist theologian arguing that in fact
Wesley's theology was one of activity rather than passivity.
For Cannon, man's freedom to decide whether or not to respond
to the divine initiative made man the "sole determinative factor
in the decision of his own justification," and that a response
of faith indicated human activity--indeed human *initiative*--in
the process of redemption.[94] In Cannon's words:

> The usual conception of divine initiative and human
> response is of course descriptive of Wesley's teach-
> ing; but, if understood properly, the conception of
> human *initiative* and *divine* response is likewise
> descriptive of his teaching and is not alien to his
> theology. Why? Simply because divine initiative in
> bestowing common or 'preventing' grace is taken for
> granted.[95]

Cannon's view that Wesley would affirm human initiative in
the redemptive process is not shared by most contemporary Wesley
scholars. Franz Hildebrandt and Colin Williams both emphasize
with Cell Wesley's continuation of the emphases which Calvin
and Luther put on the centrality of the divine initiative.[96]
Williams, while affirming with Cannon that Wesley's theology of
redemption is marked by synergism, suggests that while man re-
sponds freely to God's grace in his redemption, this response
is not to be understood in a "semi-Pelagian" sense. From the
latter type of perspective, Williams notes,

> the downward movement of God's grace meets the upward
> movement of man's natural will so that man is seen as
> a co-operator in the work of salvation, with his natu-
> ral ability being so strengthened by grace that he is
> enabled to rise to the moral level required for salva-
> tion.[97]

For Williams, Wesley's position is synergistic only to the extent that God has given man the freedom to receive or resist grace--the divine *initiative* remains unshared.

The clearest statement of the manner in which Wesley's theology is synergistic without implying human initiative is that of Albert Outler. While disagreeing with Cell, Hildebrandt, and Williams about the relative importance of the continental reformers to Wesley's mature theological stance, he also affirms that redemption, according to Wesley, required no human initiative:

> The Christian life, in Wesley's view, is empowered
> by the energy of grace: prevenient, saving, sancti-
> fying, sacramental. Grace is always interpreted as
> something more than mere forensic pardon. Rather,
> it is experienced as actual influence--God's love,
> immanent and active in human life. Its prior initi-
> ative makes every human action a *re*-action; hence,
> it is *'preventing.'* It is a function of God's mercy
> that is over all his works; hence, it is universal.
> It can be 'resisted'; hence it is co-operant rather
> than irresistible.[98]

Outler confirms our interpretation of Wesley's mature theology as one of passivity. In the redemptive process there simply is no such thing as human initiative. *All* initiative, even that manifesting itself in the life of the Christian who has attained perfection, is *divine* initiative. Wesley himself uses words expressing the passive nature of man's response to the grace of God acting in him:

> Why, the very power to 'work together with Him' was
> from God. Therefore to Him is all the glory. Has
> not even experience taught you this? Have you not
> often felt, in a particular temptation, power either
> to resist or yield to the grace of God? And when
> you have yielded to 'work together with Him,' did
> you not find it very possible, notwithstanding, to
> give him all the glory? So that both experience
> and Scripture are against you here, and make it clear
> to every impartial inquirer, that though man has
> freedom to work or not 'work together with God,' yet
> may God have the whole glory of his salvation.[99]

In Wesley's words the co-operation with grace is a "yield-ing," not an initiative, and Outler is correct in characterizing the human response as one of *reaction*. At this point one can discern the radical difference between Wesley's early theology and his mature theology with respect to the problem of initiative.

Wesley had found his own attempts to take the initiative to be
conflictual and adaptively dysfunctional. Even given his capacities for denial and other defense mechanisms, when he took the
spiritual initiative which he believed was needed for success
in his chosen vocation, he failed to achieve the *purity of intention* which he thought to be required for realizing his goals.
"Spiritual ambition," it appears, though ostensibly directed
solely toward pleasing God, was enough to trigger an extremely
punitive response from his superego--especially when the sexual
temptations of Georgia underscored the divisions within his will.
The only option left for him was to "yield" before the strictures
of his parental introjects. We have suggested above that the
intense depression and despair which marked Wesley's experience
in the period immediately following the Georgia episode manifested a state of ego-passivity before the punitive superego.
In the preceding section of this chapter we have argued that
Wesley found under Bohler's tutelage a theology which in its
emphasis on subjective passivity rendered his cognitive formulations less conflictual through elimination of any suggestions
of initiative on his part. We now turn to a concluding examination of the psychodynamic infrastructures underlying his theology of passivity.

Ego-Activity Through a Theology of Passivity

The final issue which we must address is whether Wesley's
overt theology along with his cultivation of subjective states
of passivity constitutes a continuation of ego-passivity in the
form of compliance with superego demands at the expense of ego-
ideals. Such a conclusion would seem to be suggested by Wesley's
emphasis on resignation and "yielding" before the divine initiative. Even Albert Outler concluded that Wesley was an obsessive-
compulsive neurotic--a diagnostic category corresponding to this
particular type of ego-passivity.[100] As suggested in the beginning of this chapter, however, our conclusions are quite different. Wesley's achievement of a subjective state of passivity
need not lead us to conclude that the ego-passivity manifest in
his depression continued after his discovery and embracing of
his theology of passivity. Rapaport has noted that an apparent
passivity may mark an actual active ego state. In his words,

Yet activity may be turned into a passivity which is only ostensible, the actual control of the ego over the drive demand remaining sustained. Kris subsumed a broad segment of such processes under the concept of *regression in service of the ego*.[101]

As an illustration he quotes Kris on ecstasy and inspiration:

...the driving of the unconscious toward consciousness is experienced as an intrusion from without--an attitude of a passive nature *par excellence*. The decisive difference, however, can be formulated more clearly. In ecstasy the process results in an emotional climax only; in states of inspiration it leads to active elaboration in creation. The process is dominated by the ego and put to its own purposes--for sublimation in creative activity.[102]

Rapaport then summarizes the significance of Kris' insights for all creative processes:

Creative experiences vary from those in which the artistic or scientific invention appears in subjective experience as hallucinated, entirely 'inspired' from the outside, to those in which it appears in subjective experience as entirely the produce of 'deliberate effort.' Yet the ego integration of the creative product is characteristic of all creative processes, and this ego integration --rather than subjective experience--is decisive, whether the process in question is one of activity or one of passivity, as here defined.[103]

There can be little doubt that these insights apply to the realm of the religious as well as those of the artistic and scientific. Wesley's painful period of depression and his initial embrace of resignation and submission did mark a regression on his part. Subsequently, however, this regression proved to be a regression in service of the ego. Psychosexual initiative was shelved for the time being, but would find expression in myriad ways in later years. The retention and cultivation of subjective states of passivity in practice functioned as a much more adequate extension of Wesley's penchant for denial and rationalization as defense mechanisms. Yet with the development of the theology of passivity his denial of initiative and rationalization of the intensively active modes of his overt behavior had found a systematic framework and a historical and Biblical foundation which enabled them to function far more successfully in facilitating ego-activity, and with it, purposive movement toward the fulfillment of his ego-ideals. The rejection of the decrees of predestination had affirmed that any real authority in the divine realm had to be fair, and that the spiritual "race" was significant and worth running. The rejection of human initiative and affirmation of the divine had insured that he would not only avoid immobilizing assaults by the superego, but that through submission he would be empowered by the grace of God to work toward ends both sanctioned by the superego and representative of ego-ideals. The resigned self had found a theology which could energize his quest for exaltation.

CHAPTER V

JOHN WESLEY AND INSTITUTIONAL RELATIONSHIPS

In the foregoing chapters we have presented an interpretation of the manner in which John Wesley dealt with the problem
of authority and initiative in his personal development and in
his theological formulations. The third and last area of inquiry
which will complete our investigations into the primary sources
is that of Wesley's institutional relationships. Joachim Wach,
whose theses regarding parallels in authority structures in these
areas provide the basic issues of our study, regarded religious
leadership as an especially important field for research. Wesley,
of course, is best known for his work as the leader of the Methodist movement, yet little sophisticated interpretive work from
a psychosocial perspective has been done on the rich materials
which Wesley and his movement offer for research in this area.[1]
Our task in this chapter is a quite circumscribed one and is not
to be construed as an adequate or comprehensive account of Wesley's religious leadership. Instead, the focal question here
is that of whether the particular dynamics treated in previous
chapters are manifest in representative major areas of authority
conflict and resolution in his institutional relationships.

We have suggested that Wesley resolved his focal conflict
over the exercise of initiative through the transformation of
his conscious states from activity to passivity in order to
facilitate dynamic activity. If this is the case, and if our
hypothesis of parallels between the structures of conflict resolution in personality, thought, and institutional relationships
is accurate, then an examination of the sources should provide
us with documentation of Wesley's use of similar adaptive tactics
in both his exercise of and response to institutional authority.
In the following discussion we will focus on representative conflicts in both of these areas. The first part of our inquiry
will deal with his exercise of authority within his own movement
and the second with his much-discussed reluctance to separate
from the Church of England.

Wesley as Leader: The Rationalization of Total Power

We have discussed Wesley's discovery of his vocation and his development of a theology appropriate for his task. It is, however, widely agreed that his creative genius was manifested in the organizational mode of his religious leadership. Effective as his preaching was, the success of his movement was insured by his development of a means of continued contact and control of those who responded to him. It was one thing to respond in a positive manner to his preaching--it was quite another to try to sustain the alteration in lifestyle which was assumed to be the result of such a response. The newly converted pleaded with Wesley to continue his relationship with them and to give them guidance in this new way of living. In Wesley's words:

> They said, 'But we want you likewise to talk with us often, to direct and quicken us in our way, to give us the advices which you well know we need, and to pray with us as well as for us.' I asked, which of you desire this? Let me know your names and places of abode. They did so. But I soon found they were too many for me to talk with severally so often as they wanted it. So I told them, 'If you will all of you come together every Thursday in the evening, I will gladly spend some time with you in prayer and give you the best advice I can.'[2]

Thus was born the Wesleyan society which was soon to grow into a chief feature of the movement. He soon noted that those involved in the society continued to grow in their faith and commitment, while those without such supervision tended to lapse back into their old ways. The growing size of the society soon became unwieldy, and he decided to divide the society into small groups of ten to twelve people. These small groups were the beginning of the Methodist "class meeting." Each class had a leader whose responsibility it was to oversee the development of each member, to collect money for the poor, and to report regularly to Wesley on the condition of the group. At first the leader visited with each member in the person's home. It was quickly realized, however, that not only was this as time consuming as it had been for Wesley himself, but that the lack of privacy made frank conversation--especially confession--problematic. The classes began to meet together, joining in prayer, singing and group confession and exhortation. Wesley discovered

that this approach made possible a high level of discipline
within the movement. Those who were unwilling to participate
in this intense mutual monitoring could be identified and separated from the fellowship. Chafing under Wesley's iron hand
began even at this early stage of development:

> But, notwithstanding all these advantages, many were
> at first extremely averse to meeting thus. Some,
> viewing it in a wrong point of light, not as a priv-
> ilege (indeed an invaluable one) but rather a re-
> straint, disliked it on that account, because they
> did not love to be restrained in anything.[3]

As early as 1741 he began the practice of giving membership tickets to the members of the societies. These tickets he
viewed as letters of recommendation, and meant, as he put it,
"I believe the bearer hereof to be one that fears God and works
righteousness."[4] The practical use of these tickets was to insure that the groups could exclude any who would not conform to
the standards which Wesley had set. Each quarter the tickets
were changed, and a "disorderly" member simply did not receive
a new ticket. Wesley was conscious of the negative ways in
which this discipline of the bands and his tight rein over them
could be taken:

> The thing which I was greatly afraid of all this time,
> and which I resolved to use every possible method of
> preventing, was a narrowness of spirit, a party zeal,
> a being straitened in our own bowels; that miserable
> bigotry which makes many so unready to believe that
> there is any work of God but among themselves.[5]

Apparently there was a substantial amount of resistance to
his use of these methods of close supervision. The rules for
the societies and later the bands were quite austere, prescribing
required practices such as participation in public worship, alms-
giving, mutual assistance, and honesty and trustworthiness in
all areas of life. They also prohibited the use of alcohol or
tobacco and "immoderate" use of jewelry. Each member was to be
a model of self-denial, frugality, and commitment for the others.
Wesley clearly believed that he could tell without any real
doubt who should be dropped from the groups, provided only that
his class-leaders used "common sense" and honesty in answering
his questions about the members. Protestors argued that he
would have to have the miraculous gift of "discernment of spirits"

in order to make accurate judgments in such matters, but Wesley
saw making such judgments as a relatively simple matter:

> I visit, for instance, the class in the Close,
> of which Robert Peacock is leader. I ask, 'Does this
> and this person in your class live in drunkenness or
> any outward sin? Does he go to church, and use the
> other means of grace? Does he meet you as often as
> he has opportunity'? Now, if Robert Peacock has
> common sense, he can answer these questions truly;
> and, if he has common honesty, he will. And if not,
> some other in the class has both, and can and will
> answer for him. Where is the difficulty, then, of
> finding out if there be any disorderly walker in this
> class, and, consequently, in any other?[6]

There is little doubt that in Wesley's mind he was simply
carrying out his responsibilities to those who had asked him to
offer pastoral oversight. He saw his activities as a continuation of practices which had been carried out in the early church,
and believed himself to be responding to the initiative not only
of the people, but also of the God who had providentially placed
him in this position of leadership and responsibility. Others,
however, noted the tremendous power which he wielded over group
members, and accused him of an abuse of power reminiscent of
papal power. He noted the objections but seemed to miss the
point:

> An objection much more boldly and frequently urged is
> that 'all these bands are mere Popery.' I hope I
> need not pass an harder censure on those (most of them
> at least) who affirm this than that they talk of they
> know not what; they betray in themselves the most
> gross and shameful ignorance. Do not they yet know
> that the only Popish confession is the confession
> made by a single person to a priest?--and this it-
> self is in no wise condemned by our Church; nay,
> she recommends it in some cases. Whereas that we
> practise is the confession of several persons conjoint-
> ly, not to a priest, but to each other. Consequently
> it has no analogy at all to Popish confession. But
> the truth is, this is a stale objection, which many
> people make against anything they do not like. It
> is all Popery out of hand.[7]

It is certainly a tribute to Wesley's renewed capacities
for denial and rationalization that he was now able to interpret the complaints of Popery as relating *simply* to specific
practices which he required of the members of the bands. Had
his defenses against a realization of the extent of his raw
power in these matters been less effective, he might have been

troubled by memories of similar complaints against him when he
was not sheltered by his passive-aggressive assumptions. Take,
for example, the complaints of colonists which were made to the
Trustees of Georgia regarding his tyrannical behavior:

> All Jesuitical arts were made use of to bring the
> well concerted scheme to perfection; families were
> divided into parties; spies were engaged in many
> houses, and the servants of the families they be-
> longed to; nay, those who had given themselves up
> to his spiritual guidance (more especially women)
> were obliged to discover to him their most secret
> actions, nay even their thoughts and the subject
> of their dreams....[8]

The response of the band members was not the first and
would not be the last time that Wesley was accused of Popery.
In Georgia the colonists were quite aware that it was not any
particular practice which was perceived as being suspect, but
a whole configuration of practices which, taken together, made
it evident to them that Wesley's object was in fact a rather
total, and very "un-English" control over their lives:

> ...As there is always a strict connection betwixt
> Popery and Slavery; so the design of all this fine
> scheme seemed to the most judicious, to be calculated
> to debase and depress the minds of the people, to
> break any spirit of liberty, and humble them with
> fastings, penances, drinking of water, and a thorough
> subjection to the spiritual jurisdiction which he
> asserted was to be established in his person; and
> when this should be accomplished, the minds of people
> would be equally prepared for the receiving civil or
> ecclesiastical tyranny.[9]

Wesley's indignant decrying of the ignorance of his band
members as to what constituted true "Popery" marks his own ignoring of the real nature of their complaint. It was not the
practice of group confession which troubled them, but the power
which it and other practices implied to be grounded in his
"spiritual jurisdiction." While it is beyond the scope of this
chapter to trace Wesley's development of his organization, the
authority structure manifest in the mature as well as the early
stages of that movement can be accurately characterized as a
strict hierarchy with Wesley at the summit, controlling the
movement—to use Wesley's own apt metaphor—as an operator does
a "machine."[10] A crisis in the society in Dublin in 1771 led
Wesley to spell out the hierarchy in detail, making clear the

proper jurisdiction of each level of leadership. It now was
made up of lay-assistants, preachers, stewards, and class leaders.
An excerpt from the paper Wesley read to the society outlines the
authority issue:

Q. 1. What authority has a single leader?
He has authority to meet his class, to receive their
contributions, and to visit the sick in his class.
Q. 2. What authority have all the leaders of a society
met together?
They have authority to show their class papers to the
assistant, to deliver the money they have received to
the stewards, and to bring in the names of the sick.
Q. 3. But have they not authority to restrain the
assistant, if they think he acts improperly?
No more than any member of the society has. After
mildly speaking to him, they are to refer the thing
to Mr. W.
Q. 4. Have they not authority to hinder a person from
preaching?
None but the assistant has this authority.
Q. 5. Have they not authority to displace a particular
leader?
No more than the door-keeper has. To place and displace leaders belongs to the assistant alone.
Q. 6. Have they not authority to expel a particular
member of the society?
No; the assistant only can do this.
Q. 7. But have they not authority to regulate the
temporal and spiritual affairs of the society?
Neither the one nor the other. Temporal affairs
belong to the stewards; spiritual to the assistant.[11]

Wesley was attempting to make it clear to the society members that the only legitimate authority in the societies was
that which he had assigned and which only he or his duly appointed representative could alter. It was the very awareness
of this point that had led to the attacks on this arrangement
as being "Popery." Wesley had set up an organization with
clearly differentiated levels of status and power, giving an
increasing increment of prestige to each succeeding upward step
in the hierarchy. He rewarded those who conducted themselves
as he desired with promotion within the movement. Behavior
which ignored the rules he had made, or which questioned the
existing structures of power was deemed "disorderly" and the
culprit demoted, or worse, dismissed from the society. Wesley's
choosing Thursday evenings to begin his guidance with his "children in the faith" is significant. Thursday night had been his
turn at having the undivided attention of Susanna in the Epworth

parsonage. Susanna now provided him with his model for the
exercise of pastoral authority as well as--as we shall see be-
low--his tactics of confronting it.

On the surface it might seem that assuming the authoritative
position in this manner would smack of undue initiative on his
part and prick his tender conscience. Yet in his mind, the
machine had been set up to do the will of God and it was his
humble responsibility to see that the work was done--that the
"wheels" moved smoothly:

> In the Methodist discipline the wheels regularly
> stand thus: the assistant, the preachers, the
> stewards, the leaders, the people....But here the
> leaders, who are the lowest wheel but one, were
> got quite out of their place. They were got at the
> top of all, above the stewards, the preachers, yea,
> and above the assistant himself.[12]

The authority which was being challenged, of course, was
his own. From his point of view, however, it was God's work--
and of course God's initiatives which were being hindered:

> ...To this, chiefly, I impute the gradual decay of
> the work of God in Dublin.
> There has been a jar throughout the whole ma-
> chine. Most of the wheels were hindered in their
> motion. The stewards, the preachers, the assistant,
> all moved heavily. They felt all was not right. But
> if they saw where the fault lay, they had not strength
> to remedy it.
> But it may be effectually remedied now. Without
> rehearsing former grievances (which may all die and
> be forgotten) for the time to come, let each wheel
> keep to its own place. Let the assistant, the preach-
> ers, the stewards, the leaders, know and execute
> their several offices. Let none encroach upon another,
> but all move together in harmony and love. So shall
> the work of God flourish among you, perhaps as it
> never did before, while you all hold the unity of the
> Spirit in the bond of peace.[13]

Wesley's call for peace and order in the societies was
reminiscent of Pauline exhortations and was based on a view of
his own authority which also approached the apostolic in the
totality of its claim. Still, though the work proceeded steadily, unity and peace--especially with regard to the authority
issue--was elusive. Not only was Wesley's iron hand unresponsive
to the growing democratic tendencies expressed by his preachers,
but the very interest in a larger voice in the movement manifested an ambition in the ranks that irritated the ambitious

founder. As Wesley noted after describing the role of the preachers, "But how hard is it to abide here! Who does not wish to be a little higher? suppose, to be ordained!"[14] Wesley's "sons in the Gospel" had gradually expanded the breadth of their functions and their status within the movement had grown. In the beginning they had been called "lay-assistants," later, "helpers" as in Wesley's understanding of the practice of the early church, and finally, "lay-preachers." With a few ordained clergymen and even fewer of these lay-preachers Wesley had initiated in 1744 an organizational structure which subsequently was of great importance to the movement--the annual conference.

From the beginning Wesley had carefully avoided referring to his preachers as "ministers" and refused to allow them to administer the sacraments. Much of the pressure from the lay members of the conference to separate from the Church of England was based on these restrictions, viewed by the preachers as arbitrary. Their ambition assisted them in discerning much of the reality which Wesley's own ambition required that he deny: the extent to which their activities paralleled--perhaps even constituted--dissent. The preachers had little, if any, reluctance to become full-fledged dissenting clergymen. It was clearly Wesley's own agenda, to be discussed below, which stood between the lay-preachers and separation--and consequently between their subordinate status and the realization of their ambitions.

The issue came to a head in the Leeds conference of 1766. The preachers first sought to have Wesley admit that the Methodists were in fact dissenters and that he ought, therefore, to allow them full status as clergymen. Wesley's powers of rationalization are evident in his response:

> Q. 45. But are we not Dissenters?
> A. No: Although we call sinners to repentance in all places of God's dominion; and although we frequently use extemporary prayer, and unite together in a religious society; yet we are not Dissenters in the only sense which our law acknowledges, namely, those who renounce the service of the church. We do not, we dare not, separate from it. We are not Seceders, nor do we bear any resemblance to them. We set out upon quite opposite principles. The Seceders laid the very foundations of their work in judging and condemning others: We laid the foundations of our work in judging and condemning ourselves.[15]

The preachers must have listened in disbelief to their
leader. They had had little difficulty in discerning the many
similarities of Methodist "irregularities" to dissent. They
remembered, too, Wesley's scathing judgment and condemnation of
the typical Anglican clergyman which he uttered in response to
attacks upon his use of lay-preachers. The preachers wanted
him to acknowledge that Methodist services constituted "public
worship" and therefore dissent. He refused to draw such a conclusion:

> But some may say, 'Our own service is public worship.'
> Yes; but not such as supersedes the Church Service; it
> presupposes public prayer, like the sermons at the Uni-
> versity. If it were designed to be instead of the
> Church Service, it would be essentially defective; for
> it seldom has the four grand parts of public prayer,
> deprecation, petition, intercession, and thanksgiving.[16]

The preachers went on to demand to know why they should not
separate from the established church given the "wickedness both
of the Clergy and the people"? Wesley simply referred them to
the reasons "printed above twenty years ago, entitled, 'Reasons
Against a Separation from the Church of England.'"[17] Not being
able to get Wesley to see what they deemed to be the natural
and logical implications of his practices, they attacked what
they saw as his tyranny over them. Some of them must have remembered his criticism of Count Zinzendorf for his dictatorship
over the Moravian societies. Wesley had always resolved to
"call no man master," and now the preachers wanted to know why
they should not apply to him his criticism of and response to
the count. Wesley responded, "Count Zinzendorf loved to keep
all things close: I love to do all things openly. I will
therefore tell you all I know of the matter, taking it from the
very beginning."[18] It is not surprising that the preachers were
not pacified by his "open" discussion of the source and nature
of the power which he exercised over the preachers and societies.
We should also not be surprised by the way Wesley structured his
rationalization of that power. The same *denial of initiative*
on his part which we have documented in other areas serves as
the cornerstone of his argument. He began by calling their attention to the very beginnings of the movement in 1738 when
"two or three persons" came to him in London and asked him to
"advise and pray with them." He observed that the "desire was

on their part" and not his own. He had really, he reminisced,
wanted only to "live and die in retirement" but had seen in their
actions a divine initiative and thus could not refuse to help
them and "be guiltless before God."[19]

> Here commenced my power; namely, a power to appoint
> when, and where, and how they should meet; and to
> remove those whose lives showed that they had not
> a desire 'to flee from the wrath to come.' And
> this power remained the same, whether the people
> meeting together were twelve, or twelve hundred
> thousand.[20]

Wesley then gave his account of the origins of the office
of steward, emphasizing first that the suggestion for such an
office had come from the people, but, after the need had become
evident, it was Wesley himself--not the people--who had determined the nature of the office and who should occupy it. Next
he turned to the origins of the lay-assistants. According to
his apologia three men came to him and volunteered to serve him
as "sons in the gospel," working whenever and wherever he directed. Again he repeated his rationale:

> Observe: These likewise desired me, not I them. But
> I durst not refuse their assistance. And here com-
> menced my power, to appoint each of these when, and
> where, and how to labour; that is, while he chose to
> continue with me. For each had a power to go away
> when he pleased; as I had also, to go away from them,
> or any of them, if I saw sufficient cause. The case
> continued the same when the number of Preachers in-
> creased. I had just the same power still, to appoint
> when, and where, and how each should help me; and to
> tell any (if I saw cause), 'I do not desire your help
> any longer.' On these terms, and no others, we joined
> at first: On these we continue joined.[21]

In the course of these remarks Wesley protested repeatedly
that the preachers were doing him no *personal* favor at all,
that leadership had been thrust upon him by Providence and that
it was a great burden for him--one that he would, if he could,
give up. He then turned to the origins of the annual conference
and repeated his theme:

> Observe: I myself sent for these of my own free
> choice. And I sent for them to advise, not govern,
> me. Neither did I at any time divest myself of
> any part of the power above described, which the
> providence of God had cast upon me, without any
> design or choice of mine.[22]

Wesley had given his "open" summary of the historical development of his leadership and authority, and he left the
preachers little doubt of the totality of the autocratic power
which he was forthrightly claiming. In case they had not yet
understood his argument, he summarized it for them:

> What is that power? It is a power of admitting into,
> and excluding from, the societies under my care; of
> choosing and removing Stewards, of receiving or not
> receiving Helpers; of appointing them when, where,
> and how to help me, and of desiring any of them to
> confer with me when I see good. And as it was merely
> in obedience to the providence of God, and for the
> good of the people, that I at first accepted this
> power, which I never sought; so it is on the same
> consideration, not for profit, honour, or pleasure,
> that I use it at this day.[23]

His statement did not go unchallenged. Several of the
preachers retorted that in spite of his rationale, the totality
of his power was offensive and amounted to "shackling free-born
Englishmen." Again they likened his power and the ruthlessness
with which he exercised it to "Popery," and again Wesley responded with his standard arguments:

> 'But this is making yourself a Pope.' This carries
> no face of truth. The Pope affirms that every
> Christian must do all he bids, and believe all he
> says, under pain of damnation. I never affirmed any-
> thing that bears any the most distant resemblance to
> this. All I affirm is, the Preachers who choose to
> labour with me, choose to serve me as sons in the
> gospel. And the people who choose to be under my
> care, choose to be so under the same terms they
> were at first.[24]

The structure of and rationale for Wesley's exercise of
authority in the Methodist movement is evident. His power was
autocratic and total. Those who "elected" to either membership
or assistantship--after their decision to affiliate--surrendered
any further initiative to Wesley and became, if they remained
with him, also "resigned selves." Wesley made the rules for
the race quite evident and "rational," and, while exclusion
from his rule did not *insure* damnation, it was deemed in that
ethos to render it far more likely. Their position before
Wesley had been structured in a manner closely analogous to
that which he himself had perceived to exist between child and
parent in the Epworth parsonage and between self and God in the

post-Aldersgate period. Spiritual ambition was carefully cultivated in each of these realms, and in the movement provided
sufficient motivation for most to continue "submitting" in order
to be exalted. Wesley's mother had been fair and predictable,
so had his God, and now his exercise of authority--modeled on
these earlier examples--seemed to him to be equally above re-
proach, and criticism of it was somehow unappreciative and un-
fair:

> Therefore all talk of this kind is highly injurious
> to me, who bear the burden merely for your sake.
> And it is exceeding mischievous to the people,
> tending to confound their understanding, and to
> fill their hearts with evil surmisings and unkind
> tempers toward me; to whom they really owe more,
> for taking all this load upon me, for exercising
> this very power, for shackling myself in this man-
> ner, than for all my preaching put together: Be-
> cause preaching twice or thrice a day is no burden
> to me at all; but the care of all the Preachers and
> all the people is a burden indeed![25]

No wonder the next question was, "What reason can be assigned why so many of our Preachers contract nervous disorders"?[26]
Wesley simply could not see that he had any initiative at all,
much less that he was manifesting an "unspiritual" arrogance of
power. He had surrendered his own will to God, and now what appeared to be autocracy to these ungrateful dissidents was merely
the fair, consistent, rightful authority of God which flowed
through him without any resistance on his part. It was this
resignation before the divine initiative which indeed legitimized
his authority in the movement. Since he denied any personal,
"natural" or "worldly" authority or initiative on his part, and
since his actions were merely his obedient response to the working
of the divine initiative through him, those who opposed him could
do so only out of ignorance of the nature of his extraordinary
mission or other motives at least questionable and probably down-
right unchristian. Let us now turn to an examination of how this
same view of authority and initiative was operant in and provides
us with a key for understanding his strange relationship to the
Church of England.

Wesley and the Church of England:
Covert Rebellion and Its Denial

Of the many aspects of Wesley's religious leadership which could be scrutinized in a study utilizing psychosocial interpretation, his lifelong ambivalent relationship to the Church of England has been the most puzzling to historians and biographers. To date no attempt has been made to clarify the dynamics underlying this ambivalence. Our task in the remainder of this chapter will be to document the manner in which this relationship was grounded in Wesley's chosen adaptive strategies with respect to the problem of authority, initiative, and guilt. In the course of our discussion we will examine Wesley's interaction with three groups with respect to the issues: his family members, the bishops and clergy of the established church, and members of his own movement.

Earlier in this chapter I alluded to Susanna as a model not only for Wesley's exercise of authority but for his response to it. I have reference here to the episode discussed in a previous chapter in which Susanna in Samuel's absence held meetings in her home for parishioners who desired spiritual guidance. In this situation Samuel had as usual played the role of the impractical strict interpreter of canon law while Susanna chose to place the spiritual welfare of the parishioners before the letter of the law. Impatient with the incompetent and lazy curate whom Samuel had left in charge, she believed that her responsibility before God necessitated her attempting to do everything in her power to nurture the souls of the people--even if her actions resembled dissent. When Samuel had remonstrated with her for her actions, she did not deny his *formal* authority--as husband and parish priest--to order her forthrightly to end her activities. Nevertheless, she challenged him on the grounds of the divine authority and their mutual responsibility before it and Samuel had withdrawn his prohibitions. Susanna's Puritan heritage was never as completely suppressed as Samuel's had been, and this event, taken together with her later encouragement of Wesley's use of lay preachers, illustrates her capacity to rationalize innovation in the service of the faith as she understood it. In addition to the appeal to higher authority to counter that of her husband and narrow interpretations of

church law, the episode also illustrates her use of carefully
reasoned argument to limit the abuse of legitimate authority
and power. As we have seen, Wesley chose to emulate her response
to Samuel and developed an unequalled capacity for rationalization
as a means of defense against Samuel's--and later episcopal--
authority.

Still, she considered herself a loyal member of the Church
of England and soon after John's return from Georgia she was
troubled by reports from Samuel, Jr. concerning the irregular
thinking and behavior of his younger brothers. Her support,
even encouragement, of Wesley's "irregular" behavior came later
at the point of the initiation of lay preaching.

John Wesley's elder brother, though he did not become a
parish priest, continued the traditions of his father in another
way: his high churchmanship. In all family conflicts he tended
to take the side of his father, and he was particularly suspicious
of John's motivations and judgments. Soon after the younger
brothers' conversions Samuel received a frantic letter from one
Mrs. Hutton complaining of their fanaticism. Both John and
Charles had resided in her home for a time after returning from
Georgia and she was tremendously concerned regarding the influence
the Wesleys were having on her two children:

> But your brother John seems to be turned a wild en-
> thusiast, or fanatic; and to our very great afflic-
> tion is drawing our two children into these wild
> notions, by their great opinion of Mr. John's sanc-
> tity and judgment. It would be a great charity to
> many other honest, well-meaning, simple souls, as
> well as to my children, if you could either *confine*
> or *convert* Mr. John when he is with you; for after
> his behavior on Sunday the 28th of May, when you hear
> it, you will think him not *a quite right man*.[27]

It seems that Wesley's experience the previous week and his
subsequent witness to "salvation by faith alone" were already
causing a stir. It was evident, too, that Wesley's influence
at this point was understood as tending toward encouragement of
dissent and dangerous undermining of authority, both ecclesiastical and parental. At this point Wesley belived he had found true
humility through passivity before God. Mrs. Hutton read the
situation differently:

If there cannot be some stop put to this, and unless
he can be taught true humility, the mischief he will
do wherever he goes among the ignorant but well-mean-
ing Christians will be very great....Mr. John has
abridged the life of one *Haliburton* a Presbyterian
teacher in Scotland. My son had designed to print it,
to shew the experiences of that holy man, of indwelling, &c. Mr. Hutton and I have forbid our son being
concerned in handing such books into the world: but
if your brother John or Charles think it will tend to
promote God's glory, *they will soon convince my son
God's glory is to be preferred to his parent's com-
mands.*[28]

Samuel's answer to Mrs. Hutton evidences his willingness
to believe that John, especially, was involved in "lunacy" and
"enthusiasm." He wrote to "Jack" taking him to task for his
behavior, and a fervid exchange of letters between the brothers
ensued. Samuel, as had his father before him, felt that arguing
with John was like running his "head against a stone wall."[29]
Apparently both Samuel and his mother believed that John and
Charles were on the verge of a "formal schism" because of their
use of "extemporary" preaching and prayers, their use of the
treatise on Haliburton, and their close association with the
"raving" Whitefield.[30] After John's involvement with Whitefield
at Bristol, and after reading his younger brother's excited account of God's "confirmation" of his activities, he wrote a last
letter to John to warn him of his fears concerning John's irregular activities and his increasing conflict with and criticism
of the leadership of the Church of England:

Your distinction between the *discipline* and the *doctrine* of the church is, I think, not quite pertinent;
for surely *Episcopacy* is a matter of *doctrine* too:
but granting it otherwise, you know there is no fear
of being cast out of *our Synagogue* for any tenets
whatsoever....My knowledge of this makes me suspect
Whitfield, as if he designed to provoke persecution
by his bodings of it. He has already personally dis-
obliged the Bishops of *Gloucester* and *London*; and
doubtless will do as much by all the rest, if they
fall not down before his whimsies, and should offer
to stand in his way.[31]

Samuel was criticizing the highly irregular practice of
Whitefield--and now John--of "field-preaching" in parishes in
which they had no authority or permission to work, let alone
preach outside of "consecrated walls." He characterized the
discipline of the church as indeed very lax, but warned that

even in such circumstances there were limits to what the younger
men could expect to get away with:

> Now if he by his madness should lay himself open to
> the small remains of *discipline* among us, as by mar-
> rying without license, or any other way, and get ex-
> communicated for his pains, I am very apprehensive
> you would still stick to him as your *dear brother*; and
> so, tho' the church would not excommunicate *you*, you
> would *excommunicate the church*. Then I suppose you
> would enlarge your censure, which now takes in most
> of the inferior clergy.[32]

John, however, had been experimenting with extemporary
preaching since 1735 and with extemporary prayer since 1737 and
was convinced that the *effectiveness* of a practice in saving
souls took precedence over the formalities of canon law. In
this the influence of the Moravians had been substantial. When
in 1738 he had summarized their constitution in his journal he
noted the following passage as being especially important:

> In all things which do not immediately concern the
> inward, spiritual kingdom of Christ, we simply, and
> without contradicting, obey the higher powers. But
> with regard to conscience, the liberty of this we
> cannot suffer to be any way limited or infringed.
> And to this head we refer whatever directly or in
> itself tends to hinder the salvation of souls, or
> whatsoever things Christ and his holy apostles...
> took charge of and performed as necessary for the
> constitution and well-ordering of His Church. In
> these things we acknowledge no head but Christ; and
> are determined, God being our helper, to give us, not
> only our goods (as we did before), but life itself,
> rather than this liberty which God hath given us.[33]

If Wesley did not present this passage as a manifesto, it
expressed his sentiments exactly. He intended to "call no man
master" when it came to his responsibility to save souls. Be-
sides, he was convinced that his beliefs--which sounded so strange
to his brother Samuel and others--constituted the true faith of
the established church, and, if the clergy of the church were not
so corrupt and had not strayed from the truth, his extraordinary
measures would not have been necessary. In his last letter to
Samuel he showed himself to be unshaken by his older brother's
strictures and chided Samuel for his lack of understanding:

> O my brother, who hath bewitched you, that for fear
> of I know not what distant consequences you cannot
> rejoice at, or so much as acknowledge, the great
> power of God? How is it that you can't praise God

for saving so many souls from death...unless He will
begin this work within 'consecrated walls'? Why
should he not fill heaven and earth? You cannot, indeed you cannot confine the Most High within temples
made with hands. I do not despise them any more than
you do. But I rejoice to find that God is everywhere.
I love the rites and ceremonies of the church. But I
see, well pleased, that our great Lord can work without them. And howsoever and wheresoever a sinner is
converted from the error of his ways, nay and by whom-
soever, I thereat rejoice, yea, and will rejoice![34]

From a psychological perspective this passage illustrates
several of the dynamic threads manifest in Wesley's adaptive
response to the authority issue. Wesley obviously could not
grasp the "distant consequences" which his older brother could
not "rejoice at." His use of denial here, as ever, was massive,
and his rejection of the criticisms of his older brother parallels
in its structure and rationale both his previous *and* subsequent
usage of denial to limit the claims of authority figures upon
him. Both he and Susanna had used this tactic to counter the
elder Samuel's attempts to "restrain" them, and John would employ it with clergy and bishops alike--and later with his younger
brother Charles. Since he conveniently could not grasp the consequences of his actions, here as elsewhere John can only conclude that opposition to him is grounded in lack of understanding
or worse. He intimates that Samuel is lacking in respect for
the prerogatives of the divine initiative in that he did not
"rejoice at the great power of God" but would try to "confine
the Most High within temples made with hands." From Samuel's
point of view, of course, John was manifesting the same more or
less *covert rebellion* which had characterized his behavior since
childhood.[35] It was John that he wanted to restrain--not the
"Most High"--and it troubled him that his younger brother seemed
to have difficulty in making this distinction. John's defiant
last sentence manifested clearly the degree to which his identification with the divine initiative and prerogatives could lead
him to affirm the irregular *practices* of full-blown dissent, if
not to accept the label. Soon after this interchange Samuel
wrote to his mother to give her his best understanding of the
activities of his younger brothers and his fears regarding their
consequences. He sought to enlist her aid in discouraging them
from "joining a schism." He summarized the situation as he
understood it:

> They design separation....They are already for-
> bid all the pulpits in London, and to preach in that
> diocese is actual schism. In all likelihood it will
> come to the same all over England if the bishops have
> courage enough. They leave off the Liturgy in the
> fields....Their societies are sufficient to dissolve
> all other societies but their own....As I told Jack,
> I am not afraid the church should excommunicate him--
> discipline is at too low an ebb--but that he should
> excommunicate the church. It is pretty near it....
> Love feasts are introduced, and extemporary prayers
> and expositions of Scripture, which last are enough
> to bring in all confusion.[36]

Samuel's death soon after this interchange effectively
eliminated high church opposition within Wesley's family--at
least until Charles' resistance to John's activities grew into
a reluctant rebellion. Samuel had underestimated the degree
of the "understanding" between John and Susanna, and she would
soon join the younger brother in his work.

Opposition outside the family, however, was intense. Most
of the criticism could be easily written off and viewed as the
persecution which always occurs when God's work is truly being
done, but some came from persons Wesley respected and therefore
required careful response. One of the most notable of these
challenges came from one of his former companions at Oxford,
James Hervey. Hervey had been a consistent supporter and friend
during the Oxford period and had admired Wesley's work in Georgia.
In a significant letter of March 20, 1739, Wesley answered his
criticisms point by point and left us an important document manifesting his understanding of the nature of his role and its justification.

Hervey apparently had suggested that some of Wesley's activities raised the question of whether he remained a Christian. His
reference here was obviously to the irregular activities which
had troubled Samuel. Wesley, however, neatly sidestepped the
issue by affirming that he had for some time *admitted* that some
of his actions were not those of a Christian--that he had not
truly loved God prior to his acceptance of justification by
faith alone. Nevertheless, all of his actions had been based
on a principle which he did not, and could not now, abandon:

> If you ask on what principle, then, I acted,
> it was this: A desire to be a Christian, and a con-
> viction that, whatever I judge conducive thereto,
> that I am bound to do; wherever I judge I can best

answer this end, thither it is my duty to go. On
this principle I set out for America, on this I
visited the Moravian church, and on the same am I
ready now (God being my helper) to go to Abyssinia
or China, or whithersoever it shall please God by
this conviction to call me.[37]

Hervey had suggested also that much trouble could be avoided
if Wesley would either go back to Oxford and resume his responsibilities as a tutor or accept a parish and settle down into
parish work. Wesley's response to these suggestions must have
puzzled Hervey by the degree of passivity which they manifested.
Oxford, it seems, was out because he had no office or pupils and
no parish had been offered to him. The idea that either of these
could have been easily arranged seemed to be unavailable to him.
Hervey had been troubled by Wesley's interference in the parishes
of other clergy and asked him how he could justify his behavior
on "catholic principles." Wesley here took refuge in his commitment to "scriptural principles." He stated his understanding of
these principles:

> God in Scripture commands me, according to my power,
> to instruct the ignorant, reform the wicked, confirm
> the virtuous. Man forbids me to do this in another's
> parish: that is, in effect, to do it at all; seeing
> I have now no parish of my own, nor probably ever
> shall. Whom, then, shall I hear, God or man? 'If
> it be just to obey man rather than God, judge you.
> A dispensation of the gospel is committed to me;
> and woe is me if I preach not the gospel.[38]

We have seen above that Wesley never intended to accept the
ordinary role of a parish minister, and his decision in that
regard is one of the major assumptions which underlies the position taken in this letter. For Hervey, unaware of this, Wesley's
response must have been incomprehensible. Yet to John the choice
was simple: either preach wherever Providence led him to preach
or deny the divine initiative. In a now famous passage Wesley
then summarized his view of his "great commission":

> Suffer me now to tell you my principles in this mat-
> ter. I look upon all the world as my parish; thus
> far I mean, that in whatever part of it I am I judge
> it meet, right, and by bounden duty to declare, unto
> all that are willing to hear, the glad tidings of
> salvation. This is the work which I know God has
> called me to; and sure I am that his blessing attends
> it. Great encouragement have I, therefore, to be
> faithful in fulfilling the work He hath given me to

> do. His servant I am; and, as such, am employed
> according to the plain direction of His word--'as
> I have opportunity, doing good unto all men.' And
> his providence clearly concurs with his word, which
> has disengaged me from all things else that I might
> singly attend on this very thing, 'and go about doing
> good.39

Hervey could scarcely have taken comfort in this rationale
for Wesley's behavior. Wesley indeed seemed to be claiming a
divine carte blanche for his every whim with regard to ecclesiastical practice. Wesley himself was quite aware that it was
an extraordinary claim--he had spent a great deal of time searching for just such a mission, and now that he had found it, no
one could influence him to give it up. He believed that he not
only had found such an extraordinary role, but that he had a
secure rationale to support it. In a letter to his brother
Charles on June 23, 1739, he informed his brother of the stance
he took in response to the criticism of other clergy and made
it clear that Samuel had been right in assuming that John would
not scruple to defy even the bishops of the Church of England:

> 'But' (say they) 'it is just that you submit your-
> self to every ordinance of man for the Lord's sake.'
> True; to every ordinance of man which is not con-
> trary to the command of God.
> But if any man (bishop or other) ordain that I
> shall not do what God commands me to do, to submit
> to that ordinance would be to obey man rather than
> God.
> And to do this I have both an ordinary call and
> an extraordinary.
> My ordinary call is my ordination by the Bishop:
> 'Take thou authority to preach the word of God.'
> My extraordinary call is witnessed by the works
> God doeth by my ministry, which prove that he is
> with me of a truth in this exercise of my office.
> Perhaps this might be better expressed in another
> way: God bears witness in an *extraordinary manner*
> that my *thus exercising* my *ordinary call* is well-
> pleasing in His sight.
> But what if a bishop forbids this? I do not say,
> as St. Cyprian, *Populus a scelerato antistite
> separare se debet*.40 But I say, God being my helper,
> I will obey Him still; and if I suffer for it, His
> will be done.41

The year 1739 saw an escalation of conflict with the ecclesiastical authorities. Old statutes of Canon Law which had
fallen into disuse were brought into service in an attempt to
resist the Methodist practices of preaching in parishes without

permission. When refused a pulpit on these grounds, the Methodists would simply preach outside of the church. The behavior of the flamboyant Whitefield served to hasten what was in fact an inevitable encounter with episcopal authority. The most notable of these encounters with the bishops was John's lengthy interview with the Bishop of Bristol on August 18, 1739.[42] In it Wesley explained quite frankly his understanding of justification by faith, refused to take responsibility for Whitefield's behavior, and gave his explanation of practices in the societies. The bishop told Wesley that he had no business in his diocese, that he was not commissioned to preach there, and advised him to get out. Wesley gave the bishop his by this time standard rationale, now making explicit the manner in which his ordination as an Oxford fellow seemed to him to undergird his special role:

> Your lordship knows, being ordained a priest, by the commission I then received I am a priest of the Church universal. And being ordained as Fellow of a College, I was not limited to any particular cure, but have an indeterminate commission to preach the word of God in any part of the church of England. I do not therefore conceive that, in preaching here by this commission, I break any human law. When I am convinced I do, then it will be time to ask, 'Shall I obey God or man'? But if I am convinced, in the meanwhile, that I could advance the glory of God and the salvation of souls in any other place more than in Bristol, in that hour, by God's help, I will go hence, which till then I may not do.[43]

Such frankness and stubbornness of course did not increase Wesley's popularity with the Anglican bishops. Still, Wesley's refusal to publish the contents of these interviews taken together with his steadfast support of the Church of England on many other fronts made it evident to the bishops that the Wesley brothers were not to be categorized--or dealt with--easily. They had not sought to embarrass their superiors in public and though they were not altogether regular in their behavior they obviously could not be clearly classified as dissenters. The brothers sought to maintain contact with the bishops and took every opportunity to explain themselves and their work. The care with which they handled relations with the episcopacy was a successful tactic in that they were able in most cases to prevent a full-blown concerted attack on their movement. A number of bishops used their influence to try to hinder their work, but

these incidents were surprisingly few in number. Reminiscing
in 1789, Wesley waxed quite sanguine regarding the overall positive nature of his relations with the hierarchy:

> ...no one in England ever thought or called it leaving
> the church. It was never esteemed so by Archbishop
> Potter, with whom I had the happiness of conversing
> freely; nor by Archbishop Secker, who was thoroughly
> acquainted with every step we took; as was likewise
> Dr. Gibson, then bishop of London; and that great man
> Bishop Lowth. Nor did any of these four venerable
> men ever blame me for it in all the conversations I
> had with them. Only Archbishop Potter once said,
> 'Those gentlemen are irregular; but they have done
> good, and I pray God to bless them.'[44]

The opposition had been far more intense than Wesley charac-
terizes it here. But even allowing for the selective memory of
old age and his penchant for denial it is evident that Wesley
was as effective at limiting the power of the bishops as Susanna
had been at challenging Samuel in a similar situation. Both had
used tightly reasoned arguments from a position overtly loyal
to the established church but employing references to a higher
authority in order to intimidate--or at least confuse--the superior and to enable continuation of what in fact amounted to
covert rebellion on their part.

Though the bishops had not mounted a comprehensive attack
on the movement, opposition to the Methodists and their many
irregularities was heavy. By 1743 Wesley felt compelled to
issue a publication entitled "An Earnest Appeal to Men of Reason
and Religion" in which he sought to answer the rumors and criticisms which had been directed at him.[45] He had been accused of
undermining the established church, and in response he took each
criticism in turn and answered it. In actuality, he argued,
the church was stronger because of his movement. Each necessary
requirement for a strong church had been strengthened by his
work: encouraging a living faith, preaching the true word of
God, and encouraging attendance at the Lord's Supper. Others
had accused him of not obeying the laws of the church. He
answered first in terms of the rubrics, noting that he had been
more careful in their observation than his accusers. After a
detailed account of his practice, he retorted:

> Now, the question is not whether these Rubrics ought
> to be observed (you take this for granted in making
> the objection), but whether in fact they have been
> observed by you, or me, most. Many can witness I
> have observed them punctually, yea, sometimes at the
> hazard of my life; and as many, I fear, that you
> have not observed them at all, and that several of
> them you never pretended to observe. And is it you
> that are accusing me for not observing the Rubrics
> of the church?[46]

With regard to the Canons, Wesley simply listed five which
he knew were ignored by the clergy and suggested that those
persons who had observed these rigorously could "cast the first
stone." To those who suggested that the Methodists were not
friends to the church because they did not keep the vows of
obedience to the authorities, he used his standard rationale:

> I answer, in every individual point of an indifferent
> nature, we do and will, by the grace of God, obey the
> Governors of the church. But the testifying the gos-
> pel of the grace of God is not a point of an indif-
> ferent nature. 'The ministry which we have received
> of the Lord Jesus,' we are at all hazards to fulfill.
> It is the burden of the Lord which is laid upon us
> here; and we are 'to obey God rather than man.' Nor
> yet do we in any ways violate the promise which each
> of us made, when it was said unto him, 'Take thou
> authority to preach the word of God, in the name of
> the Father, and of the Son, and of the Holy Ghost.'
> We then promised to *submit* (mark the words) *to the*
> Godly *admonitions and injunctions of our Ordinary.*
> But we did not, could not, promise to obey such in-
> junctions as we know are contrary to the word of
> God.[47]

Wesley's irregular practices had led many to conclude that
he had already in fact left the church for the ranks of dissent. To those who asked why he had chosen to lead the Methodists out of the established church he had the following retort:

> Leave the church! What can you mean? Do we leave
> so much as the church walls? Your own eyes tell you
> we do not. Do we leave the ordinances of the church?
> You daily see and know the contrary. Do we leave the
> fundamental doctrine of the church, namely, salvation
> by faith? It is our constant theme, in public, in
> private, in writing, in conversation. Do we leave the
> practice of the church, the standard whereof are the
> the ten commandments? which are so essentially in-
> wrought in her constitution (as little as you may ap-
> prehend it), that whosoever breaks one of the least of
> these is no member of the church of England. I believe
> you do not care to put the cause on this issue. Neither
> do you mean this by leaving the church. In truth, I

cannot conceive what you mean. I doubt you cannot
conceive yourself. You have retailed a sentence
from somebody else, which you no more understand
than he. And no marvel; for it is a true observation, *Nonsense is never to be understood.*[48]

It seems that here, as well as in so many of his other conflicts, Wesley simply could not comprehend why his opponents
chose to give his work such negative interpretations. In a
sequel continuing his apologia he emphasized that he had really
not taken the initiative in beginning field preaching, but that
the innovation had been forced upon him:

Be pleased to observe: 1. That I was forbidden as by
a general consent to preach in any church (though not
by any judicial sentence) 'for preaching such doctrine'....2. That I had no desire or design to preach
in the open air till long after this prohibition.
3. That when I did, as it was no matter of choice, so
neither of premeditation. There was no scheme at all
previously formed which was to be supported thereby,
nor had I any other end in view than this--to save as
many souls as I could. 4. *Field-preaching* was therefore a sudden expedient, a thing submitted to rather
than chosen, because I thought preaching *thus* better
than *not* preaching *at all.*[49]

Again Wesley was denying that his actions manifested any
initiative on his part--he was merely responding to the divine
initiative. To another challenge that he should either obey
the church or leave it he both denied any lack of regard for
church authority or any intention to leave the church on his
own initiative:

As to your next advice, 'To have a greater regard to
the rules and orders of the church,' I *cannot*, for
I now regard them next to the word of God. And as
to your last, 'to renounce communion with the church,'
I *dare not.* Nay, but let them thrust us out. We
will not leave the ship. If you *cast us* out of it,
then our Lord will take us up.[50]

If Wesley was sure that he would never willingly *choose*
to leave the church--except, of course, as a response to the
divine initiative--his preachers began to manifest a different
point of view. At first attacks on the church from the ranks
were viewed as attacks against Wesley and some of the "disorderly"
ones were expelled from the movement. Nevertheless, the ambition
of the preachers, discussed above, was not lessened but enhanced
by Wesley's careful culling of the preachers who proved "inadequate" to their task. If they were not removed, then they were

approved as measuring up to Wesley's high standards. Since they
knew that Wesley viewed them to be in many ways superior to the
ordained clergy, they continued to question him on why he would
not choose to separate from the church and ordain them.

His power, as we have seen above, was so total as to be
able to forestall any movement toward an overt, publicly acknowledged rebellion against the church. Charles, however, was becoming increasingly frightened about the clamor of the preachers
and began to take steps to try to limit it. In 1752, he persuaded
John to have the preachers agree to a resolution "never to leave
the communion of the church of England without the consent of
all whose names are subjoined."[51] Charles was in fact afraid
that the preachers would precipitate a separation and that John
would "permit" it to occur. He had begun to wish that the
preachers could be disbanded and that, through this process,
John's dangerously inflated power could be reduced. If he had
ever really had more confidence in John's judgment and loyalty
to the Church of England than his older brother Samuel, it was
no longer the case. Two things had begun to be clear to Charles.
First, the course of the Methodist practices was heading toward
schism if in fact it was not already a reality. The pressure
on John to allow the preachers to celebrate the Lord's Supper
and to ordain them was obviously, he believed, causing his
brother to waver in his commitment to the church. Secondly,
it was evident to him that John in truth did not--perhaps could
not--perceive either the gravity of his irregular actions or
the logical consequences of the direction in which he was moving.
He urged influential friends to write to John warning him of
the dangers of allowing the preachers to celebrate the Lord's
Supper:

> What a pity such spirits should have any influence
> over my brother! They are continually urging him
> to a separation: that is, to pull down all he has
> built, to put a sword in our enemies' hands, to
> destroy the work, scatter the flock, disgrace him-
> self, and go out--like the snuff of a candle.[52]

When John did not respond to the first set of warning letters, Charles urged his cautious supporters to send him another
round as soon as possible. His developing distrust of John
was even more manifest:

> Write again, and spare not. My brother took no notice
> to me of your letter. Since the Melchisedeckians have
> been taken in I have been excluded his Cabinet Council.
> They know me too well to trust him with me. He is come
> so far as to believe a separation quite lawful, only
> not yet expedient. They are indefatigable in urging
> him to go so far that he may not be able to retreat.
> He may 'lay on hands,' say they, without separating.
> I charge you to keep it to yourself, *That I stand in
> doubt of him*.[53]

Charles had come to see through his brother's tightly reasoned and articulately presented defenses of his actions. He
no longer could see how his brother could assume such an innocuous posture and present such a claim of humility and passive
obedience--of loyalty to the church. The accumulation of practices paralleling dissent could not be ignored: independent
societies, extemporaneous prayer and preaching, an itinerant
ministry, field-preaching, the authorization of lay-preachers,
institution of a sacramental community, the building of separate
Methodist preaching houses, and the use of legal registrations
and licensing as dissenters when pressed to do so. The direction,
if not the reality, could not be mistaken.

Charles' resistance was at least temporarily effective.
Apparently the letters had forced John to admit into awareness
his proximity to separation. Charles' comment on John's retreat
is particularly interesting:

> Your letters (and some others wrote him with the
> same honesty) have had the due effect on him, and
> made him forget he was *ever inclined to their
> party*. He has spoken as strongly of late in be-
> half of the church of England as I could wish, and
> everywhere declares he never intends to leave her.[54]

John obviously appeared to have changed his direction and
presented to the Methodists a treatise entitled, "Ought We to
Separate From the Church of England." Enumerating twelve reasons for staying within the church, Wesley argued that separation
would be inexpedient:

> 1. Because it would at least be a seeming contradic-
> tion to the solemn and repeated declarations which
> we have made in all manner of ways, in preaching,
> in print, and in private conversation.
> 2. Because (on this as well as many other accounts)
> it would give huge occasion of offence to those who
> seek and desire occasion, to all the enemies of God
> and his truth.

> 3. Because it would exceedingly prejudice against us
> many who fear, yea who love, God, and thereby hinder
> their receiving so much, perhaps any farther, benefit
> from our preaching.
> 4. Because it would hinder multitudes of those who
> neither love nor fear God from hearing us at all,
> and thereby leave them in the hands of the devil.
> 5. Because it would occasion many hundreds if not
> some thousands of those who are now united with us
> to separate from us, yea and some of those who have
> a work of grace in their souls.[55]

He went on to emphasize the strife and contention which
would be created unnecessarily by separation. Such disorder
would demand time which could be better spent in promoting "practical, vital religion" in the land. In addition, the formation
of a new church would require too much time and care which could,
again, be better spent. The concluding series of reasons considered the possible impact on the success and relative influence
of the movement, items no doubt very important to him since they
function as the marks of God's sanction of his extraordinary
mission:

> Because the experiment has been so frequently tried
> already, and the success never answered the expec-
> tation. God has since the Reformation raised up
> from time to time many witnesses of pure religion.
> If these lived and died...in the churches to which
> they belonged, notwithstanding the wickedness which
> overflowed both the teachers and people therein,
> they spread the leaven of true religion far and wide,
> and were more and more useful, till they went to
> Paradise. But if upon any provocation or considera-
> tion whatever they separated and founded distinct
> parties, their influence was more and more confined;
> they grew less and less useful to others, and general-
> ly lost the spirit of religion themselves in the spirit
> of controversy.[56]

After all, Wesley pointed out, the church was in a sense
the "mother" of all that had been raised in it, and "her blem-
ishes" should be concealed as much as possible "without bringing
guilt upon our own conscience." The preachers of course believed that Wesley seemed to be concealing from himself the blem-
ishes which he had so enthusiastically pointed out to them.
They believed that he had already committed himself to separation. His answer manifests his continuing denial of initiatives
toward separation:

> If it be said, 'The doubt comes too late. You have
> done it already in appointing to preach,' we answer:
> we have not (in the sense in question) *appointed* any
> man to preach. There is not one of you who did not
> preach more or less antecedent to any appointment of
> ours. The utmost we have ever done is this: after
> we were convinced that God had *appointed* any of you
> an extraordinary preacher of repentance, we *permitted*
> you to act in connexion with us.[57]

Charles wanted to dismiss most of the preachers and secure
proper episcopal ordination for the remainder. John, however,
would have none of Charles' "bigotry" over such ecclesiastical
subtleties. Charles had considerable support from such respected
and trusted clergymen as Samuel Walker and Thomas Adam. Both
seconded Charles' claim that even the present state of affairs
was unacceptable and in fact constituted an open breach of the
order of the church.[58] From their point of view Wesley would
either have to do away with lay preaching or admit openly that
he had separated from the church. It is significant that both
of these men--generally sympathetic to Wesley's cause--in effect
were accusing him of using "disingenuity" and rationalization
to cover up both the preacher's ambitions of becoming ordained
ministers and his own of preserving the movement which he had
created and nurtured. As was usually the case, his defense
mechanisms were more convincing to himself than to his contem-
poraries. John, as we might have surmised, would not accept
their arguments and the irregular behavior of the preachers was
"permitted" to continue. A number began to serve the sacrament
without being "appointed" to do so, and, upon hearing of this,
Charles fired an angry challenge to his brother: "You must wink
very hard not to see all this. You have connived at it too, too
long."[59] In a letter to his wife he summarized the situation:

> We have allowed our lay preachers to take out licenses
> as dissenting Protestants. To the government they
> therefore say, 'We are dissenting ministers'; to the
> Methodists they say, 'We are not dissenters, but true
> members of the church of England.' To a press war-
> rant or persecuting justice they say again, 'We are
> dissenters'; to me at our next conference they will
> unsay it again. This is their sincerity; and my
> brother applauds their skillfulness--and his own.[60]

Again, however, the opposition which Charles was able to
mobilize was sufficient to stop the gathering momentum toward
open separation. At the Bristol Conference of 1760 John Wesley

was pressured into threatening dismissal of those who insisted
on ordination and administering the sacraments, and more than
two decades would pass before the crisis of authority in relation to the established church would again reach a critical phase.
Through these years, at the price of an increasing estrangement
from his brother, Charles was able to carry out a protracted
holding action against John's "submitting to be more vile" than
he already was. Samuel, Jr. had been wrong: John could *not* be
so *overtly* rebellious as to excommunicate the church. He had,
however, correctly sensed that John seemed strangely credulous
when it came to his openness to the influence of friends such
as Whitefield. Charles now had this characteristic of John
clear in his mind. His brother was capable of condoning incredi-
bly outrageous behavior by a resort to rationalizations which
made little sense to anyone but himself. Neither his rebellious
preachers nor his critics, friendly or unfriendly, could believe
that he could not see the logical consequences of his actions.
Charles wavered between believing that John was a "conniver"
and viewing him as a dupe of his ambitious associates. He was
quite sure, nevertheless, about one thing: if John would not
"excommunicate the church," his associates would not hesitate
for a moment to do so.

The surge toward separation which Charles feared had evidently gained momentum in spite of his resistance, and at the
time of the Leeds conference of 1775 radical plans were again
being submitted to John by the most trusted of his colleagues.
At that time Joseph Benson and John William Fletcher presented
to Wesley a comprehensive program which, knowing both his goals
and his reservations with regard to separation, they believed
that he would find attractive. Benson, a lay preacher, shared
the concern of many over the quality of the education and commitment of the preachers. In a plan submitted to the conference
in consultation with the presbyter Fletcher he suggested that
the less committed and qualified be dismissed, and that the remainder be either prepared for ordination at Kingswood School
or--if qualified--ordained by John and Charles Wesley, Fletcher,
and other presbyters. Fletcher's letter to Benson concerning
this proposal contains an insightful analysis of the difficulties
involved and particularly the stance of the brothers Wesley:

> My own particular objection to it respects Messrs.
> Wesley, who could not with decency take the step
> of turning bishops after their repeated declara-
> tions that they would stand by their mother to the
> last. I mention to Mr. Wesley that before he takes
> that step, it will be expedient that he desire, in
> print, the bishops to take it. It would be but
> form, I grant; it might, however, show that he would
> not break off without paying a proper deference to
> Episcopacy.[61]

That Fletcher was a careful student of the personality of
John Wesley is even more evident in his careful presentation of
his plan to the older man. In his letter to Wesley he calls on
John's sense of an extraordinary mission as a reformer while
emphasizing the possibility of remaining loyal to his beloved
"mother":

> You love the church of England, and yet you are not
> blind to her freckles, nor insensible of her shack-
> les. Your life is precarious, you have lately been
> shaken over the grave; you are spared it, it may be,
> to take yet some important step, which may influence
> generations yet unborn. What, sir, if you used your
> liberty as an Englishman, a Christian, a divine, and
> an extraordinary messenger of God? What if with bold
> modesty you took a farther step toward the reforma-
> tion of the church of England? Now sir, God has
> given you that light, that influence, and that in-
> trepidity which many...have not. You can reform,
> so far as your influence goes, without perverting;
> and, indeed, you have done it already. But have you
> done it professedly enough? Have you ever explicitly
> borne your testimony against all the defects of our
> church? Might you not do this without departing from
> your professed attachment to her? Nay, might you not,
> by this means, do her the greatest of services? If
> the mother who gave you suck were yet alive, could you
> not reverence her without reverencing her little whims
> and sinful peculiarities (if she had any)?[62]

Fletcher knew Wesley well, and was appealing to his ego-
ideals in a powerful manner. He was seeking to present John
with a way to take his previous activities to their logical conclusion without creating in himself feelings of disloyalty to
his "mother." He minimized the implications of schism by including in the plan protestations of loyalty and attempts to
secure official sanction before obeying "God rather than men."
The Methodists were to be formed into a general society--as
Fletcher put it, "a daughter church of our holy mother."[63] This
church, "the Methodist church of England," would recede from the

established church in only those defects which were unevangeli-
cal," and would defend the established church against the unjusti-
fied attacks of dissenters. The Methodists would be "willing
to submit to her in all things that are not unscriptural--approv-
ing of her ordination--partaking of her sacraments, and attending
her service at every convenient opportunity."[64] They would ask
that the bishops not consider the step as a schism, but only as
an act of reformation. Wesley would ordain the preachers only
if the bishops refused to do so. But even if this irregular
step had to be taken, they would remain "loyal" to the established
church. As evidence of their continued loyalty, one of the vows
taken at ordination would be: "Wilt thou consider thyself as a
son of the church of England, receding from her as little as possible; never railing against her clergy, and being ready to submit to her ordination, if any of the bishops will confer it upon
thee"?[65]

Little is known of Wesley's response to this plan. Doubtless it appealed strongly to his vision of his own role, yet the
fact that he did not choose to act on it at the Leeds conference
is perhaps an indication that--even with Fletcher's disclaimers
--such a program smacked too much of overt rebellion against his
"holy mother." That Wesley himself was moving toward ordination
and its schismatic consequences is, however, without question.
Rather than accepting openly the plan of Benson and Fletcher,
Wesley preferred to have "Providence" provide the initiative
through events which seemed to offer him no option but to follow conscience and the divine initiative. The challenge of the
situation of Methodists in America was to provide him with such
a clear imperative. In Wesley's view the hierarchy of the established church had been negligent in providing for the spiritual
needs of Americans. Wesley had sought ordination for men whom
he believed qualified for ministry in America but had been turned
down. In the recalcitrance of the bishops expressed in their
refusal to ordain men to meet obvious spiritual needs Wesley
had increasing evidence that the episcopal refusals would continue and were based on less than laudable motives. The bishops
had protested that his candidates were uneducated, yet men who
had received an education at Kingswood School were continually
rejected. Wesley now had his requisite "spiritual emergency."

At this point Wesley's extraordinary call was used to vali-
date an action even more radical than that which had been proposed by Benson and Fletcher. Instead of simply ordaining
presbyters for ministry in England, Wesley proposed to ordain
Thomas Coke for a role in America which was--though disguised
by terminology--in reality that of a bishop with the power to
ordain others. Coke's letter of testimonial contained the following passage:

> I have this day set apart as a superintendent, by the
> imposition of my hands and prayer (being assisted by
> other ordained ministers) Thomas Coke, Doctor of
> Civil Law, a Presbyter of the church of England, and
> a man whom I judge to be well qualified for that
> great work. And I do hereby recommend him to all
> whom it may concern as a fit person to preside over
> the flock of Christ.[66]

Coke also had authority from Wesley to confer the same
status upon Francis Asbury. In spite of the careful use of
"superintendent" instead of "bishop," the Methodists in America
quickly dispensed with what they knew to be only semantic sleight
of hand. By 1787 Asbury had begun to use the title of bishop
openly. Evidently this publicized the degree of Wesley's assertiveness to a degree quite uncomfortable for him. In an
angry letter which illustrates the degree of his denial and
rationalization of his action he wrote Asbury:

> How can you, how dare you suffer yourself to be
> called 'bishop'? I shudder, I start at the very
> thought! Men may call me a knave or a fool, a
> rascal, a scoundrel, and I am content; but they
> shall never by my consent call me a bishop! For
> my sake, for God's sake, for Christ's sake put a
> full end of this! Let the Presbyterians do what
> they please, but let the Methodists know their
> calling better.[67]

Wesley's scolding of Asbury is amusing enough given the
audacity of his own actions, but it is even more interesting
in the light of its conflict with a rationale for his behavior
which Wesley presented in 1785. In it Wesley not only called
himself a bishop, but sought at the same time to cast his
seemingly arrogant behavior in a passive light, suggesting
again that he was merely obeying the dictates of necessity and
conscience:

> I am now as firmly attached to the church of England
> as I ever was since you knew me. But meantime I
> know myself to be as real a Christian bishop as the
> archbishop of Canterbury. Yet I was always resolved,
> and am so still, never to act as such except in case
> of necessity. Such a case does not (perhaps never
> will) exist in England. This I made known to the
> bishop of London, and desired his help. But he per-
> emptorily refused it. All the other bishops were of
> the same mind; they rather because (they said) they
> had nothing to do with America. Then I saw my way
> clear, and was fully convinced what it was my duty
> to do.
>   As to the persons amongst those who offered them-
> selves, I chose those whom I judged most worthy, and
> I positively refuse to be judged herein by any man's
> conscience but my own.[68]

Not surprisingly, Charles had been excluded from the deliberations which led to the ordinations for America. On hearing of the event he put his sentiments into verse:

> So easily are bishops made
>   By man's, or woman's whim?
> Wesley his hands on Coke hath laid,
>   But who laid hands on him?[69]

Though for Charles, John's behavior was already schismatic,
he believed that some hope still existed for keeping the majority
of Methodists in England within the established church. John
had continued his irregular ordinations by ordaining ministers
for Scotland. Charles hoped to dissuade his brother from taking
the next step: ordaining Methodist preachers in England. He
warned John that, even if *he* did not intend it, his preachers
led by Coke would press for ordination and that this act would
clearly constitute all English Methodists as dissenters. John's
position on this matter is evident in a letter written in 1786:
"The alteration which has been made in America and Scotland has
nothing to do with our kingdom. I believe I shall not separate
from the church of England till my soul separates from my body."[70]

The act which Charles had feared finally materialized in
1788. In ordaining Alexander Mather, Wesley seems from all
available evidence to have intended to create an English counterpart to Coke--in effect an English Methodist bishop. That by
1788 Wesley realized--at least intermittantly--that Methodism
would eventually separate from the Church of England is incon-
testable. Yet when Coke proposed a formal separation to the

conference Wesley made it evident that as long as he lived no
formal separation would be allowed. He gave the conference a
summary of the principles which he had adhered to over the years
and which he fully intended to act upon the rest of his life:

> (1) That, in a course of fifty years, we had neither
> premeditately nor willingly varied from it in one
> article either of doctrine or discipline; (2) That
> we were not yet conscious of varying from it in any
> point of doctrine; (3) That we have in a course of
> years, out of necessity, not choice, slowly and
> warily varied in some points of discipline, by
> preaching in the fields, by extemporary prayer, by
> employing lay preachers, by forming and regulating
> societies, and by holding yearly conferences. But
> we did none of these things till we were convinced
> we could no longer omit them at the peril of our
> souls.[71]

Though he did not mention his ordinations he viewed them
in the same manner as manifesting *variation* not separation. Until his death he continued to claim that in spite of what anyone
else might say he remained a loyal churchman. As he put it in
a letter to Henry Moore: "I am a church of England man; and,
as I said fifty years ago so I say still, in the church I will
live and die, unless I am thrust out."[72]

In the epilogue to his encyclopedic treatment of Wesley's
relationship to the Church of England Frank Baker draws a number of insightful conclusions about that relationship. First,
Wesley's separatist actions in the last seven years were neither
"crazy whims" nor the result of the pressure of the preachers
on a weakened old man. They were, rather, "the logical culmination of all that had gone before."[73] Baker discerned a method
in Wesley's apparent madness:

> Frequently he had claimed that in his relations with
> the church of England he followed two principles:
> to stay as close as possible to her doctrines and
> discipline and worship, but to make variations in
> these whenever and wherever this was demanded by
> the peculiar work of God to which he was called.
> This really amounted to one master principle, of
> course: he would follow the dictates of his own
> conscience, his own reading of the will of God for
> the opportunities and challenges of each changing
> situation.[74]

Here Baker is acknowledging Wesley's total reliance upon
and commitment to what we have called the divine initiative.

He admits that Wesley was a dictator in his own exercise of authority, but claims that "No one could show that John Wesley lived for his own pleasure or profit or prestige: he lived unshakeably and unstintingly for the glory of God."[75]

> Although many of his words and actions during eighty years of supposed loyalty to his beloved church appear somewhat bizarre in a churchman; although he frequently shifted ground in his constant protestations of never separating from the church; although he certainly founded a great daughter church in spite of those protestations—and toward the end knew that he was doing it; although he was (in a word) inconsistent in his relationships with the church of England, yet throughout his life was revealed a higher consistency: it was stamped with the hallmark of 'following providence as it slowly opened out.'[76]

One can certainly agree that from John Wesley's subjective point of view the principle of consistency which runs through not only his dictatorship in the movement but also his relationship with the Anglican church was his passive response to the leadership of providence—of the divine initiative. Wesley certainly did not live for physical pleasure or material profit. In contradiction to Baker's point of view, however, prestige was quite another matter. What Baker fails to see is that Wesley's very passive obedience to his self-interpreted divine initiative was in fact the chief instrumentality through which Wesley attained the greatness which had been one of his central ego-ideals since childhood. His carefully cultivated and protected subjective passivity throughout his life masked a prodiguous manifestation of dynamic ego-activity and a consequent flood of creative energy. His relationship with the Church of England was less inconsistent than Baker supposes. Given his adaptive style, Wesley was psychologically incapable of a conscious awareness of the long-range implications of his actions. Such an awareness would have sabotaged, not facilitated, the realization of his goals. His careful avoidance of a subjective awareness of "premeditation" or "choice" in his "variations" from accepted church practice in all of the occasions which we have examined manifest the same dynamic pattern. When protests by Charles or others penetrated his system of denial and rationalization he simply retreated to previous positions which were

more *manifestly* passive until he could find more adequate ways
to rationalize his actions as merely *reactive* to the leading of
the divine initiative. Though he could defy the "tarnished"
authority of the church as expressed in the views of his brothers
and particularly in the *paternal* expressions of the bishops, the
maternal claim of the "mother church" remained potent for him
until the end. Associations with the legitimate and just maternal authority no doubt played a part in his incapacity to "excommunicate the church." Susanna had exercised authority fairly,
had resisted "calling any man master," and had remained loyal
to the church. Wesley had simply taken the model for authority
dynamics which he had learned in the Epworth parsonage and applied it consistently in each of his institutional relationships.
In so doing he had not only been able to avoid the immobilizing
guilt which accompanies "self-will," but also had realized
Susanna's--and his own--goal of a providential, *most* extraordinary role: spiritual father to the world. Though not papal
in its rationale, his understanding of his vocation rivaled
papal authority in its global vision and far surpassed it, in
Wesley's view, in its legitimacy.

CHAPTER VI

EXALTATION THROUGH RESIGNATION: CONCLUDING REFLECTIONS ON AUTHORITY AND INITIATIVE IN THE LIFE AND THOUGHT OF JOHN WESLEY

The focal task for this study has been that of carrying forward the work of Max Weber and Joachim Wach on the problem of the structure and dynamics of authority in religious leadership. Our intent has been to contribute to the "sustained interpretation" and investigation in this area which had been envisioned by Wach by studying intensively the career of one religious leader with regard to the manner in which his style of authority is expressed psychologically, theologically, and sociologically. The life and thought of John Wesley has provided us with extensive materials for a lengthy case study. In an attempt to reintegrate psychological interpretation into its rightful place in serious work in religious inquiry, I have analyzed the reasons for what I have referred to elsewhere as the eclipse of psychological method in *Religionswissenschaft*. I have suggested that religious scholars--exemplified by Wach--followed Dilthey in his frustrated retreat from psychological interpretation, a retreat which was necessitated by the lack of an adequate "descriptive and analytical psychology" appropriate to the task of the *Geisteswissenschaften*. Convinced that the psychoanalytic ego psychology of Erik Erikson and others can facilitate a creative regression in our understanding of the contribution of psychological interpretation, I have adapted Erikson's approach for this study. Furthermore, I have suggested that such a method should be understood not as an alien intrusion by the psychologizers, but as a perspective easily integrated into cultural and religious hermeneutics.

This concluding discussion addresses three important remaining tasks. First, I summarize the results of our intensive study of Wesley in the light of the problem of authority, clarifying the manner in which our findings support Wach's thesis. Second, I relate this inquiry to related discussions in the work of Wach, Weber, and others. Third and finally, I suggest some further theoretical development which must be accomplished before the methodological reintegration envisioned by this study can be elaborated and consolidated.

John Wesley and the Problem of Authority

Our use of psychoanalytic ego psychology has enabled us to perceive the dynamic infrastructures which are manifest in Wesley's personality, thought, and institutional relationships. Wach's contention was, quite simply, that through the sensitive application of *Verstehen* a meaningful coherence can be discerned between the experiences, expressions, and events which constitute these different aspects of the career of the leader. Extant studies of Wesley have often suggested that such a meaningful correspondence can be seen in his life and work but have failed to establish and elaborate the structure and dynamics of the relationship. In the foregoing discussion we have established that such a *Sinnzusammenhang* clearly exists, and though we have by no means completed the task of elaboration, we have presented sufficient data and interpretations to support Wach's assumption. Let us recall a few of the basic parameters of coherence which have been elucidated above.

First, we have presented some of the developmental factors which were influential in Wesley's goal of an extraordinary role for his life. With the help of recent formulations in ego psychology we have shown that Wesley's basic style of adaptation need not be reduced to a neurotic style, dominated by overly severe parental introjects. Rather, we have shown that his ambitions can be understood as manifesting to a large degree a quest for the fulfillment of ego-ideals and not simply the reaction to the dictates of a punitive superego. Nevertheless, we did demonstrate the manner in which the socio-cultural reality in which he lived, mediated in different ways through both Samuel and Susanna, made the polarity of initiative vs. guilt the fundamental conflict of his life.

Samuel Wesley had abandoned the ranks of dissent in the hope, at least in part, of a successful career in the traditional hierarchy of the Anglican church. His hopes, and those of his wife Susanna, had been unfulfilled. John Wesley spent his early years in a quest for a role in which he might achieve the

distinction which had eluded his father. His precocious ambition, fostered by his mother, became problematic when he realized
the intensity of the conflict between his personal and spiritual
athleticism and his mother's declarations for humility and against
self-will. The serious conflict between initiative and guilt
which this double-bind engendered came to a crisis point in the
Georgia episode. Toward the end of the Georgia experience he
was immobilized by this conflict and regressed into a state of
passive resignation awaiting divine aid. This regression was
to prove to be a creative regression which ultimately led to
the resolution of his immobilizing conflict.

The means whereby he was enabled to overcome his guilt lay
in his discovery of a viable theology of passivity. This theology
enabled him to bolster his considerable capacities for denial and
rationalization and, consequently, to cultivate a continual state
of subjective passivity. Thereafter, intensive activity and ag-
gressiveness on his part was experienced as being merely reactive
to the unquestionable claims of the divine initiative. Predestination was rejected because of the question it raised concerning
the efficacy of free response to divine initiative, and the conception of perfection was embraced because of its exemplification
of pure passivity.

The beginnings of the revival gave Wesley for the first
time an opportunity to envision a role for himself which was
sufficiently extraordinary in nature and comprehensive in scope
to promise fulfillment of his sense of a special destiny. The
positive response to his ministrations was perceived as God's
confirmation of his special vocation, and his adult ego-identity
was complete. Clearly, now, he was God's man, and his parish
extended to the ends of the earth. Though both friends and
enemies feared that he would "excommunicate the church," he had
no such *conscious* design. He deemed himself simply to be following the leadings of providence in each discrete situation.
Though others could see it clearly, Wesley did not discern until
the end of his ministry the inner logic of the direction in which
he was moving. Friends and opponents alike were astounded by
his constant claims of loyalty to his "mother" church while his
"variations" increased in the degree of their irregularity. He
denied any plan of separation and any personal initiative or
premeditation in the unfolding of his innovations.

In his movement he had created and formalized a hierarchy
of status and prestige which provided opportunities for upward
mobility for those without access to the accepted channels of
a traditional society. The lowliest member of the societies
could, by membership alone, be a part of a religious elite,
while the lay-assistants and preachers could rate themselves
as at least the equal--and more often the superior--of an Anglican clergyman. Responding to the caution of more conservative
colleagues Wesley resisted pressure from his preachers to secede.
Toward the end, however, he realized that a Methodist separation
after his death was inevitable and took steps to provide for a
legitimate succession. In making possible the realization of
his own special destiny he had given birth to an institution
through which many of the dispossessed were able to find an alternative which promised hope and a role which offered a chance
for personal development.

The interpreter working from a psychosocial perspective
quickly discerns two conflicting orientations to authority and
initiative which are manifest in the data elaborated in the foregoing chapters. The first, from Wesley's subjective point of
view, is unjust, irrational, and therefore illegitimate. If
Wesley had listed these in a hierarchy, the concept of a Calvinist
deity would have been at the top. We have seen that from his
standpoint, predestination would have rendered his pure passivity
irrelevant and ineffectual. It is evident that Wesley's spiritual
athleticism was crucial in this judgment, though it had by 1738
been transformed into a passive mode. Next in the hierarchy
would have been the uncooperative bishops of the Church of England. They represented for Wesley "bad fathers" in the faith,
and were perceived as getting in the way of the fulfillment of
his God-given special mission. From his perspective they lacked
both purity of motive and a rational approach to the problems
of church and people. Wesley's own father stands in the line
of these "bad fathers" and was always perceived by Wesley as
unjust, irrational, and as somewhat of a failure in his calling.

"Tainted brothers" in the faith included his brother Samuel
who took the place of the father as the representative of the
conservative establishment. All Anglican clergymen in the opposition to Methodism fall into this category, and in the later

phase even the recalcitrant Charles was no doubt considered by
Wesley to be representing the interests of the establishment to
the detriment of God's action through Methodism.

The other discernible hierarchy of authority was Wesley's
own--and it clearly reflects the moral order of the Epworth
nursery as Wesley perceived it. Its authority is total in its
claim, but is nevertheless just, rational, and therefore legitimate. Though to participate in this order successfully required
the transformation of subjectivity into a passive mode, one
could always know what the rules were and what it would take to
be successful in terms of them. Even the smallest and weakest
individual would find a rung on the developmental ladder which
his foot could reach. If he responded to the claims of the
authority, he could be assured of and confirmed in his progress.
At the top of this hierarchy would be the Wesleyan God, jealously
guarding all initiative, but ever faithful to reward the person
who seeks to surrender his self-will and resign himself to the
divine initiative. Second would be the established church as
"mother" which was in fact the victim of the "bad fathers" but
still deserved the services of loyal sons who could rescue her
from the negative influences of both impure fathers and sons.

Next, of course, would be Susanna who served as a model
for Wesley in his understanding of both church and authority.
She, like the Anglican church, had been abused by the unjust,
insensitive, irrational paternal authority, yet offered a new
order to those under her care. While she sought no open break
with Samuel, she made every attempt to limit the destructiveness
of Samuel's behavior both for her and her children. She believed
she knew what correct behavior entailed, and did not allow the
children any expressions of self-will. Nevertheless, they found
her intrusive, total claims to be reassuring--not in the sense
that they could relax in the bliss of completion, but that at
least they knew concretely what was expected of them and could
tell when they had made progress toward complete perfection in
development. Instead of being immobilized by fear or confusion,
they were energized to work.

John Wesley included in his personality, thought, and
leadership a comprehensive configuration of this pattern of
authority. His conception of the divine provided a God who,

though not tolerating conscious self-will, would consistently reward passive obedience. The most insignificant person could, through the cultivation of passive responsiveness and resignation to the divine initiative, be exalted. Wesley had always envisioned his exaltation into a special, extraordinary role--and he did not find the rejection of conscious self-will to be too high a price to pay for success. Following his mother's suggestion, he made religion the business of his life. Like Susanna, he considered himself to be the representative of the claims of God's initiative. Like Susanna he resisted, with passive aggression if at all possible, the destructive contamination of his business by those whose authority is legitimate by tradition but called into question by their faulty thinking and impure motivation. And like Susanna he expected total obedience by those who were his children in the faith. His initiatives, he believed, came from a just and reasonable God. As the mediator of God's claim, he could not tolerate self-will and disobedience from his subordinates. He had provided a carefully rationalized salvation machine--the Methodist movement--through which even the most insignificant person could find a place, receive guidelines and directives, and begin to make progress up the ladder of spiritual success. Success at the price of surrender of conscious self-will was more attractive than no success at all, and Wesley was flooded with volunteers who were willing to try their degree of capacity for response to the divine initiative. Each person allowed to remain in the movement had achieved status as a member of a spiritual elite, and there was the possibility of becoming a class leader, trustee, or perhaps even a lay-preacher.

This second paradigm for authority, gleaned by Wesley from the Epworth nursery and elaborated into the Methodist theology and institutions, no doubt offered a significant adaptive option for those for whom the traditional structures of authority seemed unjust and insensitive to their growing ambitions and aspirations. For those who had experienced a childhood under the enervating tutelage of ambivalent parents and grown to adulthood in a culture marked by increasingly ineffectual traditional authority structures, Wesley's rational Methodist machine offered them an immediate identity and a reasonable hope for the future. Energies

previously immobilized or expended in self-destructive behavior
were now released and channeled through a new moral order.

The price for this new chance was as heavy for those who
voluntarily associated with the Methodist movement as it had
been for Wesley himself. Developing egos functioning in this
cultural context faced an extremely difficult task. The memory
of a traumatic revolution and regicide weighed heavily on all
Englishmen and no doubt complicated the normal resolution of
the conflict of initiative and guilt. Wesley, as we have seen,
was acutely aware of the bitter fruits of past rebellions--both
religious and political. Civil war had played a large role in
the history of his family and, as Bernard Semmel has noted, the
civil war in his soul cannot be fully understood without setting
it in this context. His mother had carefully concealed and under-
played her rebellions, and Wesley learned that rebellions had
best be covert, denied and rationalized as true loyalty. In
this context self-will and pleasure had been associated and the
conscious presence of either brought on severe attacks of guilt.
The price of initiative, then, was massive denial and rationalization. For ego-activity to be a real possibility, guilt had to
be assuaged through the cultivation of subjective passivity and
objective asceticism.

Toward the end of his life, his exaltation accomplished,
Wesley allowed himself to realize that he had created the beginnings of a new establishment, and that his work as a reformer
would inevitably result in formal separation. Though pleased
with his accomplishments, he had begun to wonder about the future
significance of the movement. Others, he realized, had found
in Methodism an alternative ladder for spiritual development but
in the process of the climb seemed to have lost their vision of
the goal of spiritual perfection. He had seen that the lifestyle
which he advocated "would necessarily produce both Industry and
Frugality," that these virtues "cannot but produce Riches."
Nevertheless, he noted, "as Riches increase, so will Pride, Anger
and Love of the world in all its branches."[1] He feared that as
Methodists continued to accumulate riches true religious commitment would die. Was this why, he pondered, "in the nature of
things," that no "revival of true Religion" can "continue long"?[2]

Wach and Weber: Correlates to
the Present Study

A close scrutiny of Wach's *Sociology of Religion* indicates
that he had come to conclusions closely related to our own. In
times of great cultural change, he noted, traditional symbols
are often reinterpreted to serve as a new basis for community
and social reintegration:

> In other words, if the traditional symbols are to
> serve further as a basis for communality, they
> will have to be more precisely defined. There
> are often factors which lead to a repetition, on
> a higher level, of religious integration as de-
> scribed above: a smaller, more intensive religious
> elite is formed (*ecclesiola in ecclesia*), bound
> together by deeper experiences, by stricter pre-
> cepts, or by stricter organization than the one
> open to the masses. The reaction of the outside
> world which tends to unite the members of the new
> group more intensely should also not be overlooked.[3]

In discussing religious protest, he noted that protests of
the Puritan type were "determined by individual psychological
attitudes and theological convictions, on one hand, and historical, political, and economic conditions, on the other."[4] Such
protests are "often encouraged by the needs, claims, and demands
of professional, economic, or social groups."[5] In a discussion
clearly applicable to Wesley and Methodism he notes the factors
determining the development of protesting groups:

> Apparently the personal charisma of a leader power-
> ful enough to attract and unite a group of followers
> is essential; a certain amount of creativity on the
> part of the leader also is necessary as well as
> clarity of principles and a conception of the re-
> ligious community, which will allow for the develop-
> ment of a permanent organization within or without
> the larger religious body. The problem inevitably
> arises whether the new group can realize its ideals
> within the framework of the larger society, as
> *ecclesiola in ecclesia*, as in the case with the
> monastic orders and brotherhoods, or whether a new
> community must needs be formed.[6]

Wach, indeed, was not without substantial knowledge of the
history and sociology of Methodism. He noted that the protest
of John Wesley gave rise to the Methodist movement and traced
the development of the sociological forms of Methodism from
collegium pietatis to *fraternitas* to independent church.[7] Though
he did place Wesley in the category of religious reformer, his

most relevant comments are, like those above, general ones that
are given real meaning in a concrete study. We have, for example, cited the role of Wesley's personal ambition as a contributing factor in the development of Methodism. In a discussion
of the formation of sect groups Wach includes a similar insight:

> 'In the villages,' says a student of the Skidi Pawnee
> Indians, 'were always many ambitious men unable to
> attain membership in the regular organizations. It
> is never difficult to secure a following, no public
> functions at first, no official recognition. Yet
> in time of need they might render service that would
> give them social prestige.' Such motives contribute
> in more complex cultures quite frequently to the
> growth of sects.[8]

Wach also noted the manner in which a sect appeals to its
adherents by offering them prestige through exclusivity, and
that rigorous asceticism is often one of the means through which
this exclusivity is maintained:

> We agree with Troeltsch that a sect, as distinct from
> the independent group in general, is marked by its
> selective character ('religious elite'), places in-
> tensity above universality, and tends to maintain
> uncompromising radical attitudes, demanding the
> maximum from its members in their relations to God,
> the world, and men. Sectarian standards of morality
> are often times very high and austere; religious
> sincerity frequently distinguishes its members favor-
> ably from the masses who belong to the ecclesiastical
> bodies.[9]

Wach, then, was aware of the factor of prestige which influences not only the leader--in our case, Wesley--but also the
adherents to his movement. He asked, "Are there any criteria
by which it can be determined which types of personalities command religious authority more readily than others"?[10] In answer
to this query he suggests that authority is given to those who
can generate prestige through gifts: physiological, spiritual,
moral, or intellectual.[11] On the basis of our study we are enabled to emphasize more than Wach the role of the subjective
need to excel--to find a role sufficiently extraordinary to
satisfy the personal ambitions of the religious leader.

Wach also discussed the tendency of the claims of a leader
to expand as he realizes a larger degree of success:

> The prestige of a religious leader may even bring
> about a change in his self-interpretation and in
> his claim. We may state it paradoxically by say-
> ing that, from a sociological point of view, the
> effect produces the cause. The history of a num-
> ber of *homines religiosi* and of sectarianism all
> over the world illustrates this point.[12]

Certainly Wach could use Wesley as an example of this phenomenon. We have seen above that Wesley's perception of his
successes at each point in his ministry led to the expansion of
his claims. His growing conviction that he had the authority
of a bishop is a case in point. We can also see here the relevance of Erikson for Wach's sociological interpretations in this
matter. Erikson's contributions toward an understanding of the
psychodynamics of confirmation dovetail nicely with Wach's ob-
servations and in fact render the phenomenon far less "para-
doxical."

For his orientation in this area Wach is clearly heavily
indebted to Weber's extensive work on the problem of religious
authority. Though he does not specifically mention Wesley in
this connection, he would no doubt classify Wesley's authority
as "charismatic" based largely on his personal appeal. He
stresses the totalistic quality of the charismatic leader's
claim on the loyalty of his followers--a characteristic which
we have seen to be present in Wesley's leadership.[13] With regard to the relationship between asceticism and religious authority he mentioned Weber's use of the term "virtuosos" to characterize the achievement of prestige through renunciation.[14]
Wesley was without doubt such a "virtuoso" and we have referred
to this quality as manifesting his "spiritual athleticism."
Given Wach's awareness of the role of Methodism as a response
to the needs of an industrial era it is surprising that he did
not specifically relate the phenomenon of the Methodist movement to either the work of Weber or Elie Halevy on the role of
Methodism as a factor in the development of modernization in
England.[15]

Though Weber tended to view Methodism as just another expression of Puritanism and did not inquire into any special role
which it may have played in the modernization process, he was
by no means unaware of Methodism as an expression of his thesis
on the religious foundations of worldly asceticism. In a comment

on the rationalization of the world, Weber noted the significant
ties:

> The moral conduct of the average man was thus deprived
> of its planless and unsystematic character and sub-
> jected to a consistent method for conduct as a whole.
> It is no accident that the name of Methodists stuck
> to the participants in the last great revival of
> Puritan ideas in the eighteenth century just as the
> term Precisians, which has the same meaning, was ap-
> plied to their spiritual ancestors in the seventeenth
> century.[16]

In a discussion of the secularizing influence of wealth,
he traces the problem to the monastic asceticism of the Middle
Ages, and then suggests that the "great revival of Methodism,
which preceded the expansion of English industry toward the end
of the eighteenth century, may well be compared with such a
monastic reform."[17] He then chose to use the quote from Wesley's
"Thoughts on Methodism," cited in the preceding section of this
chapter, to serve as a summary, or "motto" as he put it, for
his basic thesis:

> I fear, wherever riches have increased, the essence
> of religion has decreased in the same proportion.
> Therefore I do not see how it is possible, in the
> nature of things, for any revival of true religion
> to continue long. For religion must necessarily pro-
> duce both industry and frugality, and these cannot
> but produce riches. But as riches increase, so will
> pride, anger, and love of the world in all its
> branches. How then is it possible that Methodism, that
> is, a religion of the heart, though it flourishes
> now as a green bay tree, should continue in this
> state? For the Methodists in every place grow dil-
> igent and frugal; consequently they increase in
> goods. Hence they proportionately increase in pride,
> in anger, in the desire of the flesh, the desire of
> the eyes, and the pride of life. So, although the
> form of religion remains, the spirit is swiftly van-
> ishing away. Is there no way to prevent this--this
> continual decay of pure religion? We ought not to
> prevent people from being diligent and frugal; *we
> must exhort all Christians to gain all they can, and
> to save all they can; that is, in effect, to grow
> rich.*[18]

Weber, stating his agreement with Wesley, then concludes
that:

> the full economic effect of those great religious
> movements, whose significance for economic develop-
> ment lay above all in their ascetic educative in-
> fluence, generally came only after the peak of the
> purely religious enthusiasm was past.[19]

The intensity of the search for the Kingdom of God, Weber concluded, was transformed slowly into intense utilitarian worldli-
ness.

In attempting to locate Methodism in his schema of religious
asceticism. Weber relates it to Continental Pietism and suggests
that it combines a still ascetic emotionalism with an "increasing
indifference to or repudiation of the dogmatic basis" of Calvi-
nistic asceticism:

> The name in itself shows what impressed contemporar-
> ies as characteristic of its adherents: the method-
> ical, systematic nature of conduct for the purpose
> of attaining the *certitudo salutis*. This was from
> the beginning the centre of religious aspiration
> for this movement also, and remained so.[20]

Weber was a bit puzzled about the manner in which Methodism
was able to combine asceticism and emotionalism, calling the
combination a "peculiar alliance."[21] He observed that Calvinism
had considered emotions to be illusory, but that in Methodism
the only sure basis for the *certitudo salutis* lay in the realm
of feeling. He considered Wesley's position a "foundation of
uncertainty" for the ascetic ethic, but concluded that it remained essentially Puritan in its practice, with the concepts
of regeneration and sanctification serving it "as a sort of
makeshift for the doctrine of predestination."[22] After Methodism
awakened emotion, Weber suggests, it did not allow one to enjoy
it--as in the pietism of Zinzendorf--but immediately directed
the released energy into "a rational struggle for perfection."[23]
Weber then summarized his view of Methodism:

> The fundamentally Calvinist character of its religious
> feeling here remained decisive. The emotional ex-
> citement took the form of enthusiasm which was only
> occasionally, but then powerfully stirred, but which
> by no means destroyed the otherwise rational character
> of conduct. The regeneration of Methodism thus cre-
> ated only a supplement to the pure doctrine of works,
> a religious basis for ascetic conduct after the doc-
> trine of predestination had been given up. The signs
> given by conduct which formed an indispensable means
> of ascertaining true conversion, even its condition as
> Wesley occasionally says, were in fact just the same
> as those of Calvinism. As a late product we can, in
> the following discussion, generally neglect Methodism,
> as it added nothing new to the development of the idea
> of calling.[24]

We will have occasion to comment further on Weber's assessment of Methodism shortly. Before proceeding, however, we should note the similarity of his assessment of the practical results of Wesleyan theology to our conclusions above regarding the dynamic infrastructures of Wesley's theological position. We have differed, of course, as to the reasons for the essentially "Calvinist" effect of Wesley's position, emphasizing rather the dynamic effects of his retention of passivity before the divine initiative. Again, we will comment on this further in the conclusion to this section. Another aspect of Weber's position which immediately catches the eye of the ego psychologist is his characterization of the psychological effects of the traditions of Christian asceticism. He emphasizes the increase of a capacity for "active self-control" which was present in both rational monasticism and Puritanism:

> To put it in our terms: The Puritan, like every rational type of asceticism, tried to enable a man to maintain and act upon his constant motives, especially those which it taught him itself, against the emotions. In this formal psychological sense of the term it tried to make him into a personality. Contrary to many popular ideas, the end of this asceticism was to be able to lead an alert, intelligent life: the most urgent task the destruction of spontaneous, impulsive enjoyment, the most important means was to bring order into the conduct of its adherents. All these important points are emphasized in the rules of Catholic monasticism as strongly as in the principles of conduct of the Calvinists. On this methodical control over the whole man rests the enormous expansive power of both, especially the ability of Calvinism as against Lutheranism to defend the cause of Protestantism as the church militant.[25]

The interpreter using psychoanalytic ego psychology recognizes immediately here the description of the energizing and adaptive effects of asceticism. Weber's comments here are similar to those of an ego psychologist describing a facilitation of ego-activity. We have shown in our study the manner in which the spiritual athlete can generate prodiguous quantities of activity, self-control, and mastery while denying that such constitute personal ambition or self-will. We have also gone beyond Weber in suggesting some possible connection between the adoption of asceticism as a means for resolving the conflicts of initiative vs. guilt and the release of creative energies.

We have identified asceticism as a formidable weapon in the
arsenal of the ego when confronted with a sadistic superego.
It can therefore be seen as a defense against rather than as an
expression of punitive parental introjects.

If, as Weber says, Methodism added nothing new to the development of the idea of calling, still his decision to de-
emphasize the role of Methodism in the modernization process
has recently been called into question. Following the lead of
Elie Halevy, Bernard Semmel has suggested that Methodism was
far more important in the transition to a modern order than
Weber and others have believed:

> The Calvinist sects, it has been argued by Max
> Weber and others, had helped to produce 'modern'
> men fitted to the purposes of emerging seventeenth-
> century commercial society. I suggest that evan-
> gelical religion in the eighteenth century probably
> accomplished for masses of men what sixteenth- and
> seventeenth-century Calvinism could only confirm for
> a relative few. Particularly in its Wesleyan,
> Arminian Methodist form, in seeking to reconcile
> God and the masses 'alienated from God,' it may have
> performed the service of mediating between the ideals
> of the old society and those of the new.[26]

Semmel sees in the Methodist movement a "popular revolution"
which, instead of being repressive and reactionary, was in fact
a religious counterpart to the French Revolution in its libera-
ting and transforming effects. He views the movement as a
culmination of a "Protestant Counter-Reformation," a revolt
against the views of Luther and Calvin. He argues that Wesley's
theology was the "theological form taken by the liberal ideology
of the time."[27] He seeks to relate Wesley's "Arminianism" to
this major cultural shift:

> In the eighteenth century, England proved able to
> make this transformation relatively peacefully,
> despite the great pressures which seemed to be
> pushing her toward violent revolution. I shall
> examine how the special character of the 'new man'
> envisioned and to some extent created by Wesley's
> evangelical Arminianism *might* have helped--that is
> all we can safely say--to bridge the gap between
> the traditional and the modern orders without
> tumultuous upheaval, while at the same time promot-
> ing the ideals which would be most useful to the
> new society.[28]

Semmel is sufficiently sure of the importance of Methodism for the process of modernization that his next paragraph belies his protestations of tentativeness:

> It was Arminianism, particularly in its Wesleyan, evangelical form, which bore the revolutionary message of liberty and equality--of free will and universal salvation--in the shape best able to appeal to masses of men who aspired to personal autonomy but who were still rooted in a strong dependence, a deep internal attachment to traditional values....
> In the new industrial society the traditional paternalism of master and man was no more. Large numbers of men found themselves alienated from their patrimonies and expected vocations; the evangelists of the day proclaimed them 'alienated from God' as well. The lower classes, stumblingly aware of their presumed equality in law and in the eyes of their Savior, began the long move from the old dependence upon paternal favor to a growing demand for autonomy, which had early repercussions in politics.[29]

As we have noted above, Wesley himself did believe that the doctrine of predestination destroyed the basis for certainty of exaltation through resignation. Still, it is beyond the scope of our study to undertake a systematic analysis of the relative merits of Weber and Semmel on the question of Methodism and modernization. On the basis of the above discussion, however, two things seem clear. First, we can conclude from our study that there may be a common psychosocial dynamic underlying both Puritanism and Methodism with regard to the problem of authority and initiative. Among other things this dynamic may be grounded in the facilitation of ego-activity and initiative by means of the cultivation of a theology of passivity and an attendant subjective denial of human initiative or aggression. Second, though Semmel may be overemphasizing the role of Wesley's "Arminian" theology, it is clear that much more work needs to be done on the question of the role of Wesley and Methodism in the modernization process. We see, therefore, that the question of authority and initiative in the life and thought of John Wesley is one which has significance far beyond the confines of this study. With further research perhaps this psychosocial interpretation of Wesley may make a significant contribution to this wider discussion.

John Wesley and the Problem of Reductionism:
An Eriksonian Perspective

Before returning to the more general theoretical and methodological issues with which I will close this study it is necessary to re-focus on the issue of Erikson and reductionism as it
is manifest in this interpretation of John Wesley. We have seen
that Wach was most concerned with resisting the type of psychological interpretation which concluded that religious activity
was "only" a kind of repressed sexuality. There is no doubt
that Wach was criticizing certain Freudian attitudes toward religious phenomena which are grounded in what Erikson has called
"originology." Erikson writes:

> In its determination to be sparing with teleological
> assumptions, psychoanalysis has gone to the opposite
> extreme and developed a kind of originology--a term
> which I hope is sufficiently awkward to make a point
> without suggesting itself for general use. I mean
> by it a habit of thinking which reduces every human
> situation to an analogy with an earlier one, and
> most of all to that earliest, simplest, and most in-
> fantile precursor which is assumed to be its 'origin.'[30]

Clearly, for Freud, religious phenomena are "caused" by
the fact that oedipal conflicts have not been adequately resolved. They are, as he put it, "to be understood *only* on the
model of neurotic symptoms...."[31] Accordingly, the objects of
religious activity are merely substitutions for or equivalences
of the objects of early libidinal cathexis. For Erikson, however, interpretation cannot be grounded in such an over-simplified
"causal" analysis. Indeed, as Browning has put it, "Erikson does
not think in causal terms at all."[32] As I noted in the discussion of Erikson's interpretive methodology, he constantly focuses
on behavior which can be seen to have configurational similarity
in different contexts. This does not mean, of course, that
Erikson is unconcerned with either the developmental processes
which are manifest early in a child's development or the significance of child-rearing practices. On the contrary, Erikson pays
a great deal of attention to the modes of action which are of
fundamental importance for the child at each state of development.
These patterns of activity, called "organ modes" by Erikson, offer a way for the child to learn to pattern his social interaction. They are "...patterns of going at things, modes of

approach, modes of seeking relationships...."[33] The process of
human development is seen as an ongoing exercise in mutual activation between the child and those who have the responsibility
for introducing him to the realities of the cultural milieu in
which he will live. As Erikson has put it, "As a child's radius
of awareness, co-ordination, and responsiveness expands, he meets
the educative patterns of his culture, and thus learns the basic
modalities of human existence."[34] By emphasizing the reciprocal
interaction between bodily modes and the environment Erikson
has made possible an interpretation of religious behavior which
views such behavior as an important means of both personal and
cultural adaptation. Religion, then, need not be seen as either
neurotic or regressive, and the "objects" with which a mature
religious leader occupies himself are more than reactive attempts
to find a substitute for the lost love objects of infancy. In
a discussion of Erikson's understanding of the *homo religiosus*
Nelson Thayer has emphasized the creative and synthesizing cultural role of the religious leader. He notes that for Erikson,

> Cultures require religious leadership because each
> culture has its own version of estrangement of fun-
> damental sin and needs to see that and how life is
> possible in spite of it....Religious leadership, like
> other aspects of religion, facilitates the synthetic
> function of the ego. By functioning as an ego ideal,
> the religious leader provides an integrating image
> which assists his contemporaries to be open to the
> unconscious and historical forces within a given cul-
> ture and integrate them, to synthesize them within an
> ideology and framework of action which enables mean-
> ingful life to go on in spite of the perception of
> its radical contingency.[35]

My interpretation of Wesley has been an attempt to follow
Erikson in focusing on configurations, on the modal analogies
which may be discerned among the various expressions of the
religious leader's search for creative adaptation. To be sure,
Wesley's childhood experience in the Epworth rectory was an important factor in the development of his emerging style of
adaptation. In a remarkable way his parents were representa-
tives of cultural traditions basic to a problematic historical
situation. The conflicts between Samuel and Susanna provided
him with an important preview of the issues which would occupy
his energies for the rest of his life. There is no doubt that
by successfully confronting the conflicts of his childhood John

Wesley had made a significant step toward developing a "mode of approach" to the problem of initiative versus guilt which with further elaboration was to have great significance for his cultural milieu. The key words here, however, are "further elaboration." When Wesley later confronted the bishop of Bristol the encounter was more than a repetition of his earlier conflicts with Samuel. Similarly, his mature theology of passivity was more than a recapitulation of thought patterns learned under the tutelage of Susanna. As he grew to maturity Wesley was stimulated by the ecclesiastical and theological realities of his day to continue his search for a creative solution to the problem of how one can initiate action without being immobilized by feelings of guilt. His mature solution was not a reactive repetition of patterns determined by childhood experiences. *It was, rather, a creative development of a mode of approach which, once a successful tactic in learning to be a child in the Epworth rectory, with elaboration became a successful tactic in learning to be a man in eighteenth century England.* Through his life and work, then, John Wesley as a *homo religiosus* offered thousands of his fellow countrymen an ideology and a framework of action which could release their own creative energies and enable them to face the myriad tasks of life in a new age.

One should not conclude on the basis of the above discussion that my rejection of a reactive and regressive reading of the role of psychological processes in the development of Wesley's leadership constitutes a de-emphasis of the role of psychodynamic factors in such leadership. Indeed, psychoanalytic ego psychology enables us to see how determinative such dynamic processes are in the development of a *homo religiosus*. Wesley's creative solution to the modal conflict of his milieu was not determined by historical and sociological forces inexorably working themselves out through a passive personality. To be sure, the conflicted traditions of his cultural heritage provided a context which not only elicited his creative energies but also offered appropriate channels for their expression. But it was the adaptive and synthesizing function of Wesley's ego which enabled him to transform and renew those traditions through his religious leadership.

Beyond the Classics: Creative Regression
and Methodological Reintegration in
Religionswissenschaft

In the introduction to this study I went to some lengths
to trace the historical and systematic factors which have contributed to the continued eclipse of psychological interpretation
in *Religionswissenschaft*. It was noted that Dilthey's frustrated search for an adequate psychological method led to his turn
to hermeneutics and *Verstehen* as a substitute for the understanding of human experience and expressions. This turn, I maintained,
influenced Wach and, through him, later historians and phenome-
nologists of religion toward severe reservations regarding the
usefulness of psychological interpretation.

It is significant that Weber, Wach's master in the field
of *verstehende Soziologie* , has been criticized on similar
grounds by Talcott Parsons. Weber, Parsons argues, did not believe his interpretation of the role of motives in human action
was "psychology."[36] Psychology as such was no more important
to sociology than was geology or physics. Weber seems to have
thought of psychology in terms of natural science and therefore
concluded that it was not relevant for the application of "subjective categories."[37] In a sentence germaine to my earlier
discussion of Dilthey, Parsons comments that Weber "does, to be
sure, mention in passing a branch of *verstehende* psychology
which would be more closely related to sociology, but does not
elaborate on it."[38] Given the psychology of his day, Weber's
"*Sinnzusammenhänge* were not psychological entities precisely
because they included situational elements which were variable
on the level of the situation and of the definition of the
situation."[39] Parsons suggests that Weber was remiss in neglecting the importance of psychological interpretation:

> In this, it seems, through misunderstanding of the
> methodological situation, he went too far. If,
> in order to clarify many of his problems, it is
> necessary to place the structural elements implied
> in his formulations of ideal types in their context
> of a generalized system of social structure, it is
> by the same logic necessary to clarify the nature
> of the unit of reference, the 'actor.' It cannot
> be true that the conceptual scheme in terms of
> which this unit is treated is no more closely rele-
> vant to sociology than any other dealing with the
> conditions of action. For the actor is the unit

of systems of action, and the frame of reference
and other categories, in terms of which this unit
is treated, are inherently part of the same theoretical system as categories on the level of types
of action or social structure. Hence in some sense,
a 'psychology' is an essential *part of* (not, note,
'basis' or 'set of assumptions for') a theory of
social action.[40]

Parsons is here calling for the same type of methodological reintegration which I have envisioned in this study. The
fact that one cannot justify totalistic claims for a psychology
should not lead to its exclusion from fundamental method in
either societal or religious hermeneutics. Unlike Weber, Wach
was at least aware of this, though he made no real progress in
its realization. In the following passage Parsons projected
for inquiry into human action the type of extension into psychological interpretation which I have suggested for the tradition
of *Religionswissenschaft*:

Weber was fundamentally right that the adequate concrete motive *always* involved the situational elements
which are specifically non-psychological. By doing,
however, what Weber failed to do, taking a concrete,
in a sense institutional, starting point, and then
using the resources of modern psychology to complete
the analysis on its psychological side, it is undoubtedly possible to develop a far more adequate
analysis of concrete motivation than either psychology or the social sciences have, for the most part,
previously commanded.[41]

From the development of Parsons' work it is evident that
he has realized the promise of recent developments in ego psychology as a component in such a comprehensive analysis. One
characteristic of psychoanalytic ego psychology which may have
recommended it to Parsons is the ease with which it can be related to the systems analysis which has played such an important
role in his theoretical formulations.[42] Erikson's work in
particular can be said to focus on the "systemic" qualities of
both the individual organism and its social world and goes far
toward illuminating the "flow-patterns" which can be expected
as the various levels in the hierarchy of systems interact.

It can at this point be argued, however, that even Erikson
has not fully grasped the importance of the concept of "system"
for the problems of interpretation of culture and personality.
In this area he could learn not just from Parsons but also from

Ludwig von Bertalanffy and other prominent theorists in the field of general systems theory.[43] For maximum usefulness as a multi-dimensional conceptual framework for psychosocial interpretation, the systemic conceptuality should be expanded into a comprehensive metatheoretical model on the order of general systems theory. Such a development would go far toward meeting the call by Yankelovich and Barrett for a fundamental epistemological reconstruction for psychoanalytic interpretation.[44] It should be noted, for example, that in Erikson's use of parallels between patterns of action for interpretive purposes, and in Dilthey's use of the *Analogieschluss*, both scholars prefigure the kind of "isomorphic thinking" suggested by von Bertalanffy.[45] What, after all is more congruent with von Bertalanffy's concepts than the idea of discerning similar "patterns" in the "flow of energy" in different structures at different levels in a hierarchy of systems? This mode of thinking is, I believe, employed implicitly in psychosocial interpretation much more widely than is commonly understood. A use of the general systems paradigm for an interpretive conceptual framework could assist us in making explicit the assumptions upon which many of our interpretive methods in practice, seem to be grounded.

I am not suggesting here that if Erikson's ego psychology is, with or without revision, a fulfillment of Dilthey's descriptive and analytical psychology, then the turn to a wider historical and sociological hermeneutic was unnecessary. On the contrary, the comments of Talcott Parsons at the beginning of this section were included precisely for the purpose of giving needed perspective on this issue. Like Wach, Parsons sees the necessity for an adequate psychological component in a wider "general theory of action" but realizes that psychosocial interpretation requires a comprehensive metatheory which can give an orienting perspective to inquiry into a diverse range of issues.

Significantly, major theorists in other fields have shared fundamental components of the theoretical and methodological reconstruction envisioned here. Robert Berkhofer, Jr. in history, Laura Thompson in cultural anthropology, Roy Grinker in psychiatry, Kenneth Boulding in economics, and many others are making important steps beyond both disciplinary myopia and

contrived "interdisciplinary" models.[46] The project shared by
these scholars is quite simply, as Yankelovich and Barrett have
so aptly put it, "a radical extension of holistic thinking to
cover virtually every aspect of human experience, from the most
minutely elaborated personality traits to the broadest social
institutions."[47]

Unfortunately, the myriad disciplines of *Religionswissenschaft*, contrary to the vision of Joachim Wach, seem in the absence of any contemporary integrative vision to be growing further
apart. The recent *Beyond the Classics? Essays in the Scientific
Study of Religion* is a sad case in point.[48] The perspectives of
the history and phenomenology of religion are excluded altogether,
and even among the otherwise excellent essays one discerns no
consciousness of a metatheoretical "spine" which might have given,
if not the reality, at least an appearance of a "sense of form
and order." Some theorists, if confronted with this, would undoubtedly suggest that methodological "perspectivalism" could
be discerned as an underlying structure. A scrutiny of the current methodological morass in religious studies, however, reveals
beyond the shadow of a doubt that this "perspectivalism" continues to be without an adequate root-metaphor which could enable
it to be more than a myopic surrender to methodological atomism.

I am convinced that the post-modern systems paradigm of
general systems theory and, more recently, systems philosophy
can, if applied to the problems of hermeneutics in religious
studies, go far toward the revitalization of hermeneutical theory
--both special and general--called for by Wach. In commenting
on the need for a unified method for *Religionswissenschaft*, Wach
himself has anticipated the position taken in this conclusion:

> After dwelling upon the nature and the task of com-
> parative studies in religion, we can now discuss the
> method to be followed. Much controversy has been
> carried on in the last decades between two schools
> of thought. One has insisted that the method of
> religious studies is totally *sui generis* and in no
> way comparable or related to methods in other
> fields of knowledge. The other school has main-
> tained that, irrespective of the character of the
> subject matter to be investigated, the only legiti-
> mate method is the so-called 'scientific method.'...
> Both these approaches have been found wanting; in
> the present era of the comparative study of religion
> a new synthesis is being worked out.[49]

Wach's vision of this "new synthesis" has not yet, as is
seen above, been realized. Recent publications which purport
to present the current state of the study of religion make it
quite clear that the two schools of thought have remained as
methodologically and theoretically discrete as ever.[50] Nevertheless, Wach went further in sketching the outlines of his
vision. He suggested that a rejection of unqualified pluralism
or dualism in method must form one foundation of his new synthesis since "all idealism and all naturalism--including materialism
--stand or fall with methodological monism."[51] But the second
and equally important foundation was that "the method be adequate
for the subject matter."[52] Most important to the position taken
here, however, is Wach's identification of a "metaphysical concept" which he believed to be most adequate for his understanding
of religious hermeneutics:

> A positivistic age could cherish the notion of a uni-
> versally applicable technique of inquiry. Religion
> was to be studied exactly as any phenomenon of the
> inorganic or organic world. With the above-mentioned
> qualification that the method must fit the subject
> matter, the new era has shown a growing demand for a
> metaphysical concept which would do justice to the
> nature of phenomena of the spiritual as well as of
> the physical world....The tremendous success of the
> philosophy of Alfred North Whitehead in the Anglo-
> Saxon world can be explained in terms of this need.
> It has been widely felt that he has provided a co-
> herent system for understanding nature, mind, and
> spirit.[53]

Ervin Laszlo has characterized the manner in which general
systems theory and systems philosophy relate to both the White-
headian tradition and to the contemporary integrative task:

> The philosophy capable of performing this task evolved
> in slow progression from the philosophy of real uni-
> versals of Plato and the categorical scheme of Aris-
> totle, through scholastic metaphysics in the Middle
> Ages, to the modern process philosophies of Bergson,
> Lloyd Morgan, Samuel Alexander, and Alfred North
> Whitehead. Systems philosophy is a logical next
> step in this progression. It reintegrates the con-
> cept of enduring universals with transient processes
> within a non-bifurcated, hierarchically differentiated
> realm of invariant *systems*, as the ultimate actuali-
> ties of self-structuring nature. Its data come from
> the empirical sciences; its problems from the history
> of philosophy; and its concepts from modern systems
> research.[54]

Laszlo echoes Wach in his assumption that a new humility and respect will naturally accompany progress in methodological sophistication. If we can employ general systems theory and systems philosophy to revitalize the great tradition in philosophical hermeneutics, perhaps a significant step can be made toward the metatheoretical and methodological synthesis which Wach hoped for. We may be enabled to gain a new appreciation not only for the richness and complexity of the religious phenomenon, but also for each other as communicating and cooperating colleagues in a common interpretive enterprise.

NOTES

CHAPTER I

[1]Joachim Wach, *Sociology of Religion* (Chicago: University of Chicago Press, 1944), p. 344.

[2]*Ibid.*

[3]Richard W. Scheimann, "Wach's Theory of the Science of Religion" (Ph.D. dissertation, University of Chicago, 1963), p. 272.

[4]*Ibid.*, pp. 272-73.

[5]Albert Outler, ed., *John Wesley* New York: Oxford University Press, 1964), p. 37.

[6]There is currently a good deal of confusion about the appropriate use of the term. Originally a term for the "general science of religions" or "science of religions" it has of late been identified with the discipline of the history of religions, and those interested in the "scientific study of religions" are not included.

[7]Joseph Kitagawa, "The Life and Thought of Joachim Wach," in Joachim Wach, *The Comparative Study of Religions*, ed. with an introduction by Joseph M. Kitagawa (New York: Columbia University Press, 1958), p. xxiii.

[8]*Ibid.*, pp. xxiii-xxiv.

[9]*Ibid.*, p. 23.

[10]Joachim Wach, *Types of Religious Experience, Christian and Non-Christian* (Chicago: University of Chicago Press, 1951), pp. 28-29.

[11]Joachim Wach, "Das Religiose Gefuhl" in *Das Problem der Kultur, Vortrage des Institut fur Geschichte der Medizin an der Universitat Leipzig* 4 (1931): 9-33.

[12]Joachim Wach, "'Nur.' Gedanken uber den Psychologizismus," *Zeitschrift fur Missionskunde und Religionswissenschaft* 29 (1924): 211.

[13]*Ibid.*, p. 213.

[14]See the excellent discussion of the lack of Dilthey scholarship in Anglo-American circles in Kurt Muller-Vollmer, *Toward A Phenomenological Theory of Literature: A Study of Wilhelm Dilthey's Poetik* (The Hague: Mouton and Company, 1963), pp. 29-32.

[15]Richard E. Palmer, *Hermeneutics: Interpretation Theory in Schleiermacher, Dilthey, Heidegger, and Gadamer* (Evanston: Northwestern University Press, 1969), p. 98.

[16]Eugene T. Gendlin, "Wilhelm Dilthey and the Problem of Comprehending Human Significance in the Science of Man" (Master's thesis, University of Chicago, 1950), p. 25.

[17]*Ibid.*, p. 26.

[18]*Ibid.*, p. 28.

[19]*Ibid.*

[20]H. A. Hodges, *Wilhelm Dilthey: An Introduction* (London: Routledge and Kegan Paul, 1944), p. 84.

[21]H. A. Hodges, *The Philosophy of Wilhelm Dilthey* (London: Routledge and Kegan Paul, 1952), p. 4.

[22]*Ibid.*, p. 23.

[23]Hodges, *Wilhelm Dilthey: An Introduction*, pp. 42-43.

[24]*Ibid.*, p. 45.

[25]Hodges, *The Philosophy of Wilhelm Dilthey*, pp. 208-11.

[26]Scheimann, "Wach's Theory of the Science of Religion," p. 244. Scheimann's entire work is a comprehensive analysis of the foundational influence of Dilthey's approach to *Geisteswissenschaft* on Wach's methodological paradigm for *Religionswissenschaft*.

[27]Erik H. Erikson, *Young Man Luther, A Study in Psychoanalysis and History* (New York: W. W. Norton & Company, Inc., 1958). See the extensive discussion of this book in Robert Coles, *Erik H. Erikson, The Growth of His Work* (Boston: Little, Brown and Company, 1970), pp. 202-54.

[28]Erikson, *Young Man Luther*, pp. 253-54.

[29]*Ibid.*, p. 254.

[30]*Ibid.*

[31]Erik H. Erikson, *Identity and the Life Cycle* (New York: International Universities Press, 1959), p. 48.

[32]*Ibid.*, p. 49.

[33]Erik H. Erikson, "On the Nature of Psycho-Historical Evidence: In Search of Gandhi," *Daedalus*, Summer, 1968, pp. 695-730; the latter article was published as a chapter in *Insight and Responsibility* (New York: W. W. Norton & Company, Inc., 1964), pp. 47-80.

[34]Erikson, *Insight and Responsibility*, p. 59.

[35]*Ibid.*

[36]Erikson, "On the Nature of Psycho-Historical Evidence," p. 709.

[37]*Ibid.*, pp. 702-13.

[38]Max Horkheimer, "The Relation Between Psychology and Sociology in the Work of Wilhelm Dilthey," *Studies in Philosophy and Social Science* 8 (1939): 440.

[39]*Ibid.*, p. 441.

[40]Cf. Heinz Hartmann, *Ego Psychology and the Problem of Adaptation* (New York: International Universities Press, Inc., 1939), pp. 23-24.

[41]Erikson, *Young Man Luther*, p. 77.

[42]Coles, *Erik H. Erikson, The Growth of His Work*, pp. 215-16.

[43]Don S. Browning, "Body and Existence: A Problem in Interpretation," Chicago, 1968. (Mimeographed.)

[44]*Ibid.*, p. 35.

[45]Daniel Yankelovich and William Barrett, *Ego and Instinct: The Psychoanalytic View of Human Nature--Revised* (New York: Random House, 1970).

[46]*Ibid.*, p. 309.

[47]*Ibid.*, p. 310.

[48]*Ibid.*, p. 311.

[49]*Ibid.*

[50]*Ibid.*, pp. 311-12.

[51]*Ibid.*, pp. 313-19.

[52]*Ibid.*, p. 319.

[53]*Ibid.* See page 434 for an indication of a growing awareness on the part of the authors that they have been heavily dependent upon Erikson for their "new" perspective.

[54]*Ibid.*, p. 328.

[55]*Ibid.*, p. 329.

[56]*Ibid.*

[57]*Ibid.*, p. 331.

[58]*Ibid.*, p. 332.

[59]*Ibid.* This is especially evident in their discussion of Erikson's *Young Man Luther* on pages 145-50.

[1]William R. Cannon, *The Theology of John Wesley* (New York: Abindgon-Cokesbury Press, 1946), p. 13.

[2]Albert Outler, ed., *John Wesley* (New York: Oxford University Press, 1964), p. 37.

[3]Wesley scholars Albert Outler and Richard Heitzenrater have argued convincingly that an exhaustive psychobiography of Wesley should await the completion of critical editing now in process on Wesley's *Works*. The conclusions of the present study will necessarily require re-evaluation in the light of currently unavailable biographical data. Professor Heitzenrater, for example, is currently deciphering heretofore untranslated diaries.

[4]Herbert R. Loring, "A Comparison of the Biographies of John Wesley Since 1850 in the Light of Biographical and Critical Materials" (Ph.D. diss., Boston University, 1951), pp. xix-xx.

[5]Albert Outler, personal letter, 25 November 1970.

[6]Outler, *John Wesley*, pp. 13-18.

[7]*Ibid.*, p. 14.

[8]*Ibid.*

[9]*Ibid.*, p. 17.

[10]*Ibid.*

[11]*Ibid.*, pp. 17-18.

[12]Erik H. Erikson, *Identity: Youth and Crisis* (New York: W. W. Norton & Co., 1968), p. 73.

[13]*International Encyclopedia of the Social Sciences*, 1968 ed., s.v. "Psychosocial Identity," by Erik H. Erikson.

[14]*Ibid.*

[15]*Ibid.*

[16]*Ibid.*

[17]*Ibid.*

[18]Erikson, *Identity and the Life Cycle*, pp. 112-13.

[19]*Ibid.*, pp. 113-14.

[20]Erikson, *Identity: Youth and Crisis*, p. 49.

[21] *Ibid.*

[22] Erikson, *Identity and the Life Cycle*, p. 116.

[23] Erikson, *Identity: Youth and Crisis*, p. 50.

[24] Erikson, *Identity and the Life Cycle*, p. 91.

[25] *International Encyclopedia of the Social Sciences*, 1968 ed., s.v. "Psychosocial Identity," by Erik H. Erikson.

[26] Erik H. Erikson, ed., *The Challenge of Youth* (New York: Doubleday, 1965), pp. 22-23.

[27] *Ibid.*

[28] *Ibid.*, pp. 23-24.

[29] Erikson, *Identity: Youth and Crisis*, p. 59.

[30] *Ibid.*, p. 54.

[31] Erikson, *The Challenge of Youth*, p. 13. See his *Identity: Youth and Crisis*, p. 212, for his reasons for substituting identity *confusion* for the earlier identity diffusion.

[32] *Ibid.*

[33] *Ibid.*

[34] Erikson, *Identity: Youth and Crisis*, pp. 156-58.

[35] *Ibid.*, pp. 159-61.

[36] *Ibid.*

[37] Adam Clarke, *Memoirs of the Wesley Family* (London: J. & T. Clarke, 1823), p. 94.

[38] Martin Schmidt, *John Wesley, A Theological Biography*, 2 vols. (Nashville: Abingdon Press, 1962), 1:20.

[39] *Ibid.*, p. 21.

[40] *Ibid.*, p. 23.

[41] *Ibid.*, pp. 23-24.

[42] *Ibid.*, p. 27.

[43] *Ibid.*, p. 30.

[44] *Ibid.*, p. 31.

[45] Clarke, *Memoirs*, pp. 24-32.

[46] Schmidt, *John Wesley*, 1:37-39.

[47]*The Journal of the Rev. John Wesley, A.M.*, ed. Nehemiah Curnock, 8 vols. (London: Epworth Press, 1909), 1:42 (hereafter cited as *Journal*).

[48]*Ibid.*

[49]Schmidt, *John Wesley*, 1:37. See also *Journal* 5:120-24.

[50]John S. Simon, *John Wesley and the Religious Societies* (London: Epworth Press, 1921), p. 31.

[51]Clarke, *Memoirs*, p. 24.

[52]*Ibid.*, pp. 25-32.

[53]*Ibid.*, p. 39.

[54]Simon, *Religious Societies*, p. 44.

[55]Frank Baker, *John Wesley and the Church of England* (New York: Abingdon Press, 1970), pp. 266-67.

[56]Clarke, *Memoirs*, p. 236.

[57]*Ibid.*

[58]*Ibid.*, p. 237.

[59]*Ibid.*

[60]Schmidt, *John Wesley*, 1:43.

[61]*Ibid.*

[62]Simon, *Religious Societies*, p. 44.

[63]Schmidt, *John Wesley*, 1:42.

[64]John Wesley, *A Christian Library*, 2nd ed., 30 vols. (London: Printed by T. Cordeux, for T. Blanshard, 1819-26).

[65]V. H. H. Green, *The Young Mr. Wesley* (London: Edward Arnold, 1961), p. 42.

[66]G. Elsie Harrison, *Son to Susanna* (Nashville: Cokesbury Press, 1938), 1:44. Although not a critical biography, Harrison's interpretation of Wesley contains several illuminating psychological insights.

[67]Green, *Young Mr. Wesley*, p. 43.

[68]Schmidt, *John Wesley*, 1:41-44.

[69]*Ibid.*, p. 43.

[70]Green, *Young Mr. Wesley*, p. 44.

[71]*Ibid.*

[72]Maldwyn Edwards, *Family Circle: A Study of the Epworth Household in Relation to John and Charles Wesley* (London: The Epworth Press, 1949), pp. 1-22.

[73]Green, *Young Mr. Wesley*, p. 47.

[74]*Ibid.*

[75]Edwards, *Family Circle*, p. 29.

[76]*Ibid.*, pp. 1-22.

[77]Green, *Young Mr. Wesley*, p. 47.

[78]Harrison, *Son to Susanna*, pp. 204-6.

[79]Edwards, *Family Circle*, p. 52.

[80]*Ibid.*, p. 53.

[81]*Ibid.*, p. 54.

[82]*Ibid.*, pp. 54-55.

[83]*Ibid.*, pp. 55-56.

[84]Harrison, *Son to Susanna*, p. 34.

[85]*Ibid.*

[86]Clarke, *Memoirs*, pp. 94-95.

[87]Green, *Young Mr. Wesley*, p. 50.

[88]*Ibid.*

[89]*Ibid.*

[90]*Ibid.*

[91]*Ibid.*, p. 58.

[92]*Journal*, 3:34-39.

[93]*Ibid.*

[94]*Ibid.*

[95]*Ibid.*

[96]Harrison, *Son to Susanna*, p. 19.

[97]Rebecca L. Harmon, *Susanna: Mother of the Wesleys* (Nashville: Abingdon Press, 1968), p. 53.

[98]Harrison, *Son to Susanna*, p. 29.

[99]*Ibid.*, p. 35.

[100]Green, *Young Mr. Wesley*, p. 54.

[101]*Ibid.*

[102]*Ibid.*

[103]*Ibid.*, p. 51.

[104]*Ibid.*, pp. 51-52.

[105]*Ibid.*, p. 52.

[106]Harrison, *Son to Susanna*, p. 33.

[107]Schmidt, *John Wesley*, 1:57.

[108]*Ibid.*, pp. 48-58.

[109]V. H. H. Green, *John Wesley* (London: Thomas Nelson and Sons, 1964), pp. 11-12.

[110]*Ibid.*

[111]*Ibid.*, p. 13.

[112]Green, *Young Mr. Wesley*, p. 209.

[113]Green, *John Wesley*, p. 16.

[114]*Ibid.*, p. 17.

[115]Green, *Young Mr. Wesley*, p. 208.

[116]*Ibid.*

[117]*Ibid.*

[118]*Ibid.*, p. 213.

[119]*Ibid.*, p. 210.

[120]*Ibid.*, p. 105.

[121]*Ibid.*, p. 106.

[122]*Ibid.*

[123]*Ibid.*

[124]*Ibid.*

[125]Schmidt, *John Wesley*, 1:112.

[126]*The Letters of the Rev. John Wesley, A.M.*, ed. John Telford, 8 vols. (London: Epworth Press, 1931), 1:79 (hereafter cited as *Letters*).

[127]Green, *Young Mr. Wesley*, p. 219.

[128]*Ibid.*, p. 225.

[129]*Ibid.*, p. 226.

[130]Schmidt, *John Wesley*, 1:133.

[131]Harrison, *Son to Susanna*, p. 70.

[132]Edwards, *Family Circle*, pp. 154-73.

[133]*Ibid.*, p. 160.

[134]Green, *Young Mr. Wesley*, p. 110.

[135]*Ibid.*

[136]*Ibid.*, p. 111.

[137]*Ibid.*

[138]Schmidt, *John Wesley*, 1:119.

[139]*Letters*, 1:134.

[140]Green, *Young Mr. Wesley*, p. 242.

[141]*Letters*, 1:166-78.

[142]*Ibid.*

[143]*Ibid.*

[144]*Ibid.*, pp. 179-80.

[145]See the chart listing the births and deaths of the nineteen Wesley children in Harmon, *Susanna*, pp. 6-7.

[146]Cf. the similar dynamics discussed in Albert J. Lubin, *Stranger on the Earth: A Psychological Biography of Vincent Van Gogh* (New York: Holt, Rinehart and Winston, 1972), pp. 88-90. The theme of the significance of the deceased sibling is an important thread in Lubin's interpretive narrative. Some have suggested that Tyerman and the majority of Wesley biographers have been in error in ascribing a middle name to him. Even if this objection is proven accurate the psychodynamic situation remains fundamentally the same.

[147]Edwards, *Family Circle*, p. 51.

[148]Green, *Young Mr. Wesley*, p. 50.

[149]Edwards, *Family Circle*, pp. 11-12.

[150]*Ibid.*, p. 29.

[151]*Ibid.*

[152]Green, *Young Mr. Wesley*, pp. 254-55.

CHAPTER III

[1]*Letters*, 1:199.

[2]*Journal*, 1:291-92.

[3]*Ibid.*, p. 292.

[4]*Ibid.*, p. 293.

[5]*Ibid.*, p. 294.

[6]*Ibid.*

[7]*Ibid.*

[8]*Ibid.*, pp. 280-81.

[9]*Ibid.*, p. 285.

[10]*Ibid.*, p. 286.

[11]*Ibid.*, p. 287.

[12]*Ibid.*, pp. 290-91.

[13]*Ibid.*, p. 294.

[14]*Ibid.*

[15]*Ibid.*, p. 298.

[16]*Ibid.*

[17]*Ibid.*

[18]*Ibid.*, p. 300.

[19]*Ibid.*, p. 324.

[20]*Ibid.*, p. 315.

[21]*Ibid.*

[22]*Ibid.*, p. 316.

[23]*Ibid.*, p. 317.

[24]*Ibid.*

[25]*Ibid.*, pp. 317-18.

[26]*Ibid.*, p. 318.

[27]*Ibid.*, p. 319.

[28]*Ibid.*, p. 320.

[29]*Ibid.*, p. 323.

[30]*Ibid.*

[31]*Ibid.*

[32]*Ibid.*, p. 324.

[33]*Ibid.*, p. 325.

[34]*Ibid.*

[35]*Ibid.*, pp. 325-26.

[36]*Ibid.*, p. 326.

[37]*Ibid.*, p. 327.

[38]*Ibid.*

[39]*Ibid.*, p. 328.

[40]*Ibid.*, pp. 328-29.

[41]*Ibid.*, p. 329.

[42]*Ibid.*, p. 330.

[43]*Ibid.*

[44]*Ibid.*, pp. 330-31.

[45]*Ibid.*, p. 333.

[46]*Ibid.*

[47]*Ibid.*, pp. 333-34.

[48]*Ibid.*, pp. 334-35.

[49]*Ibid.*, p. 335.

[50]*Ibid.*, pp. 335-36.

[51]*Ibid.*, p. 337.

[52]*Ibid.*

[53]*Ibid.*, p. 366.

[54]*Ibid.*, pp. 368-69.

[55]*Ibid.*, p. 376.

[56]*Ibid.*, p. 377.

[57]Patrick Tailfer *et al.*, *A True and Historical Narrative of the Colony of Georgia*, ed. Clarence L. Ver Steeg (Athens: University of Georgia Press, 1960), pp. 67-68.

[58]*Ibid.*, pp. 70-71.

[59]*Journal*, 1:399.

[60]*Ibid.*, p. 400.

[61]*Ibid.*

[62]*Ibid.*, p. 413.

[63]Erikson, *Identity and the Life Cycle*, pp. 74-82.

[64]*Journal*, 1:151.

[65]*Ibid.*, pp. 415-16.

[66]*Ibid.*, p. 418.

[67]*Ibid.*, p. 421.

[68]*Ibid.*, pp. 423-24.

[69]*Ibid.*, p. 424.

[70]I am indebted to Donald Capps for insight into the importance of resignation in Wesley's psychodynamics and for the designation of Wesley as a "resigned self." See Donald Capps and Walter H. Capps, eds., *The Religious Personality* (Belmont, California: Wadsworth Publishing Co., Inc., 1970), pp. 46-61.

[71]*Journal*, 1:432.

[72]*Ibid.*, pp. 437-39.

[73]*Ibid.*, pp. 435-36.

[74]*Ibid.*, pp. 462-63.

[75]*Ibid.*, p. 436.

[76]Schmidt, *John Wesley*, 1:226.

[77]*Journal*, 1:440.

[78]*Ibid.*, pp. 441-42.

[79]*Ibid.*, p. 442.

[80]*Ibid.*, p. 447.

[81]*Ibid.*

[82]*Ibid.*, p. 454.

[83] *Ibid.*

[84] *Ibid.*, pp. 454-55.

[85] *Ibid.*, p. 459.

[86] *Ibid.*, pp. 471-62.

[87] *Ibid.*, pp. 463-64.

[88] *Ibid.*, pp. 464-65.

[89] *Ibid.*, pp. 465-72.

[90] *Ibid.*, p. 472.

[91] *Ibid.*, p. 471.

[92] *Ibid.*, pp. 475-76.

[93] *Ibid.*, p. 476.

[94] *Ibid.*, p. 477.

[95] Outler, *John Wesley*, pp. 51-53.

[96] William R. Cannon, *The Theology of John Wesley* (New York: Abingdon-Cokesbury Press, 1946), pp. 54-60.

[97] *Letters*, 1:258.

[98] *Journal*, 1:478.

[99] *Ibid.*, pp. 482-83.

[100] *Journal*, 2:13.

[101] *Ibid.*, pp. 28-36.

[102] *Letters*, 1:252-54.

[103] Schmidt, *John Wesley*, 1:298.

[104] *Ibid.*, p. 299.

[105] *Journal*, 2:28.

[106] *Letters*, 1:258.

[107] Luke Tyerman, *The Life and Times of the Rev. John Wesley, A.M.*, 3 vols. (New York: Harper and Brothers, 1872), 1:20.

[108] *Journal*, 2:91.

[109] *Ibid.*, pp. 79-80.

[110] *Ibid.*, p. 84.

[111]*Ibid.*, pp. 89-91.

[112]*Ibid.*, p. 91.

[113]*Ibid.*, p. 116.

[114]*Ibid.*

[115]*Ibid.*

[116]*Ibid.*

[117]*Ibid.*, pp. 125-26.

[118]*Ibid.*, p. 126.

[119]Erikson, *The Challenge of Youth*, pp. 23-24.

[120]*Journal*, 2:156.

[121]*Ibid.*, pp. 159-66.

[122]*Letters*, 1:252.

[123]*Journal*, 2:167.

[124]*Ibid.*, p. 168.

[125]*Ibid.*, pp. 172-73.

[126]*Ibid.*, pp. 173-92.

[127]*Letters*, 1:308.

[128]*Ibid.*, pp. 309-10.

[129]*Ibid.*, p. 310.

NOTES

CHAPTER IV

[1]To my knowledge the literature on authority and initiative has not yet been co-ordinated with the literature on ego
activity and passivity. It is, I believe, a logical and illuminating correlation. The appropriateness of associating these
concepts has been confirmed by my consultant in ego psychology,
Dr. Donald Stolar of the Neuro-Psychiatric Institute, Center for
the Health Sciences, University of California at Los Angeles.

[2]See David Rapaport's essay "A Historical Survey of Psychoanalytic Ego Psychology" in Erikson's *Identity and the Life Cycle*,
pp. 5-17.

[3]David Rapaport, "The Autonomy of the Ego," in *The Collected Papers of David Rapaport*, ed. by Merton M. Gill (New
York: Basic Books, Inc., 1967), pp. 357-67. See also the following related articles in the same volume: "Some Metapsychological Considerations Concerning Activity and Passivity," pp.
530-69; "A Theoretical Analysis of the Superego Concept," pp.
685-710; and "The Theory of Ego Autonomy: A Generalization,"
pp. 722-44.

[4]Donald Stolar and Erika Fromm, "A Further Extension of
Rapaport's Theory of Activity and Passivity of the Ego," *Pro-
ceedings*, 81st Annual Convention of the American Psychological
Association (1973): 501-02.

[5]*Ibid.*, p. 501.

[6]*Ibid.*, p. 502.

[7]Rapaport, "Some Metapsychological Considerations Concerning Activity and Passivity," pp. 560-61.

[8]*Ibid.*; p. 556.

[9]See Roy Schafer, "Ideals, Ego Ideals, and Ideal Self,"
in R. R. Holt, ed., *Motives and Thought: Psychoanalytic Essays
in Honor of David Rapaport* (New York: International Universities
Press, Inc., 1967), pp. 131-74.

[10]Richard Hooker, *Works*, 3 vols. (Oxford: Clarendon Press,
1874), 3:486.

[11]William Laud, *A Relation of the Conference Between
William Laud, Then Lord Bishop of St. Davide, Now Lord Arch-
bishop of Canterbury and Mr. Fisher, the Jesuit with an Answer
to Such Exception as A. C. Takes Against It* (London: Richard
Badger, 1639), pp. 74-75.

[12]Lancelot Andrewes, *Works*, 11 vols. (Oxford: John Henry
Parker, 1841-1854), 2:156-57; 3:186-202; and 6:21.

[13]Henry Hammond, *Miscellaneous Theological Works*, 3 vols. (Oxford: John Henry Parker, 1849), 2:138-40.

[14]George Bull, *Harmonia Apostolica* (Oxford: John Henry Parker, 1844), pp. 16-18.

[15]*Ibid.*, p. 58.

[16]John Kirk, *The Mother of the Wesleys* (London: Henry James Tresidder, 1864), p. 31.

[17]Cannon, *The Theology of John Wesley*, pp. 45-48.

[18]Quoted in V. H. H. Green, *The Young Mr. Wesley*, p. 66. See also Clarke, *Memoirs*, pp. 201-04.

[19]Green, *The Young Mr. Wesley*, p. 66.

[20]*Ibid.*, p. 67.

[21]*Ibid.*, pp. 67-68.

[22]*Letters*, 1:19.

[23]*Ibid.*, p. 20.

[24]*Ibid.*, p. 22.

[25]*Ibid.*, pp. 15-16.

[26]*Ibid.*, p. 16.

[27]Quoted in J. Brazier Green, *John Wesley and William Law* (London: The Epworth Press, 1945), p. 27.

[28]*The Works of the Reverend John Wesley*, ed. Thomas Jackson, 3rd ed., 14 vols. (London: Wesleyan Conference Office, 1872), 11:367 (hereafter cited as *Works*).

[29]Green, *John Wesley and William Law*, p. 39.

[30]*Journal*, 1:467.

[31]Green, *John Wesley and William Law*, p. 58.

[32]*Letters*, 1:22-23.

[33]*Ibid.*, p. 70.

[34]*Ibid.*, p. 71.

[35]*Ibid.*, pp. 71-72.

[36]*Ibid.*, p. 71.

[37]*Journal*, 1:423-24.

[38]*Ibid.*, p. 442.

[39]*Letters*, 1:239.

[40]*Ibid.*

[41]Green, *John Wesley and William Law*, p. 68.

[42]*Letters*, 1:241-42.

[43]*Ibid.*, p. 242.

[44]*Ibid.*, p. 244.

[45]George C. Cell, *The Rediscovery of John Wesley* (New York: Henry Holt and Company, 1935), p. 201.

[46]Quoted in *Ibid.*, pp. 201-02.

[47]*Ibid.*, p. 202.

[48]*Journal*, 1:476.

[49]*Ibid.*, p. 483.

[50]*Works*, 5:7.

[51]*Ibid.*, pp. 10-12.

[52]*Ibid.*, p. 16.

[53]Other sermons were equally important statements of his emerging theological stance.

[54]*Ibid.*, p. 99.

[55]*Ibid.*

[56]*Ibid.*, p. 102.

[57]*Ibid.*, p. 104.

[58]*Ibid.*, pp. 106-7.

[59]*Ibid.*, 6:509.

[60]*Ibid.*, p. 512.

[61]*Ibid.*, 7:187.

[62]*Ibid.*, 5:57.

[63]*Ibid.*, p. 62.

[64]Colin W. Williams, *John Wesley's Theology Today* (New York: Abingdon Press, 1960), pp. 65-66.

[65]*Works*, 8:275-76.

[66]*Ibid.*

[67] *Ibid.*, pp. 5-6.

[68] *Ibid.*, 5:223-24.

[69] *Ibid.*, 6:70-71.

[70] *Ibid.*, 5:111.

[71] *Ibid.*, p. 119.

[72] *Ibid.*, p. 120.

[73] *Ibid.*, p. 155.

[74] *Ibid.*, 6:488.

[75] *Letters*, 8:238.

[76] *Ibid.*, 5:20.

[77] *Works*, 11:366-446.

[78] *Ibid.*, p. 374.

[79] *Ibid.*, p. 417.

[80] *Ibid.*, p. 378.

[81] *Ibid.*, p. 379.

[82] *Ibid.*, p. 384.

[83] Maximin Piette, *John Wesley in the Evolution of Protestantism* (New York: Sheed and Ward, 1937).

[84] Quoted in Cell, *Rediscovery of John Wesley*, p. 114.

[85] *Ibid.*, p. 361.

[86] *Ibid.*

[87] Cannon, *Theology of John Wesley*, p. 223.

[88] Harald Lindström, *Wesley and Sanctification* (New York: Abingdon Press, 1946), pp. 136-37.

[89] Cell's intention was clearly to promote a Calvinist reading of Wesley's theology.

[90] Cell, *Rediscovery of John Wesley*, p. 269.

[91] *Ibid.*, pp. 270-71.

[92] Cannon, *Theology of John Wesley*, p. 106.

[93] *Ibid.*, p. 115.

[94] *Ibid.*, p. 117.

[95]*Ibid.*, p. 116.

[96]Cf. Franz Hildebrandt, *From Luther to Wesley* (London: Lutterworth Press, 1951) and Williams, *John Wesley's Theology Today*.

[97]Williams, *John Wesley's Theology Today*, p. 72.

[98]Outler, *John Wesley*, p. 33.

[99]*Works*, 10:230.

[100]Outler, personal letter, 25 November 1970.

[101]Rapaport, "Some Metapsychological Considerations Concerning Activity and Passivity," p. 556.

[102]*Ibid.* The quote is from Ernst Kris, *Psychoanalytic Explorations in Art* (New York: International Universities Press, 1952), p. 302.

[103]Rapaport, "Some Metapsychological Considerations Concerning Activity and Passivity," p. 557.

CHAPTER V

[1]Most if not all of the studies of Methodism have been manifestations of "filial piety." There are some indications now, however, that serious scholarly inquiry into the significance of the Methodist tradition may be beginning. See, for example, the recent stimulating monograph by Bernard Semmel, *The Methodist Revolution* (New York: Basic Books, 1973). Semmel's book should serve as an important stimulus for further research.

[2]*Letters*, 2:294.

[3]*Ibid.*, p. 298.

[4]*Ibid.*, p. 300.

[5]*Ibid.*, pp. 300-1.

[6]*Journal*, 3:285.

[7]*Works*, 8:259.

[8]Tailfer *et al.*, *A True and Historical Narrative of the Colony of Georgia*, p. 70.

[9]*Ibid.*, p. 69.

[10]*Journal*, 5:405.

[11]*Ibid.*

[12]*Ibid.*, p. 406.

[13]*Ibid.*

[14]*Works*, 8:309.

[15]*Ibid.*, p. 321.

[16]*Ibid.*, pp. 321-22.

[17]*Ibid.*, p. 322.

[18]*Ibid.*, p. 310.

[19]*Ibid.*, p. 311.

[20]*Ibid.*

[21]*Ibid.*, p. 312.

[22]*Ibid.*

[23] *Ibid.*

[24] *Ibid.*, p. 313.

[25] *Ibid.*

[26] *Ibid.*

[27] Clarke, *Memoirs*, p. 398.

[28] *Ibid.*, p. 399.

[29] *Ibid.*, p. 411.

[30] *Ibid.*, p. 421.

[31] *Ibid.*, p. 425.

[32] *Ibid.*

[33] *Journal*, 2:53.

[34] Quoted in Baker, *John Wesley and the Church of England*, p. 57.

[35] Covert rebellion is a designation often used by clinicians to refer to behavior which challenges the restraints of authority without admitting intent to do so.

[36] Joseph Priestly, ed., *Original Letters by the Rev. John Wesley and His Friends, Illustrative of His Early History* (Birmingham: Pearson, 1791), pp. 110-11.

[37] *Letters*, 1:285.

[38] *Ibid.*, pp. 285-86.

[39] *Ibid.*, p. 286.

[40] "The people ought to separate themselves from a wicked bishop."

[41] *Letters*, 1:322-23.

[42] This encounter is of course reminiscent of the encounter in 1661 between Wesley's paternal grandfather and the Bishop of Bristol.

[43] *Journal*, 2:257.

[44] *Letters*, 8:141.

[45] *Works*, 8:1-42.

[46] *Ibid.*, p. 33.

[47] *Ibid.*, pp. 34-35.

[48] *Ibid.*, p. 35.

[49] *Ibid.*, pp. 112-13.

[50] *Ibid.*, p. 119.

[51] *Journal*, 4:8-11.

[52] Quoted in Tyerman, *Life and Times of the Rev. John Wesley, A.M.*, 2:201-2.

[53] *Ibid.*, p. 202.

[54] *Ibid.*, p. 203.

[55] Quoted in Baker, *John Wesley and the Church of England*, pp. 334-35.

[56] *Ibid.*, pp. 335-36.

[57] *Ibid.*, p. 332.

[58] *Ibid.*, p. 170.

[59] Quoted in *Ibid.*, p. 175.

[60] *Ibid.*, pp. 175-76.

[61] *Journal*, 8:330.

[62] *Ibid.*, pp. 331-32.

[63] *Ibid.*, p. 332.

[64] *Ibid.*

[65] *Ibid.*, p. 333.

[66] *Journal*, 7:16 (facsimile insert).

[67] *Letters*, 8:91.

[68] *Ibid.*, 7:262.

[69] Quoted in Baker, *John Wesley and the Church of England*, p. 273.

[70] *Letters*, 7:321.

[71] *Journal*, 7:422.

[72] *Letters*, 8:58.

[73] Baker, *John Wesley and the Church of England*, p. 324.

[74] *Ibid.*

[75] *Ibid.*, p. 325.

[76] *Ibid.*

NOTES

CHAPTER VI

[1]John Wesley, "Thoughts Upon Methodism," *Arminian Magazine* 10 (March 1787): 156.

[2]*Ibid.*

[3]Wach, *Sociology of Religion*, p. 36.

[4]*Ibid.*, pp. 158-59.

[5]*Ibid.*, p. 236.

[6]*Ibid.*, p. 166.

[7]*Ibid.*, p. 176.

[8]*Ibid.*, p. 198.

[9]*Ibid.*

[10]*Ibid.*, p. 334.

[11]*Ibid.*

[12]*Ibid.*, p. 338.

[13]*Ibid.*, p. 337.

[14]*Ibid.*, p. 336.

[15]*Ibid.*, pp. 276-77.

[16]Max Weber, *The Protestant Ethic and the Spirit of Capitalism* (New York: Charles Scribner's Sons, 1958), p. 117. See also the discussion of Wesley's relationship to Puritanism in Robert C. Monk, *John Wesley: His Puritan Heritage* (New York: Abingdon Press, 1966).

[17]Weber, *Protestant Ethic*, pp. 174-75.

[18]*Ibid.*

[19]*Ibid.*, p. 176.

[20]*Ibid.*, p. 139.

[21]*Ibid.*, p. 140.

[22]*Ibid.*, pp. 142-43.

[23]*Ibid.*, p. 143.

[24] *Ibid.*

[25] *Ibid.*, pp. 119-20.

[26] Semmel, *The Methodist Revolution*, pp. 8-9.

[27] *Ibid.*, p. 7.

[28] *Ibid.*, p. 8.

[29] *Ibid.*

[30] Erikson, *Young Man Luther*, p. 18.

[31] Sigmund Freud, *Moses and Monotheism*, in *The Complete Psychological Works of Sigmund Freud*, ed. James Strachey, 24 vols. (London: Hogarth Press, 1961), 23:58.

[32] Browning, *Body and Existence*, p. 26.

[33] Erikson, *Childhood and Society*, p. 69.

[34] *Ibid.*

[35] Nelson S. T. Thayer, "The Place of Religion in Erik H. Erikson's Theory of Human Development" (Ph.D. dissertation, University of Chicago, 1973), pp. 166-67.

[36] Talcott Parsons, "Weber's Methodology of Social Science," in *Max Weber: The Theory of Social and Economic Organization*, ed. by Talcott Parsons (New York: Oxford University Press, 1947), p. 25.

[37] *Ibid.*

[38] *Ibid.*

[39] *Ibid.*, p. 26.

[40] *Ibid.*

[41] *Ibid.*, p. 27.

[42] See the extensive application of systems conceptuality in Talcott Parsons, *The Social System* (New York: The Free Press of Glencoe, 1964).

[43] See my introduction to the systems paradigm in "Process Philosophy and General Systems Theory: A Review Article," *Process Studies* 4, no. 4 (Winter 1974): 291-300.

[44] Yankelovich and Barrett, *Ego and Instinct*, p. 312.

[45] Ludwig von Bertalanffy, *General System Theory: Foundations, Development, Applications* (New York: George Braziller, 1968), pp. 80-86.

[46]In addition to references in my review article see especially Laura Thompson, *Toward a Science of Mankind* (New York: McGraw-Hill Book Company, Inc., 1961) and Robert F. Berkhofer, Jr., *A Behavioral Approach to Historical Analysis* (New York: The Free Press, 1969).

[47]Yankelovich and Barrett, *Ego and Instinct*, p. 312.

[48]Charles Y. Glock and Phillip E. Hammond, eds. *Beyond the Classics? Essays in the Scientific Study of Religion* (New York: Harper and Row, 1973).

[49]Wach, *The Comparative Study of Religions*, p. 14.

[50]In addition to the Glock and Hammond volume mentioned above see Allan W. Eister, ed., *Changing Perspectives in the Scientific Study of Religion* (New York: John Wiley and Sons, 1974).

[51]Wach, *The Comparative Study of Religions*, p. 14.

[52]*Ibid.*, p. 15.

[53]*Ibid.*, pp. 15-16.

[54]Ervin Laszlo, *Introduction to Systems Philosophy: Toward a New Paradigm of Contemporary Thought* (New York: Gordon and Breach, 1972), p. 12.

SELECTED BIBLIOGRAPHY

Baker, Frank. *John Wesley and the Church of England*. New York:
 Abingdon Press, 1970.

von Bertalanffy, Ludwig. *General System Theory*: *Foundations,*
 Development, Applications. New York: George Braziller,
 1968.

Blanck, Gertrude and Blanck, Rubin. *Ego Psychology*: *Theory*
 and Practice. New York: Columbia University Press, 1974.

Browning, Don S. "Body and Existence: A Problem in Interpretation." Chicago, 1968. (Mimeographed.)

Cannon, William R. *The Theology of John Wesley*. New York:
 Abingdon-Cokesbury Press, 1946.

Capps, Donald and Capps, Walter H., eds. *The Religious Person-*
 ality. Belmont, California: Wadsworth Publishing Co.,
 Inc., 1970.

Cell, George C. *The Rediscovery of John Wesley*. New York:
 Henry Holt and Company, 1935.

Clarke, Adam. *Memoirs of the Wesley Family*. London: J. & T.
 Clarke, 1823.

Coles, Robert. *Erik H. Erikson, The Growth of His Work*. Boston:
 Little, Brown and Company, 1970.

Deschner, John. *Wesley's Christology*. Dallas: Southern
 Methodist University Press, 1960.

Edwards, Maldwyn. *Family Circle*: *A Study of the Epworth House-*
 hold in Relation to John and Charles Wesley. London: The
 Epworth Press, 1949.

Eisenstadt, S. N., ed. *The Protestant Ethic and Modernization*:
 A Comparative View. New York: Basic Books, Inc., 1968.

Erikson, Erik. "Autobiographic Notes on the Identity Crisis."
 Daedalus. Fall, 1970.

_____. *Childhood and Society*. New York: W. W. Norton &
 Company, Inc., 1969.

_____. *Gandhi's Truth*. New York: W. W. Norton & Company,
 Inc., 1969.

_____. *Identity and the Life Cycle*. New York: International
 Universities Press, Inc., 1959.

_____. *Identity Youth and Crisis*. New York: W. W. Norton
 & Company, Inc., 1968.

241

Erikson, Erik. *Insight and Responsibility*. New York: W. W. Norton & Company, Inc., 1964.

_____. "On the Nature of Psycho-Historical Evidence: In Search of Gandhi." *Daedalus*, Summer, 1968, pp. 695-730.

_____. *Young Man Luther, A Study in Psychoanalysis and History*. New York: W. W. Norton & Company, Inc., 1958.

_____. "Youth: Fidelity and Diversity." *The Challenge of Youth*. Edited by Erik Erikson. New York: Doubleday & Company, 1965.

Freud, Sigmund. *Moses and Monotheism. The Complete Psychological Works of Sigmund Freud*. Edited by James Strachey. Vol. 23. London: Hogarth Press, 1961.

Gendlin, Eugene T. "Wilhelm Dilthey and the Problem of Comprehending Human Significance in the Science of Man." Master's Thesis, University of Chicago, 1950.

Green, J. Brazier. *John Wesley and William Law*. London: The Epworth Press, 1945.

Green, V. H. H. *John Wesley*. London: Thomas Nelson and Sons, 1964.

_____. *The Young Mr. Wesley*. London: Edward Arnold, 1961.

Harmon, Rebecca L. *Susanna: Mother of the Wesleys*. Nashville: Abingdon Press, 1968.

Harrison, G. Elsie. *Son to Susanna*. Nashville: Cokesbury Press, 1938.

Hartmann, Heinz. *Ego Psychology and the Problem of Adaptation*. New York: International Universities Press, Inc., 1939.

_____. *Essays in Ego Psychology*. New York: International Universities Press, Inc., 1964.

Hildebrandt, Franz. *From Luther to Wesley*. London: Lutterworth Press, 1951.

Hirsch, E. D. *Validity in Interpretation*. New Haven: Yale University Press, 1967.

Hodges, H. A. *Wilhelm Dilthey: An Introduction*. London: Routledge and Kegan Paul, 1944.

_____. *The Philosophy of Wilhelm Dilthey*. London: Routledge and Kegan Paul, 1952.

Holt, R. R., ed. *Motives and Thought: Psychoanalytic Essays in Honor of David Rapaport*. New York: International Universities Press, Inc., 1967.

Ihde, Don. *Hermeneutic Phenomenology: The Philosophy of Paul Ricoeur*. Evanston: Northwestern University Press, 1971.

Kris, Ernst. *Psychoanalytic Explorations in Art*. New York: International Universities Press, Inc., 1952.

Laszlo, Ervin. *Introduction to Systems Philosophy: Toward a New Paradigm of Contemporary Thought*. New York: Gordon and Breach, 1972.

_____. *The Systems View of the World: The Natural Philosophy of the New Developments in the Sciences*.

Lindström, Harald. *Wesley and Sanctification*. New York: Abingdon Press, 1946.

Little, David. *The New Order in Old England*. New York: Harper & Row, 1967.

Lonergan, Bernard J. F. *Insight: A Study of Human Understanding*. New York: Longmans, Green, and Co., 1957.

Loring, Herbert R. "A Comparison of the Biographies of John Wesley Since 1850 in the Light of Biographical and Critical Materials." Ph.D. dissertation, Boston University, 1951.

Lubin, Albert J. *Stranger on the Earth: A Psychological Biography of Vincent Van Gogh*. New York: Holt, Rinehart, and Winston, 1972.

Merleau-Ponty, Maurice. *The Phenomenology of Perception*. Translated by Colin Smith. New York: The Humanities Press, Inc., 1962.

Monk, Robert C. *John Wesley: His Puritan Heritage*. New York: Abingdon Press, 1966.

Muller-Vollmer, Kurt. *Toward A Phenomenological Theory of Literature: A Study of Wilhelm Dilthey's Poetik*. The Hague: Mouton and Company, 1963.

Outler, Albert C., ed. *John Wesley*. New York: Oxford University Press, 1964.

Palmer, Richard E. *Hermeneutics: Interpretation Theory in Schleiermacher, Dilthey, Heidegger, and Gadamer*. Evanston: Northwestern University Press, 1969.

Parsons, Talcott. *The Social System*. New York: The Free Press of Glencoe, 1964.

Piette, Maximin. *John Wesley in the Evolution of Protestantism*. New York: Sheed and Ward, 1937.

Priestly, Joseph, ed. *Original Letters by the Rev. John Wesley and His Friends, Illustrative of His Early History*. Birmingham: Pearson, 1791.

Rapaport, David. *The Collected Papers of David Rapaport*. Edited by Merton M. Gill. New York: Basic Books, Inc., 1967.

Rasmussen, David M. *Mythic-Symbolic Language and Philosophical Anthropology*. The Hague: Martinus Nijhoff, 1971.

Ricoeur, Paul. *Freud and Philosophy: an Essay on Interpretation*. New Haven: Yale University Press, 1970.

Scheimann, Richard W. "Wach's Theory of the Science of Religion." Ph.D. dissertation, University of Chicago, 1963.

Schmidt, Martin. *John Wesley, A Theological Biography*. 2 vols. Nashville: Abingdon Press, 1962.

Semmel, Bernard. *The Methodist Revolution*. New York: Basic Books, Inc., 1973.

Simon, John S. *John Wesley and the Religious Societies*. London: Epworth Press, 1921.

_____. *John Wesley and the Methodist Societies*. London: Epworth Press, 1923.

_____. *John Wesley and the Advance of Methodism*. London: Epworth Press, 1925.

Southey, Robert. *The Life of Wesley; and the Rise and Progress of Methodism*. 2 vols. London: Longmans, 1820.

Stephen, Sir Leslie. *History of English Thought in the Eighteenth Century*. 2 vols. London: Smith, Elder, 1902.

Thayer, Nelson S. T. "The Place of Religion in Erik H. Erikson's Theory of Human Development." Ph.D. dissertation, University of Chicago, 1973.

Thompson, E. P. *The Making of the English Working Class*. New York: Pantheon Books, 1964.

Tyerman, Luke. *The Life and Times of the Rev. John Wesley, A.M.* 3 vols. New York: Harper and Brothers, 1872.

_____. *The Oxford Methodists*. New York: Harper and Brothers, 1873.

_____. *Wesley's Designated Successor: The Life, Letters, and Literary Labour of the Rev. John William Fletcher*. New York: Philips and Hunt, 1883.

Wach, Joachim. *Sociology of Religion*. Chicago: University of Chicago Press, 1944.

_____. *Types of Religious Experience, Christian and Non-Christian*. Chicago: University of Chicago Press, 1951.

_____. *The Comparative Study of Religions*. Edited with an Introduction by Joseph M. Kitagawa. New York: Columbia University Press, 1958.

Walzer, Michael. *The Revolution of the Saints: A Study in the Origin of Radical Politics*. New York: Atheneum, 1968.

Weber, Max. *Max Weber: The Theory of Social and Economic Organization*. Edited by Talcott Parsons. New York: Oxford University Press, 1947.

_____. *The Protestant Ethic and the Spirit of Capitalism*. New York: Charles Scribner's Sons, 1958.